SAT 22 FEB 2014

Gordon MacRae

Gordon MacRae at home, mid-1950s. Photograph courtesy of Warner Bros. Inc.

Gordon MacRae

A BIO-BIBLIOGRAPHY

BRUCE R. LEIBY

Bio-Bibliographies in the Performing Arts, Number 17
James R. Parish, Series Adviser

GREENWOOD PRESS
New York • Westport, Connecticut • London

Library of Congress Cataloging-in-Publication Data

Leiby, Bruce R.
   Gordon MacRae : a bio-bibliography / Bruce R. Leiby.
      p.   cm. — (Bio-bibliographies in the performing arts, ISSN
   0892-5550 ; no. 17)
   Includes indexes.
   ISBN 0-313-26633-6 (alk. paper)
      1. MacRae, Gordon—Bibliography.   2. MacRae, Gordon—Discography.
   I. Title. II. Series.
   ML134.5.M3L4   1991
   016.78242'164'092—dc20   90-29291

British Library Cataloguing in Publication Data is available.

Library of Congress Catalog Card Number: 90-29291
ISBN: 978-0-313-26633-1

First published in 1991

Greenwood Press, 88 Post Road West, Westport, CT 06881
An imprint of Greenwood Publishing Group, Inc.

Printed in the United States of America

The paper used in this book complies with the
Permanent Paper Standard issued by the National
Information Standards Organization (Z39.48-1984).

10 9 8 7 6 5 4 3 2 1

Every reasonable effort has been made to trace the owners of copyright materials in this book,
but in some instances this has proven impossible. The author and publisher will be glad to
receive information leading to more complete acknowledgments in subsequent printings of the
book and in the meantime extend their apologies for any omissions.

I would like to dedicate this book to its subject, Gordon MacRae; to Mrs. Myra Chipman, who inspired me to write; to my beloved wife, Linda; and last but not least to our loving parents.

Contents

Acknowledgments

There are a number of people I would like to thank for
their help in the preparation of this book. I would like
to thank the celebrities and authors with whom I have
corresponded, my editors, Marilyn Brownstein, Mary Blair,
and Mark Kane, series adviser James Robert Parish, my
attorney, Eugene Renz, Ray Stanich, Robert Young, Jr.,
Milton Moore, Jr., Andy Hanson, Irv Steinberg, Jerome
Abeles, the Rodgers & Hammerstein Organization, Shirley
Jones, Marty Ingels, Hugh Downs, KQED-TV and Power/Rector
Productions, Warner Brothers, the Philadelphia Free Library,
my wife Linda, and the many others who have also provided
photos, information and memorabilia.

Introduction

Gordon Albert MacRae was not only the possessor of one of
the world's best voices that could handle any kind of song
from pop to operetta, but he was also a man for all media
with achievements in all areas open to a singer. He became
a six letterman of show business with credits in stage,
radio, films, television, recordings, and night clubs and
concerts.
    The purpose of this book is two-fold. It is a tribute
to its subject as well as the first in-depth study of
MacRae's life and career to be chronicled to date in one
place for the use of libraries, researchers, fans, and
students of film, radio, theatre, television, and music.
    The first section is a biographical and career
overview with quotes from persons I have corresponded with
who either worked with or knew Mr. MacRae.
    Following the biography is a separate section on each
of the media in which he was involved. Each credit in the
section is numbered and assigned a letter: S (Stage), R
(Radio), F (Filmography), T (Television), D (Discography),
SM (Sheet Music), NC (Night Clubs and Concerts), B
(Bibliography). The indexes reflect this numbering system.
    The stage section is arranged chronologically with
different productions of the same show listed together.
The show is designated as to whether it was a stock or
Broadway production. Each entry, when possible, includes
date, theatre, place, credits, cast(with character name),
synopsis, songs(MacRae's songs designated), review, and a
comment.
    The third section, radio, is arranged alphabetically
giving the show, and when possible, network, date, and
information as to cast, credits and songs. There is also a
complete RAILROAD HOUR LOG. Shows I have found available on
tape from collectors are noted.
    The filmography lists films chronologically giving
production company, date of release, length, detailed
credits, detailed cast(with character name), synopsis,
songs(with performer), a review followed by some sources
for additional reviews and where applicable a comment.
Only black and white films are designated (BW): all others
are in color. The abbreviation Vita stands for Vitaphone

Corporation (a part of Warner Brothers). OKLAHOMA,
CAROUSEL, and THE PILOT are on video, but I have found most
of MacRae's other movies on video from collectors or they
can be taped by VCR owners.
     The television section is also arranged in
chronological order with show, and where possible, network,
date, cast, credits, and songs by MacRae. His series also
includes days and times shown, as well as an episodic
listing with songs and or guests. The shows I have found on
video are noted.
     In the discography, the 78s and 45s are arranged in
chronological order. The LPs, compilation records,
cassettes, 8-tracks, and CDs are arranged alphabetically.
The singles include date, record label and number, and where
possible, orchestra and singing group. Charted and gold
records are noted. The charted records include date
charted, peak position, and length of time charted. LPs
also give record label and number, size, date, orchestra,
songs by side, producer(when known), and singers or choruses
accompanying MacRae. Various versions of a record are also
noted. If a corresponding cassette or CD exists, a cross
reference is given. Songs listed on compilation records are
only those by MacRae.
     A partial sheet music list is given with date. If it
is a song that pertains to a film, the date of the film
version is given and not necessarily the publication date
of the song.
     The night club and concert section is arranged
chronologically giving club(room played if known) or place
of concert with date, and where known, orchestra, others
appearing on the bill, songs and impressions by MacRae, and
a review.
     An annotated bibliography follows and is split into
two parts with newspapers and magazines making up the
first part, and books the second. Bibliography entries
B416 and B417 attribute Mr. MacRae with additional film and
Broadway credits, which he could have done, but since they
do not appear anywhere else in the MacRae information, I was
uncertain if the actor appearing in them was the same
MacRae, as he would have been very young at the time. I
did not list them in their respective sections but placed
them in the bibliography so, the reader would be aware of
their existence.
     Three alphabetical indexes finish the book. The first
is a song index followed by a title and general index.
     This work attempts to provide the researcher in need
of more information, a good foundation on which to build.
     Although I tried to be as thorough, accurate, and
complete as possible, there may have been some errors or
omissions and I would welcome any corrections or additions.

Gordon MacRae

1

Biography

Gordon Albert MacRae started out as a young performer, and developed into a six letterman of show business, after having achieved success in all fields available to a singer: theatre, radio, records, motion pictures, television, night clubs, and even the world of big bands.

An affinity towards show business came naturally to Gordon, who was born of Scottish descent, on March 12, 1921, to William Lamont MacRae--a pioneer radio performer (WGY Schenectady, New York), inventor (sold an invention to Eastman Kodak), and manufacturer--and Helen Violet (Sonn) MacRae, a concert pianist and teacher, in East Orange, New Jersey. The MacRae family did not remain in East Orange long, for by the age of two, Gordon with his parents and sister, June, had moved to Buffalo, then to Syracuse, New York. Within two years, young Gordon was leading the kindergarten band at the Charles Andrew School.

At six, MacRae developed an ear infection of the mastoid. At that time, there were no sulfa drugs available to help fight the infection. His doctors did not have much hope for his recovery. Prayer played a vital part in helping the family through this troubling period. Miraculously, the mastoiditis cleared up. Gordon came out of his coma and recovered fully.

William MacRae, like most fathers, wanted his son to become a good citizen with a normal job. He hoped that Gordon would follow in his footsteps and eventually take over his manufacturing business upon his retirement. Gordon, wishing to please his father, worked in the machine shop after school, on Saturdays, and during school vacations, but was unhappy in this line of work.

Once when William was home ill for a few weeks, he heard Gordon singing. He soon realized that music was his son's forte. With this realization, he gave Gordon his blessing to become an entertainer if that was what he wanted. He made sure Gordon realized that it was not going to be easy and a lot of hard work would be involved. William gave Gordon some advice that would prove invaluable in later years. "Son," he said, "if you feel like singing, sing. Sing all the time, wherever you are."[1]

At age seven, Gordon awakened at 4 a.m. and walked to

the Netherland Dairy in Syracuse to earn some extra money, peddling milk in horse-drawn wagons. By the age of eleven, Gordon would rush over to the local radio station after school to work as a master of ceremonies. At age twelve, he spent a summer at Camp Ropoia in Maine, swimming, playing tennis, and singing campfire songs. The next summer he worked in a New Hampshire hotel. At fourteen, he distinguished himself by making his debut with the Children's Theatre of Syracuse University.

As a youngster, MacRae played the part of Joe Penner, who was a member of the Miller family. Because of his performance, he became a Miller Talent Winner and was offered $2.50 per show to repeat his role. While attending Nottingham High School, Gordon became a charter member of the school's drama club, playing the part of Dandy in MARRIED FOR MONEY. Once he played a black butler and did not appear until later in the show. While watching back stage, he became interested in the show and nearly missed his cue.

MacRae was a good student and earned grades in the 90s throughout high school. He completed his high school education at Deerfield Academy in Massachusetts. There the headmaster, Dr. Frank Boyden, took an interest in MacRae, teaching him tolerance, good manners, and sportsmanship. Next to his immediate family, Boyden had the greatest early influence on Gordon. While at Deerfield, MacRae made many appearances with the school glee club. One late afternoon, in the new music room, Gordon was engrossed in listening to Dvoak's "New World Symphony" when a boy told him he had missed the bus and that Dr. Boyden would drive him to Hartford, Connecticut where he was to sing the solo "Standing in the Need of Prayer" with the choir.

MacRae had always shown an interest in sports. During his school days, he played football (No. 18), basketball, hockey, track, lacrosse (No. 48), and baseball. The National Rifle Association awarded him the First Class Marksman Medal. He also won a swimming medal.

Gordon wanted to broaden his musical talent so he learned to play the piano, clarinet, and the saxophone--all proficiently. While in high school, he made personal appearances with a hillbilly quartet and was billed as Mortimer Q. MacRae, further demonstrating his versatility. He already had three years of radio experience behind him by the time he was featured weekly on MINIATURE MINSTRELS on station WFBL, singing such songs for writer-producer Bill Lundigan as "If I Had a Million Dollars."

After graduating from high school, Gordon planned to attend Amherst. He felt that it was a good idea to get a general education behind him before starting a musical career. Before sending his son off to college, William MacRae wanted him to expand his education, so he sent him on a 43-day trip to Europe, sponsored by the YMCA. However, before Gordon could enroll at Amherst, William died, and Gordon had to give up his college plans and go to work.

At nineteen, the readers of <u>Picture Magazine</u> voted MacRae the winner of a talent contest. The prize was a two-week engagement at the New York World Fair's famed Trylon and Peresphere Outdoor Dancing Pavilion, earning $50 a week singing for the Harry James and Les Brown bands. Ironically, Mike Todd, who later invented the Todd-AO process used in the film OKLAHOMA, owned the place where Gordon performed. The experience was not a long one, but quite educational. Even though no offers came from the engagements, MacRae knew that he definitely wanted a career in show business. Gordon felt that learning more about the legitimate stage would help his career. So on September 24, 1940, he borrowed his mother's car and drove from Scarsdale to the Millpond Playhouse on Long Island. Arriving with him was an actor who later became known as Jeff Chandler.

MacRae worked for Christopher Morley in exchange for five dollars a week, plus room and board. While at the playhouse, Gordon met Sheila Margot Stephens, who was a young, pretty, blonde born in London, England, on September 24, 1924. She was the daughter of Louis and Winifred (Baker) Stephens.

Sheila had had acting experience since grade school. She and her family had only arrived in the United States in 1938. Shortly thereafter, she took the job of acting secretary at the playhouse.

MacRae auditioned for, and won the part of Deiphobus, a warrior, in the play entitled THE TROJAN HORSE, in which Miss Stephens played Helen of Troy. Gordon and Sheila did not immediately become friends because she thought he was too brash. Many people, even in later years, thought he was conceited. In reality, he was a confident young man who spoke his mind and knew exactly where he was going.

Sheila's mother and sister lived near the playhouse and would drop by frequently to watch rehearsals. Paula and her mother were impressed with Gordon and suggested Sheila invite him home for dinner. Sheila was reluctant at first. The playhouse director, whom she liked, had just left for another job. To help forget him, she decided that maybe her mother's idea was not so bad after all. Gradually the ice between Gordon and Sheila began to melt, and she soon became interested in the handsome baritone. He drove her into New York City for drama lessons. They would have lunch, stroll up Fifth Avenue, visit the zoo, or watch skaters at the Rockefeller Plaza ice rink.

When autumn came and the Millpond group broke up, Gordon went to New York and got a job as a page for NBC, earning $16 a week. One day, George Jackson, a scout for band leader Horace Heidt, overheard MacRae singing in a lounge. Jackson explained that Heidt was losing one of his singers. Would Gordon be interested in auditioning? Gordon assured him that he would. After Heidt heard MacRae sing, he offered him a job as a replacement for Ed, of the Don Juans (at $50 a week), from 1940 to 1942.

Agent Dick Dorso discovered MacRae singing for Heidt at $65 a week. Dorso felt that MacRae sounded like Frank Sinatra, as did others, and convinced him the competition would be difficult. If he wanted to succeed, he should use his natural voice. Gordon continued to seek Dorso's advice even after Dorso's office had gone out of business. Later when Larry Cotton left Heidt's band, MacRae replaced him at $150 a week. Heidt did a lot to help shape the singer's

career. During his stay with the band, Gordon continued to
see Sheila whenever he could. Very much in love, they were
frequently separated whenever the band went on tour. The
couple missed each other, which did not help Gordon's morale
or concentration.

The Heidt band stayed over in Cleveland for a couple
of days. Mrs. Heidt called Sheila's parents, promising to
chaperone if they let Sheila visit. So on May 17, 1941,
Sheila arrived on the train to visit Gordon. Larry Cotton
met her at the station, as Gordon was busy in rehearsals.
The rehearsals were still in progress when they arrived at
the theatre. Sheila went over to talk with Horace Heidt,
who told her that May 21 was his birthday and suggested that
it would be nice if it became her wedding date. "I've got
an ulterior motive for all this. He's unhappy away from you
and his mind is not on his work."[2] Heidt was also afraid
that while the band was touring during the next year, Gordon
and Sheila might drift apart.

Gordon and Sheila decided to take Heidt's suggestion
and go ahead with plans to marry. When the couple applied
for the marriage license, they learned of a ten-day resi-
dency requirement. As the band was traveling, this was
impossible. The clerks searched through the statutes for
special dispensations, and they finally got the license.
They were married on May 21, 1941 in Cleveland, Ohio.
Frankie Carle played the wedding march and Larry Cotton sang
"Ave Maria." Horace gave Sheila away, and he and his wife,
Adeline, were best man and matron of honor. Reverend
Herman Klahr performed the ceremony. Sheila was seventeen,
Gordon twenty. The wedding took place at 9:00 a.m. They
did three shows and a disc jockey show before going home at
3:00 a.m.

Like other newly married couples, Gordon and Sheila had
adjustments to make. They had to join together two
distinctly different personalities. On their honeymoon
they traveled with the band. Gordon liked to spend time
with the band, including staying at the same hotel. Sheila
wanted them to be alone. At the suggestion of Gordon's
mother, Sheila mapped out tours of historic and scenic
interest for Gordon's spare time, which gave them their
time together. There were also financial problems. They
sometimes had to do without necessities, either because
Gordon bought expensive gifts for Sheila, or because money
was short. During these times, they would have to ask for
help from his mother.

MacRae recorded "Heavenly Hide Away," "When Your Lips
Met Mine," "Be Honest With Me," and "Where the Mountains
Meet the Sky" for Heidt's band on the Columbia label. The
band also sponsored a War Bond Drive at Wittenberg College.
He agreed to appear to sing "The Star Spangled Banner."
The audience had to rescue him. He soon learned all four
verses.

In September 1942, Gordon felt he had gone as far as
he could with the Heidt band. He hesitated to leave, as
Heidt had been good to him and for his career. Gordon
also did not know how he would support himself and Sheila,
as they had been unable to save any money, and he had no job
prospects. Sheila urged him to make the change, volun-

teering to go back to work if necessary. Gordon agreed,
feeling that it was time to move on. He then negotiated his
release from the band.

MacRae was offered three jobs after leaving Heidt; one
to join a choir, another to join Benny Goodman, and the
third, a small part in the Broadway production of JUNIOR
MISS. He chose the Tommy Arbuckle role in JUNIOR MISS in
1943, marking his Broadway debut. While doing the show, he
also began singing with Ray Block's radio chorus.

Ray Block introduced MacRae to CBS moguls, who hired
him in case Frank Sinatra might get sick or find a better
job. About this time, Gordon learned that Sinatra was
planning to leave his CBS radio spot to join YOUR HIT PARADE.
Gordon was hired to replace him. He stayed with the show
for six months until he was drafted in June 1943, and became
bombardier instructor at Ellington Field, Texas.

During the band years, Gordon and Sheila had spent a
lot of nights on trains, planes, and buses, and now they
spent a lot of time in and near Air Force bases. There was
a formal dance one night at the Texas base. Sheila was
expecting their first child and could not fit into her
gowns, so she pieced them together, making a new one. While
Sheila followed Gordon from base to base, she managed to
find work on local radio stations as well as teaching
dramatics at the University of Texas, in order to supplement
Gordon's $75 a month. She continued working until she had
to retire when Meredith Lynn was born on May 30, 1945.

While earning his navigator wings at Ellington Field,
Texas, MacRae flew in a Lockheed trainer. The pilot swerved
into a speed bank that sent MacRae sailing to the back of
the plane. Before he could open the escape door, the pilot
straightened the plane. He later realized had he opened the
door, the jump could have proven fatal as his chute was on
incorrectly. Sheila had gone to New York after Meredith was
born to stay with her mother. She was interested in
astrology and one day had a feeling she needed to fly to the
Carolinas where Gordon was stationed. He was to have flown
to Mitchell Field the next day and been picked up by Sheila.
Since she had flown to meet him, he luckily did not take the
flight, which crashed into a tree killing the men on board.
Another time, Gordon was on a navigational training flight,
when the plane experienced trouble. All had bailed out
except MacRae and the copilot (who panicked). MacRae did
not want to leave him, so he made an emergency landing at
the time of Sheila's premonition.

MacRae remained in the service until his discharge in
October 1945, as a First Lieutenant Navigator in the Air
Force. Sheila wondered if he should stay in the service
for a while longer, but Gordon felt that if he stayed it
would be too late to resume his career.

After his discharge, Gordon went to the network heads
to get his radio job back. At first, they refused because
there were other singers around, and they did not need him.
He informed them that the GI Bill required them to pay
his salary for a year. The MacRaes were advised to devise a
different idea. Sheila thought of an idea based on a show
she did in Texas. She would play Cathy, a girl in love
with Gordon. They took the idea to Wendell Adams at CBS.

Adams phoned Mr. Paley (head of CBS) and Paley instructed
Adams to take them to a studio where he would listen in.
Gordon and Sheila reminded Adams that they only had an idea
and not a script. Adams took them to a studio anyway, and
they had to ad-lib for twenty minutes. After hearing the
MacRaes, Paley told Adams to go ahead and sign them. They
were given a program called GORDON MacRAE-SONGS in 1945 at
$350 a week. On the show Sheila played a grown bobby soxer
providing lead-in dialog for Gordon's songs. The show did
well, and they were moved to a 7 p.m. time slot, given a
professional writer and an audience.

Producer Stanley Gilky wanted Gordon (alone) for THREE
TO MAKE READY. On March 7, 1946, MacRae opened on Broadway
in the Ray Bolger musical. Both the play and Gordon were a
hit. When Nancy Reagan was not on stage in LUTE SONG, she
would go watch Ray Bolger, Arthur Godfrey and MacRae in
THREE TO MAKE READY.

"We were never close friends," Arthur Godfrey recalled,
"but I have always had a great respect for his talent. He
was a very good singer. Later I heard of him now and then
through our agent, Joe Higgins. I've always had high and
warm regards for him and his equally talented family."[3]

In 1946, MacRae hosted a radio show called SKYLINE
ROOF. The MacRae's second child, Heather Allison, was born
on October 5, 1946. Gordon and his family moved into an
apartment on the East Sixties in New York. His mother and
sister remained in Newark, preferring a simpler life.

The year 1947 was a big one for MacRae. He became the
star of radio's TEXACO STAR THEATRE on March 24, 1947, for
CBS, as replacement for singer Tony Martin. In 1948, the
show moved to ABC. Gordon was now earning $400 a week. He
remained with the show until Texaco replaced him with Milton
Berle.

Later that same year, MacRae became master of
ceremonies on NBC's TEENTIMERS CLUB, which greatly increased
his popularity among the teens, and in the summer of 1947,
he starred on CBS's GULFSPRAY, as a summer replacement for
Fanny Brice.

After a mild success on the Musicraft label, Capitol
Records (then a new company) signed MacRae to an exclusive
long-term contract in August 1947. The contract (with
renewals) was to span more than twenty years. His first
recording was a "Fellow Needs a Girl" and "Body and Soul."

"We thought Gordon MacRae was the finest all-around
singer in the business," said a Capitol executive. "He
could sing anything from country western to operatic arias.
And we'd tried him on everything, but we just couldn't get
him on a hit record."[4]

MacRae was not considered a liability by Capitol,
for since that first recording, Gordon had a large and
faithful following. During his recording career, many of
his records were on the music charts, and his duets with Jo
Stafford sold over 5,000,000 copies. His operetta records
were solid sellers, and later, the soundtrack albums of
OKLAHOMA and CAROUSEL would become all-time best-sellers.
While with Capitol, MacRae played on their baseball team
with Nat Cole, Jack Smith, Andy Russell, and Stan Kenton.

Gordon's voice has often been described as virile,

sensitive, powerful, compelling, and as a rich melodious baritone, with a simple straightforward technique. His voice was a mixture of classical and crooner, which enabled him to handle any kind of song, and he had a range of three octaves.

Rudy Vallee, who later worked with him on THE RAILROAD HOUR, said, "I considered him a fine person and the possessor of one of the most glorious singing voices ever."[5]

Gordon, throughout his singing career, believed that it was important to have a good song and sing it simply, with concern and conviction. He once said, "A pop music fan wants music that is listenable or danceable, a tune that tells a story or weaves a mood, and a singer versatile enough to put the message across...if possible, the singer should try to put his or her personality into the song."[6]

When he was in New York, MacRae studied voice with William Brady. One thing he learned from his training was the importance of vocalizing daily.

Music critic and writer, George Simeon assessed Gordon as a "fine performer" and a "good singer."[7]

Gordon's repertoire came from all areas of music: show tunes, operetta, film, television, and the classics. Writer Arthur Jackson said of MacRae, "To my mind one of the finest and most versatile singers of my generation and a very nice man."[8]

Writer Rodger Kinkle summed things up by saying of Gordon, "A top all-around performer, versatile, able to go from pop to musical stage material, including light operatic. On his radio show especially, he displayed his versatile talent. Excellent voice, intonation, diction."[9]

The couple's first son, William Gordon (Gar) was born on February 11, 1948. On March 30, 1948, Gordon appeared on ABC radio on the 1947 ACADEMY AWARDS at the Shrine Auditorium in Los Angeles, where he sang the nominated song "A Gal in Calico." While Gordon was auditioning for the Broadway show LOOK MA I'M DANCING in 1948, Bill Orr, a Warner Brothers executive, heard him singing. Gordon went to Hollywood, where he met Jack Warner. After his screen test, a scene from SERENADE (which he would have liked to film), Warner Brothers signed him to an exclusive seven-year contract. He gave up three Broadway plays, LITTLE SHOW, Rodgers and Hammerstein's ALLEGRO, and the LIFE OF BOBBIE BURNS, when he decided to pursue a movie career.

Gordon stepped before the cameras for the first time in 1948, already with star billing, to film the straight drama THE BIG PUNCH, in which he played a prize fighter opposite Wayne Morris and Lois Maxwell. The film was released in June of that year.

After he signed with Warners, Joan Crawford invited MacRae to a dinner party. At the party were Clark Gable, Dinah Shore, Robert Young, Robert Taylor, George Cukor, Jack Warner, Cesar Romero, Fred Astaire, and Louella Parsons. MacRae, in a rented tuxedo, broke an expensive glass and spilled wine on Louella. All seemed to under-stand that he was in awe of the guests. He was delighted when Joan asked him to sing.

MacRae's recordings and radio appearances helped his popularity grow. The teenager of an advertising executive listened to MacRae on NBC's TEENTIMERS CLUB and spoke excitedly about Gordon one night at dinner. Taking note, her father auditioned and signed MacRae for the RAILROAD HOUR. Some 297 operatic and musical comedies were performed between 1948 and 1954 by MacRae and famous guest stars, first on ABC in a 45-minute format, then on NBC for 30 minutes. Carmen Dragon, who was the musical director for the RAILROAD HOUR, said, "It was a pleasure to work with a singer like Gordon, a real musician...who sight read vocal parts right off the bat. That was one reason why we could present a different operetta each week."[10]

"Working on the RAILROAD HOUR was delightful," said Margaret Truman, who appeared on the show in SARI. "We had a good orchestra, good conductor, plenty of rehearsal. I enjoyed it. Gordon was wonderful on and off the air. He was a very thoughtful man, a real pro....He had a great talent."[11]

Norma Zimmer, who also worked on the RAILROAD HOUR said: "It was a real 'learning' experience! We did all the fine shows with excellent orchestra, directed by Carmen Dragon--choral work by Norman Luboff....Gordon was a professional in the highest meaning, always prepared, vocally perfect, and very serious about his performance ....He was always kind to everyone." She assessed his talent as "Tops!"[12]

During what was considered the Golden Age of Radio, MacRae hosted or appeared on many radio shows. It was for his work in radio that he received a star on the Hollywood Walk of Fame, located on block eleven, at 6325 Hollywood.

Margaret Whiting, who worked with MacRae on such radio shows as CHESTERFIELD SUPPER CLUB, 1948 CHRISTMAS SEAL PARTY, RAILROAD HOUR and a recording of SOUTH PACIFIC, said, "We met at Capitol Records....I loved working with him." He had a "great sense of humor, great warmth, charm and honesty."[13]

Gordon appeared on the BOB HOPE SHOW on radio and would later work with him on television. Bob Hope said that working on the show with him was "Great. He was a pro in all aspects of the word....He worked with me on quite a few radio shows and different benefits around the country....He was on a couple of USO shows--not overseas, but domestic."[14]

The 1948 ACADEMY AWARDS was broadcast on March 24, 1949, from the Academy Theatre in Hollywood. MacRae sang the nominated song "For Every Man There's a Woman."

On August 20, 1949, Jo Stafford and Gordon MacRae's biggest hit together "Whispering Hope" hit the charts and peaked at position four. It remained there for twenty-three weeks.[15] The song was revised and arranged by Stafford's husband, Paul Weston. The song earned a gold record. Their rendition led to the song's inclusion in the repertoire of many singers. Jo Stafford's recollection of working with MacRae on radio and records was "very pleasurable." He was "a real professional on both radio and records." He had "a warm engaging personality, excellent voice and projection of lyrics."

"Stafford and MacRae" were the "most professional and easiest...to work with," Paul Weston recalled. "Both could read music, which certainly helped."[16]

MacRae's second film for Warner Brothers was LOOK FOR THE SILVER LINING, which was released in July 1949. The film was his first musical and co-starred June Haver, who was lent to Warner Brothers from Twentieth Century Fox. The film was about the life and career of follies star Marilyn Miller. According to Motion Picture Herald, Motion Picture Daily, and Film Daily, LOOK FOR THE SILVER LINING was a top grossing film of the 1948-1949 season. It also received an Academy Award nomination for the scoring of a musical picture.

In 1950, Warner Brothers starred MacRae in another non-musical entitled BACKFIRE, in which he searched for a service friend who had disappeared and been framed for murder. With him in the film were Virginia Mayo, Edmond O' Brien, Viveca Lindfors, and Sheila Stephens (Mrs. MacRae). His next assignment, in 1950, was the musical DAUGHTER OF ROSIE O'GRADY. He played restaurateur, Tony Pastor. He was reunited with June Haver, who recalled working on the two films with MacRae as "a very pleasant, professional experience." She said of MacRae: "He was a delight--witty--hardworking, considerate, devoted to his family--easy going." He was a "versatile performer-- likeable and charming." He had "a big voice." Miss Haver said her husband, Fred MacMurray, "liked his voice and thought he was a good performer."[17] Debbie Reynolds had a small part playing June Haver's younger sister.

Next in 1950, MacRae appeared in RETURN OF THE FRONTIERSMAN with Julie London and Rory Calhoun, playing a sheriff's son framed for murder. He sang two songs in the otherwise non-musical, "Underneath a Western Sky" and "Cowboy."

Warner Brothers finally realized that MacRae's forte was in musicals, so they first teamed Gordon and Doris Day in TEA FOR TWO, which was released in September of 1950. Doris played the part of a socialite, who became interested in starring on Broadway and in the show's composer, MacRae. It was based on the popular play and film NO NO NANETTE. The song "I Only Have Eyes For You" was added to the film. Doris Day thought that Gordon was one of the funniest men she knew. Often, he made her laugh and the set had to be closed down until she composed herself. Before starting production on the film, Doris appeared on THE RAILROAD HOUR to do an abbreviated version of NO NO NANETTE. According to the Motion Picture Herald, Motion Picture Daily, and Film Daily, TEA FOR TWO was a top grossing film of the 1949-1950 season. In the film was a long-time friend of MacRae, Gene Nelson. Also in the cast were Eve Arden, Billy DeWolfe, and S.Z. Sakall.

Pleased with the MacRae-Day team, Warner Brothers co-starred them again in the 1950 musical WEST POINT STORY, which also starred James Cagney, Gene Nelson, Virginia Mayo, and Alan Hale, Jr. Cagney played a Broadway director who had problems when he went to West Point to

put together their annual show. The film was released in
November of that year.
    James Cagney recalled working with MacRae: "My
acquaintance with him was purely professional. He could
sing beautifully, and he knew it, which of course one had
to....Working at Warners was just work, as were the other
jobs....I never got to know Gordon well, but what I did
know was all to the good. He knew his way about the studio
and could do what he had to do rather well."[18]
    MacRae's initial night club engagement was at the El
Rancho Vegas in late 1950. He was one of the first singers
to incorporate imitations into his act. He was to become
one of the top night club acts, playing all the top clubs,
both as a single, and later teamed with wife, Sheila. He
would later break attendance records at places like Disney
World in Florida.
    Phyllis Diller, who worked with Gordon at the
Desert Inn in November 1972, said, "I always enjoyed working
with Gordon. He was what we call 'easy', no sweat, all
those dumb ways we put it. He was a gentleman. He was a
very warm person and that quality showed in his work....He
had staying power in that he had been in the business for
years and had maintained popularity."[19]
    "I think he had a great audience appeal," said Rose
Marie. "And as far as talent, he was just about the best
singer around. No one sang the "Soliloquy" from CAROUSEL
like he did! I just thoroughly enjoyed him and his
talent."[20]
    Also that same year, MacRae was voted "Father of the
Year" by members of the Music Trade Association, an
organization that represented more than 10,000 music
dealers throughout the nation.
    During the early years of his film career, the MacRaes
purchased their first home, small but quite adequate, in
the Toluca Lake District of Hollywood.
    During his busy period at Warner Brothers, Gordon
needed someone to look after his finances, so when Marty
Melcher (Doris Day's husband) approached him about handling
his investments, along with a lawyer, Jerome Rosenthall,
MacRae agreed to become their client, as had other
celebrities. Investments were made, on paper, in oil wells
and federal land-grant bonds, for which interest deductions
were made from his income tax. Years later, the IRS
disallowed these deductions, forcing Gordon to pay $480,000
in back taxes, thus wiping out a lifetime of savings.
    MacRae made a film short in 1951 called THE SCREEN
DIRECTOR. His next feature film also was in 1951, the
musical ON MOONLIGHT BAY, based on Booth Tarkington's PENROD
stories. Day played a tomboy and MacRae an Indiana college
student. Billy Gray, Rosemary DeCamp, Leon Ames, and Mary
Wicks were also in the cast. The film, released in
July 1951, was a top grosser according to <u>Motion Picture
Herald</u>, <u>Motion Picture Daily</u>, and <u>Film Daily</u>. For a
wedding present, Gordon recorded a special album of love
songs for Doris Day and Marty Melcher, carrying out the
theme, one old, new, borrowed and blue. He broke the
master disk so the married couple would have the only copy.
    Next in 1951, Gordon wanted to do the film I'LL SEE

YOU IN MY DREAMS, but the part went to Danny Thomas.   He became TV & Screen Guide's first-place male star in September 1951 as well as seventh-place male newcomer.   The film WEST POINT STORY was awarded first place for best recent picture.   Gordon made another film that year (released in December) called STARLIFT with Doris Day and most of the studio's contract players.   The film took place at Travis Air Base, where stars entertained soldiers returning from, or leaving for Korea.

MacRae wanted to work with Lucille Norman.   Mention was made of their doing a remake of VIENNESE NIGHTS but nothing ever developed.   He was the only celebrity who regularly kept in touch with Lucille after her retirement.

Another film short made in 1952 was entitled SCREEN SNAPSHOTS NO. 205.   MacRae's next film was to be APRIL IN PARIS, but he did not receive the part.   He only made one feature film that year (released in May), the musical re-make of BROTHER RAT called ABOUT FACE.   Also in the film were Eddie Bracken and a newcomer, Joel Grey.   After com-pletion of ABOUT FACE, MacRae and some of his studio friends went to Lake Mead (behind Boulder Dam) to fish.   The motor in their rented boat stopped, forcing them to jump overboard to avoid drifting over the roaring rapids.   Some of the older men couldn't get back to shore by themselves.   MacRae got everybody back into the boat and after a wild ride they got to shore safely.

Helen MacRae Osborne (Gordon's mother had married Philip Osborne) became ill on Friday night and died suddenly the next day, July 6, 1952, before Gordon could fly in from California.

MacRae was voted one of Movie Life's top ten stars of 1952.   Louella Parsons characterized MacRae as "one of the soundest, sanest, and most talented young men in town."[21]

Around 1953, Gordon was earning about $250,000 a year, so the MacRaes moved into a $70,000 mansion at 3301 Oakdale N. Hollywood in the San Fernando valley.   It was a lovely colonial farmhouse, built in 1941 by Andrew Loomis, and sat on two wooded acres with a pool and separate studio. Gordon's grandfather, Albert H. Sonn, wrote a three-volume book entitled Early American Wrought Iron, which interested Gordon and Sheila in collecting antiques.   Their home became filled with various antiques they purchased on their travels as well as some fine reproductions actor George Montgomery made for them.

Gordon loved to swim in his pool every morning before breakfast regardless of the time of year.   The MacRaes had wanted a home convenient to Gordon's work but in an area that provided an atmosphere that would enable their children to have a normal childhood.   Their San Fernando valley home provided this.   Meredith and Heather did not like being in their parents limelight and once when Gordon and Sheila were appearing at the Fountainbleau Hotel in Miami, they hid on the floor of the limousine sent to bring them to the hotel because people were staring at them.   Gordon was the disciplinarian and his powerful singing voice projected loudly, causing the children to listen.   Meredith only remembered being spanked when, as a little girl, she turned on the gas jets.   Gordon and Sheila planned vacations and

club dates around their children. Sheila was active with
the Girl Scouts and the PTA. Their home atmosphere was such
that the MacRae children felt comfortable bringing their
friends home. Frequently a friend would spend the weekend.
When Sheila did travel with Gordon, Meredith (being the
oldest) would take on some of the responsibilities of running the home, which made her close to her brothers and
sister. Many of the special occasions and holidays are now
spent at Meredith's home.

MacRae made still another film short in 1953 entitled
SO YOU WANT A TELEVISION SET, and his first feature film,
that year, was the musical BY THE LIGHT OF THE SILVERY MOON
released in May 1953. It also was based on the PENROD
stories and was a sequel to the 1951 MacRae-Day film ON
MOONLIGHT BAY, again with the same cast. These two films
were two of Doris Day's all-time favorites. She thought
they were fun to make, and she loved the nostalgia. She
could not wait to arrive on the set. The cast was as close
as a real family. Meredith MacRae and Merv Griffin appeared
in crowd scenes. MacRae released a 10-inch album in 1953,
containing the songs from the film.

Gordon and Sheila did not believe in spoiling their
children. As a child, Meredith had seen a doll she wanted
badly. As it was not her birthday or Christmas, Gordon and
Sheila said that if she wanted it, she would have to earn
the money, even though they could have afforded to buy it
for her. Meredith earned the money doing chores around the
house and finally was able to pay for the doll, giving her
a greater appreciation for it. As an occasional treat,
Meredith was allowed to appear in some of Gordon's films as
an extra.

The MacRae-Day films (five in all) each grossed over $4
million. While at Warner Brothers, Gordon's fan mail was
second only to that of his co-star. Doris would make up
names for herself and her co-stars. She was either called
Clara Bixby or Do-Do, and she called Gordon, Norbert Kunkel.

Danny Thomas stopped by the set of BY THE LIGHT OF THE
SILVERY MOON during filming. He remembered meeting Gordon
and Sheila in 1950 and doing benefits with Gordon as well
as socializing with him. Recalling the Warner period, Mr.
Thomas said that Gordon was "a great guy--friendly, a hard-
working actor, and a good one! Gordon had a great voice--
perfect pitch--good sense of humor." In reference to Gordon
and Sheila's work in night clubs, which came later, he
said, "The team was great."[22]

Next in 1953, Warner Brothers cast him in the third
film version of the Romberg and Hammerstein operetta THE
DESERT SONG, which was released in May of 1953. The first
version was in 1929, with John Boles, and the second in
1943, with Dennis Morgan. MacRae had seen DESERT SONG as a
child and had wanted to play the Red Shadow one day. The
name Red Shadow was changed in the 1953 film, because of
the controversy surrounding the McCarthy Era. MGM loaned
Kathryn Grayson to Warner Brothers to play his romantic
lead. The desert scenes were filmed near Yuma, Arizona,
where the temperatures soared to 120 degrees.

"Making the film was fun," recalled Kathryn Grayson.
"Gordon was one of the most pleasant, cooperative artists,

with whom I ever worked. Never a show of temper...Gordon
was always courteous and kind....There were locations that
were hot and uncomfortable, but he never complained." He
was "an all around nice person....Gordon had a voice of
beautiful quality."[23]

Gordon marked his first television appearance, when he
substituted for Eddie Fisher on TUNE TIME on May 20, 1953,
for NBC-TV. He would also substitute for Jackie Gleason,
Perry Como, and Ed Sullivan on their shows. This marked
the beginning of many television appearances.

Edie Adams, who appeared on TV with MacRae (May, 1969)
on MATCH GAME, said they met around 1957 and became friends
as a result of Gordon and Sheila and Edie and Ernie Kovacs
following each other into engagements at Lake Tahoe. She
described MacRae: "He was talented, warm, the sweetest man,
a pussycat. He was a wonderful performer, actor, singer, a
teddy bear." She said that her husband Ernie Kovacs "loved
Gordon's talent and thought a lot of his great baritone."[24]

Philip Osborne (who had married MacRae's mother) was 71
when he died on August 27, 1953, in Atlanta. Philip resided
at his son Jasper's home. He was originally from Spring
Lake, New Jersey, where he had retired as a commercial
banker.

MacRae's last film for Warner Brothers was the musical
THREE SAILORS AND A GIRL released in December of 1953. MGM
loaned Jane Powell to Warner Brothers. Others in the cast
included Gene Nelson, Jack E. Leonard, and Sam Levene.
Burt Lancaster made a cameo appearance. A 10-inch album,
based on the film, was released in 1953 by Capitol Records.

Sam Levene recalled, "I remember them both, Miss
Powell and Mr. MacRae were talented and pleasant....He was
an excellent actor and very professional."[25]

In addition to the film, Jane Powell worked with
MacRae on the RAILROAD HOUR and in concerts. Jane Powell
recalled, "It was a joy" working on the film. As far as
the RAILROAD HOUR and concerts were concerned, she said of
each, "It was a nice job," and it was "nice to be with
Gordon. He was quite professional, that was why he was
still in demand."[26] According to her autobiography The
Girl Next Door...and How She Grew (1988), she had quite a
fondness for MacRae and the boyish quality he seemed to have
about him. She always found him to be quite charming.
After his death, she found herself missing him.

While in Hollywood, he received six offers to do a
Broadway musical, among them, GUYS AND DOLLS, KISS ME KATE,
and MARCO POLO, but his movie and radio work prevented him
from accepting any of the offers.

Gordon loved to play golf. Whenever he got a chance,
he would go to the Lakeside Country Club, where he was
ranked in the top five (shot 18 holes in 68) celebrity
golfers. He played with such friends as Bing Crosby
(MacRae's idol), Dean Martin, Phil Harris, Jeff Chandler,
Bob Hope, Forrest Tucker, and golf pros Ed Dudley and Harry
Cooper, among others.

"We played golf a lot of times," Bob Hope recalled.
"And he was one of the best golfers in show business. He
played in our tournaments many times."

Other friends of the family included Bill and Joy Orr

(Jack Warner's daughter), Gene and Miriam Nelson, Jo
Stafford and her husband, Paul Weston, Peter Lind Hayes and
Mary Healy, Lucille Ball and Dezi Arnaz (and later Gary
Morton), and Doris Day and her husband, Marty Melcher.
      Gordon and the family often vacationed at Lake Tahoe,
Lake Arrowhead or in Palm Springs, where they enjoyed
sailing, fishing, swimming, golfing, horseback riding and
water skiing. Occasionally, when Gordon and Sheila were in
New York, they would revisit places where they had gone
while courting or when they were first married, such as the
Blue Spruce Inn, Jones Beach, and a favorite bistro,
Epicure. These places were a reminder of the times when
Gordon was only earning $65 a week and his brother-in-law,
Duncan Van Cleef II, worked out their budget.
      Gordon enjoyed making private recordings at home for
his family, including one of Sheila's favorites, "Brahms
Lullaby" and one of their favorites, "Now We Know." The
family spent many Sunday evenings in song, around the piano,
as Gordon had done as a boy.
      Around 1954 Warner Brothers began to ease their
television restrictions. Up to then, they had a clause in
most of their stars' contracts, not permitting them to make
television appearances. It was this restriction in
Gordon's contract that prevented him from hosting a
television version of his radio show, THE RAILROAD HOUR.
The sponsors of the show made surveys and found that it
would be best to wait two years to televise the show.
Plans never materialized. Shortly afterward, Warner relaxed
its ban on television. On March 28, 1954, Gordon made a
guest appearance on CBS's GENERAL FOODS 25th ANNIVERSARY
SHOW saluting Rodgers and Hammerstein. The show was also
carried on all four networks.
      Celeste Holm's recollection of the show was that
"these broadcasts were done live, we rehearsed our numbers
separately....He behaved professionally, in that he knew
his songs, was responsive and responsible to the show as a
whole....He was a pleasant man with a lovely voice!"[27]
      Mary Martin also appeared on the show. "I certainly
have the most pleasant memories of working with him way
back there. I so admired his talent and his voice."[28]
      The MacRae's second son, Robert Bruce, was born on
April 6, 1954, at St. Joseph's Hospital. Bruce, who
weighed 10 pounds, 2½ ounces, was delivered by Dr. Abner
Moss. In May 1954, Gordon was at a food festival in
Youngstown, Ohio. For their anniversary, Sheila joined him
and they went to the church where they had been married to
listen to the bells at noon. At the church, they visited
with Rev. Dr. Herman Klahr, who had performed their
marriage ceremony. Also that year, Gordon and Sheila were
interviewed, for television, at the premiere of A STAR IS
BORN starring Judy Garland.
      Gordon felt he was stagnating at Warner Brothers and
wanted to cancel his contract. There were rumors that he
and Doris Day were feuding about not wanting to be paired
again in LUCKY ME. All of this helped facilitate his
release from a $3000 a week contract in the summer of 1954.
MacRae, with no immediate job prospects, believed that the
future would take care of itself. "What counts is that

what you're doing, you're doing well," he said, and that "you're happy in what you're doing, and it's not a chore."[29] Gordon always believed at looking ahead to the future and not back on past achievements.

It took twelve years for OKLAHOMA to reach the screen. One reason it took so long was the numerous revivals. Learning that Mike Todd was planning to use his Todd-AO process, for the first time, in the film OKLAHOMA, Gordon went about learning all the songs as well as shedding some weight. He even learned to ride and rope. He knew he had to convince Rodgers and Hammerstein that he was right for the role, but the competition would be heavy, as much of Hollywood was auditioning. Among those being considered were Paul Newman (Curly), Joanne Woodward (Laurey), Eli Wallach (Jud), and Howard Keel (Curly). Director Fred Zinneman wanted James Dean to play the lead, but Rodgers and Hammerstein vetoed the idea. Charlotte Greenwood, who had to turn down the part of Aunt Eller in the Broadway show, was able to accept the part in the film. Elsa Schreiber, a director and acting coach, helped MacRae prepare for his screen test, while her husband, George Zhdanov, prepared Robert Stack for his.

Gordon had a screen test with Shirley Jones on February 24, 1954. "When I first met him so many years ago," Miss Jones recalled, "I thought him a bit egotistic...till I got to know him."[30]

He watched the news and gossip columns for word of a decision on the role. Eventually, one did appear, saying he would sign to play Curly after he got back from a fishing trip. Jan Clayton was off camera with Oscar Hammerstein, as they watched MacRae perform on the GENERAL FOODS SHOW. She wanted to know if MacRae had been cast as Curly, and if so, why had they not told him. Hammerstein told her they wanted Gordon to lose some weight first. Two things in his favor were that Capitol Records had bought the soundtrack rights for OKLAHOMA and that the studio loved his voice.

Filming began on July 7, 1954, with a budget of $6 million. The cast rehearsed on mock sets for seven weeks at MGM. Then they moved to the San Rafael valley to the Greene Cattle Company Ranch (thirty-six miles northeast of San Nogales, Arizona) for exterior filming. Fewer signs of commercial development were evident than in sites in Oklahoma. During production, MacRae received two permanents and his hair was curled by hot irons. It rained frequently during shooting. The studio grew portable thirteen-foot stalks of corn and moved them about to needed locations. They brought in the cattle from California and even trans-planted a peach orchard.

"He was especially gracious, especially considerate, and especially professional," recalled co-star Shirley Jones. "His glorious voice was just topping on the cake--along with his handsome face!" She rated his talent as "Tops!...Screen tests were agonizing and terrible, rehearsals were needed and reassuring, filming was satisfying."

OKLAHOMA became one of Gordon's biggest films, giving a boost to his career, which resulted in his becoming an

honorary citizen of Oklahoma at ceremonies, filmed for
television, at the Hollywood Bowl. After filming for
OKLAHOMA was completed, Gordon and Sheila vacationed in
Mexico.

     In 1954, Gordon was signed by the Ted Bates Company to
host his first television series, the COLGATE COMEDY HOUR
for NBC, who wanted a show to put up against the stronger-
rated ED SULLIVAN SHOW. The show did well but was unable to
draw stronger ratings than Sullivan. MacRae received an
Emmy nomination in 1954, as best male singer on television.
His competition that year included Perry Como, Eddie Fisher,
Frankie Laine, and Tony Martin. The honors went to Perry
Como.

     MacRae recorded the theme song, "Jim Bowie" for the
1955 Republic film THE LAST COMMAND. Gordon wanted to star
in another Rodgers and Hammerstein classic, CAROUSEL and
began vigorously campaigning for the lead by bombarding
Daryl Zanick with telegrams. He even let his hair and
sideburns grow. He opened in CAROUSEL on July 13, 1955,
at the State Fair Music Hall in Dallas, Texas for a three-
week engagement. Doris Day's agent called, saying she was
interested in doing CAROUSEL. However, her film YOUNG AT
HEART, with Sinatra, was not doing well. Sid Luft said
Judy Garland was also interested but wanted the song,
"Soliloquy" turned into a duet. Frank Sinatra, however, was
signed to the Billy Bigelow role opposite Shirley Jones.

     "I wanted the part of Billy Bigelow," MacRae said.
"Frank Sinatra got it. But I still didn't give up. I had
a funny premonition something might happen."[31]

     When Sinatra learned that CAROUSEL would be filmed in
two processes, Cinemascope and Todd-AO, he left the picture.
He felt that if they were going to film in two processes,
they were actually making two films and he should be paid
accordingly. Ironically, after Sinatra's departure from the
project, Fox decided to film in one process, Cinemascope.
"Mr. Sinatra left over some creative disagreement with the
executives regarding the music," Miss Jones recalled.
"And we were all sorry to see him leave."

     The studio brought a breech of contract against
Sinatra, but it was later dropped. A new Billy Bigelow was
needed. Howard Keel was still under contract at MGM.
Gene Kelly was interested but refused to have his voice
dubbed. MacRae received a phone call from Oscar Hammerstein, who told him that Sinatra had left the film and that
if he wanted it, the part was his. Gordon readily accepted.
He would earn $150,000 for ten weeks of work.

     After being released from an engagement at Lake Tahoe,
MacRae reported to Twentieth Century Fox for some
pre-recording sessions, then was flown to Booth Bay, Maine
for on-location filming. Producer, Henry Ephron had given
Gordon his role in JUNIOR MISS, when the young man playing
the part was drafted. Henry was not sure MacRae was right
for the part, as he was considered the all-American boy.
But when rehearsals began, Ephron became confident he had
made the right choice. The song, "A Real Nice Clambake"
had originally been in OKLAHOMA as a hay ride, but was
dropped from the show and added to the score of CAROUSEL.
During the filming of CAROUSEL, Governor Edmund Muskie

visited the Booth Bay set. The company remained on location for three weeks, at a cost of $4,000,000. Bad weather cut short the filming in Maine. The company returned to the West Coast, where the "Soliloquy" sequence was shot at Zoma Beach, a craggy place beyond Malibu. When Academy Awards time occurred, Twentieth Century Fox did not want to split their votes between CAROUSEL and THE KING AND I, so they ignored CAROUSEL and supported THE KING AND I in the Academy Awards race.

OKLAHOMA'S world premiere was in New York on October 11, 1955, at the Rivoli Theatre where it played until its national release in December. The premiere ceremonies included the governor of Oklahoma (Raymond Gary) riding a white horse down the streets of New York.

"Everyone pretty much knows that he was one of America's most talented singers. He had a very strong voice. He was wonderful," actor Dennis Weaver said. "No one will ever forget that wonderful voice rising above the cornfields in OKLAHOMA singing "Oh What a Beautiful Morning."[32]

OKLAHOMA won two Academy Awards in 1955, one for best scoring of a musical and the other for best sound recording. It also had been nominated for best cinematography and film editing. OKLAHOMA became the all-time (No. 142) Top Domestic Box Office Grosser, earning $7,100,000.

On September 17, 1956, the soundtrack album of OKLAHOMA was in the number one position on the music charts and remained on the charts for 305 weeks.[33]

MacRae's name was in the headlines of the <u>Los Angeles Times</u> on December 14, 1955, when he was arrested for drunk driving. He appeared with his attorney, Samuel Norton, before Municipal Judge, Julian Beck. This marked the beginning of his long battle with alcohol that would last until 1978. During the many months of filming OKLAHOMA and CAROUSEL, MacRae successfully hid his problem from co-star Shirley Jones and others, not letting it interfere with his work.

MacRae was again voted one of <u>Movie Life's</u> top ten stars of 1955. Gordon was honored again by being nominated for another Emmy in 1955, for best male singer on television. His competition this time was Harry Belefonte, Eddie Fisher, Perry Como, and Frank Sinatra. Once again, Perry Como took the honors.

CAROUSEL premiered on February 16, 1956, at the Roxy, and became one of that year's top grossing films. That same month, on February 25, 1956, the soundtrack of CAROUSEL was on the music charts and climbed to the number two position and remained on the charts for fifty-nine weeks.

Sheila came out of retirement in March 1956 and with Gordon formed Kintail Enterprises, which produced the GORDON MacRAE SHOW for NBC. Sheila made appearances on, helped write MacRae's material for, and assisted in the production of the show. The 15-minute show, which was followed by network news, had a duplicate of MacRae's livingroom with a window overlooking a scene suitable for his songs. The show was sponsored by Lever Brothers and featured vocalists, The Cheerleaders and the Van Alexander Orchestra.

MacRae's next assignment was again for Twentieth

Century Fox, in the production of THE BEST THINGS IN LIFE
ARE FREE, which was released in September of 1956. It was
the biography of the song writing team of DeSylva, Brown,
and Henderson, who were popular on Broadway in the 1920s.
MacRae played Buddy DeSylva, Dan Dailey played Ray
Henderson, and Ernest Borgnine was Lew Brown.
     "Everything went as smooth as glass," recalled Ernest
Borgnine. I "had the time of my life--dancing and singing."
In working with MacRae, Mr. Borgnine said that it was
"marvelous" and that he was "a great guy." Mr Borgnine
assessed Gordon's talent, "In the Navy it would be termed
4.0--perfect."[34]
     THE BEST THINGS IN LIFE ARE FREE received an Academy
Award nomination for the scoring of a musical picture, and
MacRae recorded the songs from the film on an album for
Capitol Records. The film as well as MacRae were good, but
unfortunately musicals were beginning to hit a period of
decline. THE BEST THINGS IN LIFE ARE FREE became MacRae's
last film for more than twenty years. It had been suggested
by some critics that Gordon might have done well in light
comedy. MacRae had been offered a long-term picture
contract by producer Buddy Alder, but TV seemed to be the
place to be, so he turned to the small screen.
     Author, Michael Pitts said that, "In my opinion, Gordon
MacRae was an extremely talented gentleman, with a
super-fine voice and good acting abilities. He starred in
some very fine and successful films and has contributed
much through his recordings. I would rank him high on the
scale of success in show business."[35]
     In September of 1956, Gordon appeared on Custom Tailor
Guild's list of America's Ten Best Dressed Men, and the
following month, on October 6, 1956, he appeared with
Shirley Jones and other top named stars on CBS's 90-minute
salute to Cole Porter entitled FORD STAR JUBILEE'S-YOU'RE
THE TOP.
     Gordon had been offered the role of Jeff in the
Broadway production of BELLS ARE RINGING but was unable to
come to terms, so in October, MacRae became host and
occasionally appeared in his third television series, LUX
VIDEO THEATRE for NBC.
     Phil Harris, who appeared with MacRae on LUX VIDEO
THEATRE, said that Gordon was a "very good friend." I
"played a lot of golf with him....Gordon had a lot of
talent and knew how to use it."[36] Gordon had an
opportunity to make his opera debut with Dorothy Kirsten in
Bernard Herrman's opera version of WUTHERING HEIGHTS, with
Leopold Stokowski conducting, but turned it down as it did
not pay as well as films, television, or night clubs. Even
though he had trained for and would have loved the chance,
he had to consider the large family he had to support.
     At Lucille Ball's suggestion, Sheila began touring
full-time in Gordon's club act in 1957. Sheila had felt
that mothers with small children should stay at home, so
she waited until the children were older before returning to
work full-time. She had even turned down a television part
in order to attend Meredith's graduation. The couple
developed one of the most successful husband and wife teams
in show business. Sheila wrote much of the material and

handled the comedy end, while Gordon handled the songs.
Both became quite good at impressions, which included
Sheila's Zsa Zsa Gabor, Barbara Streisand, and Dinah Shore,
as well as Gordon's Arthur Godfrey, Perry Como, and Frank
Fontaine's Crazy Guggenheim, among others. Sheila's full-
time inclusion in Gordon's act resulted from her sitting
ringside at a Cocoanut Grove show in August 1957, where
Gordon, in what appeared an unscheduled interruption in his
act, indulged in a playful exchange with Sheila. During
Gordon and Sheila's first appearance in Las Vegas (1953),
their children joined them for the early show. Meredith
sang, "Carry Me Back to Old Virginny" and Heather and Gar
sang, "How Much is That Doggie in the Window." Gordon and
Sheila appeared at the Broadmoor Hotel in Colorado Springs
(1954), where Sammy Cahn arranged songs from Gordon's films,
with Sheila playing MacRae's various partners.
     Gordon bought the rights to the drama MEANS TO AN END
to be produced by his company Kintail Enterprises with him
starring as a district attorney. He also made an unsold
television pilot entitled NO PLACE LIKE HOME. It was to
feature Gordon and Sheila in a domestic comedy about a show
business couple.
     On July 8, 1958, the soundtrack of OKLAHOMA earned a
gold record. Gordon performed his hit single "The Secret"
on the DICK CLARK SATURDAY NIGHT BEECHNUT SHOW after phoning
Clark and asking him if he could appear on the show, as it
was one of Meredith's favorites.
     "He was a wonderful man," recalled Dick Clark. "And I
enjoyed meeting him."[37]
     The television show BAT MASTERSON made its debut in
October 1958. Later during its run, when NBC and Gene
Barry were having some problems, the network considered
MacRae as a possible replacement for Mr. Barry. Also, that
same month, 77 SUNSET STRIP marked its television debut.
Gordon had been considered for a role on the ABC show but
felt he should stay with singing. He later realized that in
order to stay on top, he needed to diversify his talents.
On December 9, 1958, Gordon starred on the CBS special THE
GIFT OF THE MAGI with Sally Ann Howes, Howard St. John, and
Bibi Osterwald, playing the part of James Dillingham Young.
     Gordon and Sheila toured in the musical REDHEAD in
1959, and in April 1960, Gordon and Sheila released their
only album together entitled OUR LOVE STORY. Also, that
same year, the MacRae family toured in the musical ANNIE GET
YOUR GUN.
     The soundtrack of CAROUSEL became Gordon's third gold
record on July 15, 1964. Also that month, the MacRaes
toured in the musical BELLS ARE RINGING at Melodyland and
the Valley Music Theatre.
     On February 25, 1965, Meredith married Richard Berger
(a CPA), whom she had met at UCLA. The couple had a large
wedding. Freddy Martin and his orchestra provided the
music. As Meredith walked down the isle, Gordon sang to
her "The Lord's Prayer" and "Ich Liebe Dich." Reverend
Samuel Allison performed the ceremony. Heather was maid of
honor and Paul Block was best man. The couple honeymooned
in Carmel, San Francisco, and resided in Studio City.
Gordon and Sheila felt that Meredith and Richard were too

young, and that Meredith had only dated a few young men
before she had met Richard.   Among her dates were Doris
Day's son, Terry Melcher, and actors Bill Bixby and Tim
Considine.   In the summer of 1965, the MacRaes fulfilled
their engagement at the Nugget in Sparks, Nevada on July
23, 1965.   Gordon and Sheila continued their television and
night club work until Sheila took a role in GUYS AND DOLLS
in 1965, then later joined CBS's THE JACKIE GLEASON SHOW,
playing Alice Kramden in the Honeymooner sketches.   MacRae
continued the night club and television circuit as a
single.
     "Both Sheila MacRae and Gordon MacRae were talented
and wonderful people!" remembered Jackie Gleason.   "They
were both very popular with audiences, both young and
old...deservedly so!"[38]
     The JACKIE GLEASON SHOW was used as a stepping stone
by Sheila to separate from Gordon.   Sheila felt that she
could make the move now, as the children were pretty much
on their own or at least old enough to understand.
Meredith was married, Bruce was away in boarding school in
New York, Gar was attending the University of Miami, and
Heather was at the Colorado Womans College in Denver, where
she stayed for two years before dropping out to pursue a
Broadway career.   Sheila flew to California to close their
home there.   Many had hopes of a reconciliation.   However,
the film capital and fans were shocked when Sheila flew to
Juarez, Mexico to obtain a divorce from Gordon, on April
17, 1967, on the grounds of incompatibility of character,
thus ending their twenty-five years of marriage.   Factors
contributing to the divorce included MacRae's drinking
problem, his gambling, and the back taxes owed on the
investments declared taxable by the IRS.   The divorce was a
friendly one.   Sheila attended Gordon's opening at the
Waldorf Astoria on April 26, 1967.   They also did a benefit
for Israel at Madison Square Garden.   They both attended
daughter, Heather's Broadway opening of WHERE I BELONG.
     Meredith was not only saddened by the divorce of her
parents, but shortly after divorced her husband, Richard
Berger.   She went on to join the cast of MY THREE SONS in
its fifth season.   She played Sally, the fiancée of Fred
MacMurray's oldest son, Mike, played by Tim Considine.
Meredith later went on to play Billie Jo on Paul Henning's
PETTICOAT JUNCTION.
     June Haver said that her husband, Fred MacMurray,
"Tells me she was a fine actress, a pro," and that "he
enjoyed working with her."
     After divorcing Gordon, Sheila married Ron Wayne, who
was the producer of THE JACKIE GLEASON SHOW, in August
1967, at her Sutton Place house in Manhattan.   Gordon
phoned Sheila the morning of her wedding to wish her well.
The couple were introduced by Marge and Irving Cowan.   All
of the children attended the wedding.   Sheila and Ron would
later be divorced.
     Gordon was living in his Sutton Place townhouse in New
York, where he met a former boyfriend of Elizabeth Lambert
Schrafft.   Knowing that Gordon was available, he suggested
Gordon meet Liz.   After trying to reach her several times,
he finally made a date on June 15, 1967, about 100 days

before they would be married. In August of 1967, Elizabeth
divorced motel and candy czar, George Schrafft in Palm
Beach, Florida on grounds of extreme cruelty. Gordon and
Elizabeth applied for a marriage license in July of 1967,
and were wed on September 25, 1967, at St. Peter's Lutheran
Church in Manhattan. More than 1000 fans tried to come to
the wedding. Toots Shor was his best man and social figure,
Mrs William Smoper was Elizabeth's matron of honor. Among
the guests at their El Morocco reception were his children
and Lyndon Johnson's sister. Gordon and Elizabeth preferred
to stay home for an evening of television, whereas Sheila
and Ron enjoyed the night life.
     MacRae went on tour in OKLAHOMA, appearing at such
places as the Valley Forge Music Fair in Devon,
Pennsylvania in August 1967. The theatre was part of a
chain owned by Lee Guber and Shelly Gross.
     When the tour ended, Gordon went to Broadway to do
I DO! I DO! with Carol Lawrence. They began working their
way into the show (October 18, 1967) doing matinee
performances. Then on December 4, 1967, they replaced
Robert Preston and Mary Martin, who went on tour with the
show.
     "Our professional paths had not crossed," Mary Martin
remembered, "except when he and Carol Lawrence followed
Bob and me on Broadway in I DO! I DO! And I regret I did
not get to see them in it. But he certainly had continued
his talented career, and of course, he was a charmer."
     Gordon MacRae and Carol Lawrence performed an
abbreviated version of the show for Lynda Bird Johnson at
her wedding eve dinner as well as a dinner honoring
Vice-President Humphrey and Supreme Court Justice, Earl
Warren. They also appeared on the ED SULLIVAN SHOW on
August 4, 1968, to perform excerpts from I DO! I DO!
     During the run of the Broadway show in 1968, Amanda
Mercedes MacRae was born to Gordon and Elizabeth. Gordon
felt like a new man, promising to put his drinking problem
behind him. He showered Amanda with gifts. He mentioned,
in later years, that he was glad he had had more time to
spend with Amanda while she was growing up then he had had
with his other children. The run of I DO! I DO! was cut
short, in 1968, because of an Actor's Equity strike. The
show had run 560 performances. MacRae had always hoped that
he and co-star, Carol Lawrence would get to do a film
version of I DO! I DO! but that dream never materialized.
     Gordon co-hosted the MIKE DOUGLAS SHOW in Philadelphia
for the week, beginning September 3, 1968. His wife,
Elizabeth was a guest on the show with many top-named
stars.
     We "met...when he flew to Cleveland to do the show,"
recalled Mike Douglas. "He had always been very
professional and a real gentleman. We had all enjoyed
working with him....The ladies in the audience loved
him."[39]
     He was honored, that year, when he became recipient of
the Star of the Season Award from the March of Dimes.
     In 1969, MacRae released his last album under his
Capitol contract entitled ONLY LOVE, which he promoted on
the JOEY BISHOP SHOW. Meredith met actor Greg Mullavey

whose father, Greg, Sr., was a scout for the Dodger Baseball
Organization, at Esalen Institute at Big Sur. The institute
was a school that taught couples how to fight. Meredith and
Greg won an award as the couple most likely to succeed.
Meredith and Greg were married at the Pacific Palisades on
April 19, 1969. Brother Turyananda performed the ceremony.
Nancy Thatcher (Meredith's roommate) was matron of honor and
Greg's brother, Terry, was best man.

Bob Newhart, who appeared with Gordon on THE DEAN
MARTIN SHOW on May 15, 1969, recalled that "Gordon and I
went back as friends for a long time....During rehearsals
there was always a lot of joking and of course, golf
talk....Gordon had always been a consummate professional,
always on time, always prepared, a perfectionist. We had a
saying--'You can't fool the camera'! Gordon was a nice
considerate man and that came through to the audience."[40]

Gordon made a syndicated special for Screen Gems called
the GORDON MacRAE SHOW, which aired on June 21, 1969, with
guests Barbara McNair and Rich Little. The following month
on July 14, 1969, MacRae, Alisha Kashi, and Scott Jacoby
toured in the musical GOLDEN RAINBOW at such places as the
Valley Forge Music Fair in Devon, Pennsylvania. MacRae
ended the year by being a guest on GUY LOMBARDO'S NEW YEAR'S
EVE PARTY at the Waldorf Astoria.

William Gordon MacRae married Megan Handschumacker in
1970. The ceremonies took place at St. Albans Episcopal
Church in Westwood, New York. Megan's twin sister, Karen,
was maid of honor and John Peterson was best man. Megan's
father, Albert G. Handschumacker, was President of Aeronco
Inc., which was an aerospace firm. Her mother, Ann Meritt
Handschumacker, was from Pasadena. Gordon, Jr. and his
wife, Megan, would make Gordon and Sheila grandparents with
sons Zachariah (Zak), Joshua, and Jeremy.

MacRae performed in a live concert entitled A
CELEBRATION OF RICHARD RODGERS at New York's Imperial
Theatre, on March 26, 1972, and toured with Molly Picon in
MILK AND HONEY on January 4, 1973.

On May 30, 1974, Gordon appeared with other top stars
on the CBS special GRAMMY SALUTES OSCAR, hosted by Gene
Kelly. Gene Kelly and MacRae first met on THE RAILROAD
HOUR, when Kelly appeared on the show in THE RED MILL on
January 10, 1949. Mr. Kelly recalled working on the shows
as "lots of fun." His recollection of working with Gordon
was that he was "good to work with--very professional." He
assessed MacRae's talent and audience appeal as
"excellent!"[41]

A change of pace assignment for MacRae was the
dramatic appearance, on September 22, 1974, as murderer,
Sheriff Rodney on the NBC series McCLOUD in the episode,
"Barefoot Girls of Bleeker Street."

"Gordy was fun to work with," recalled star Dennis
Weaver. He was "very professional and always prepared.
We thought it would be interesting casting, not type
casting."

Shelly Winters, who also appeared on the season
opener, recalled working on the show as "marvelous. The
cast and star were wonderful."[42]

Gordon and Elizabeth had a home in Lincoln, Nebraska.

Gordon had a blue and white license plate made with "Gordo" on it, for which it cost him $50 and $25 annually. Gordon had a major role in fund raising for the Arthritis Foundation in 1974, for which he won the 17th Annual KMTV Public Service Award presented to him at a banquet in Omaha, on February 3, 1975, by Nebraska Governor J.J. Exon.

On January 6, 1975, he appeared on a segment of the CBS BICENTENNIAL MINUTES, and on June 16, 1975, he hosted an episode of the syndicated series VAUDEVILLE. That same year, Gordon became a grandfather again when his daughter, Meredith, and her husband, Greg Mullavey became the proud parents of daughter Allison.

On May 4, 1976, MacRae appeared before a live audience at Capitol Records to record the part of Thomas Jefferson and sing with Bob Hope the song, "Freedom Policy" on the Bob Hope album, AMERICA IS 200 YEARS OLD AND THERE'S STILL HOPE.

"It was a big recording studio at Capitol Records," remembered Phyllis Diller, "and every comic in the world was there, plus some very fine singers like Gordon MacRae."

Gordon kept his hand in politics by appearing at various Republican functions including luncheons and the Republican National Convention in Kansas City on August 7, 1976, where he sang the "Star Spangled Banner," as he had done at the World Series several years before.

"He was very active on my behalf and a very affirmative spokesman urging my election," President Gerald R. Ford recalled. "His involvement resulted from our long-standing friendship, and the similarity of our views on policies affecting our nation at home and abroad. I loved to listen to Gordon perform and I was told by experts he had a superb voice. Certainly his long and successful career was testimony as to his talent."[43]

Gordon began touring in AN EVENING OF RODGERS AND HAMMERSTEIN. His appearances included the Veterans Memorial Auditorium in Providence, Rhode Island on April 16, 1977, with the Rhode Island Festival Pops. Theatrical agent-producer, Jerry Grant organized a road show aimed at retirement condominiums and apartments in Florida. He booked top-named older stars, such as Gordon, to entertain a selective and sophisticated audience on what was called the Condo Circuit. Gordon started a two week engagement on August 4, 1977, at the Fairmont Hotel's posh Venetian Room, marking his first appearance there in five years. His son, Bruce, showed a slide presentation the first week and became his father's conductor the second week. Daughter Meredith surprised her father on opening night by dropping by unexpectedly. He was to follow the Fairmont engagement with AN EVENING OF RODGERS AND HAMMERSTEIN on August 21, 1977, at Temple University Music Festival in Ambler, Pennsylvania with Joyce Hall, his conductor, Gordon Munford, and the Pittsburgh Symphony, but illness forced him to cancel.

In 1978, MacRae toured in PAINT YOUR WAGON in Flint, Michigan and was guest soloist on a Christmas album with the Boys Town Choir entitled CHRISTMAS AT BOYS TOWN. Gordon and daughter, Meredith appeared on GOOD MORNING AMERICA on October 16, 1978, to announce that he would

begin shooting THE PILOT, his first feature film in
twenty-two years. The film starred Cliff Robertson (who
also directed) as a pilot with a drinking problem. MacRae
played Chief Pilot, Joe Barnes. Others in the cast
included Frank Converse, Diane Baker, Dana Andrews, Milo O'
Shea, and Ed Binns.

Gordon appeared in Greenville, South Carolina on
October 25, 1978, to do a concert but was too drunk to
remember the lyrics to songs.

"I think I'll always have a special place in my heart
for Greenville, because it was there I finally came to my
senses when I hit rock bottom," MacRae said later when he
returned to Greenville on June 14, 1983, to do a concert
sponsored by the North Greenville Alcoholism Treatment
Program.[44] On October 28, 1978, he missed a scheduled
singing appearance aboard the SS Statendam and the SS
Rotterdam, because he was too sick from drinking. On
November 3, 1978, Gordon sought treatment for his drinking
problem at the Independence Center at Lincoln General
Hospital, where he stayed until December 29, 1978.

"When alcohol began to interfere with my family, my
home life, and my career, I decided to call it quits,"
MacRae said. "I had twenty-three years of good drinking
from 1955 to 1978. If I wouldn't have quit when I did, I
would be dead."[45]

Upon his release from the hospital, he got his life
back together again as a recovering alcoholic. He remained
sober for the rest of his life, and the battle against
alcoholism became one of the causes he supported.

The PILOT began a gradual release in 1979, and that
year, MacRae appeared on OVER EASY on October 23, 1979,
with his son, Bruce, who performed "Forever Young," a song
he had written for and dedicated to Gordon. Also in 1979,
Gordon toured in SHENANDOAH.

MacRae appeared with daughter Meredith on the
HOLLYWOOD AUTISTIC CHILDRENS' TELETHON on January 15, 1980,
and he began touring the night club circuit in 4 GUYS 4.
The act included Dick Haymes (later replaced, due to
illness, by Jack Carter), Donald O' Connor, and Billy
Daniels. The act appeared at the Sahara, in Reno, on
January 13, 1980.

Gordon became the spokesperson for OPRYLAND USA for
the season beginning on March 31, 1980, and he also
appeared in the West Coast production of the Lee Guber and
Shelly Gross show THE BIG BROADCAST OF 1944. Included in
the cast were Harry James, Dennis Day, Don Wilson,
Hildegarde, Fran Warren, and the Ink Spots.

MacRae appeared on the NBC special 100 YEARS OF GOLDEN
HITS on July 19, 1981. The show had been recorded in 1978,
but did not air until 1981, celebrating the invention of
the phonograph and the evolvement of the music industry.
Later, on September 22, 1981, PBS broadcast AN AMERICAN
ORIGINAL: THE OREGON SYMPHONY ORCHESTRA. Gordon was guest
soloist at the concert recorded at the Portland Civic
Auditorium.

Gordon continued his cause against alcoholism by being
the guest speaker, in 1981, at the Sixth Annual Awareness
Dinner in Akron, Ohio. He was also a guest on the NBC

special BOB HOPE PRESENTS A CELEBRATION WITH STARS OF
COMEDY AND MUSIC, on October 22, 1981, marking the
dedication of the President Gerald R. Ford Museum. On the
show he sang "New York, New York."

MacRae was to have appeared on the televised Bob Hope
Desert Classic on January 16, 1982, but suffered a stroke
while reading in bed. When the book fell, he leaned over
to pick it up but found that he could not get back up. He
spent a month in the hospital. When he returned to work in
September 1982, his left arm was in a sling, and he walked
with a slight limp. The doctors had told him that he would
not be able to work again, but he did not let that stop him.
He continued to keep busy. He did a concert, with other
stars, at the Holiday House in Pittsburgh, on November
3, 1982, and a concert with Anna Maria Alberghetti at the
Mishler Theatre in Altoona, Pennsylvania, also in
November 1982. He also appeared on the television special
NEW YEARS EVE BIG BAND CELEBRATION broadcast on December
31, 1982, from Catalina Island.

Gordon became the honorary chairman of the National
Council on Alcoholism in 1983. MacRae had previously
sponsored the GORDON MacRAE CELEBRITY GOLF CLASSIC held at
the Paradise Valley Country Club in Las Vegas, the proceeds
of which went to help benefit the National Council on
Alcoholism. Celebrities playing in the tournament included
Bob Hope, Betty Ford, and Joe DiMaggio. President Ford, who
was campaigning for Ronald Reagan at the time, joined the
celebrities at the Sands Hotel for a dinner.

Gordon performed, in May 1983, at the Claridge Hotel
and Casino in Atlantic City. He appeared in the Palace
Room with Martha Raye. He joked about his arm being in a
sling, saying you should see the other guy. Then he told
the audience about his stroke. He told jokes and sang new
songs as well as songs associated with him. He did a
medley called the "Late Late Show," which included songs
from his films. He looked and sounded better than ever.
He performed a song he said he had written and was to
record with Capitol Records, but to this date nothing has
materialized.

On March 9, 1985, PBS aired RODGERS & HAMMERSTEIN THE
SOUND OF AMERICAN MUSIC with hostess Mary Martin. Stars
from both the Broadway shows and films were shown in film
clips and many were interviewed. Gordon was among the
stars interviewed concerning his roles in OKLAHOMA and
CAROUSEL. He mentioned learning to ride and rope. He said
that the smoke house scene in OKLAHOMA was filmed quickly,
because it was one of the most rehearsed scenes. He also
said that had he been involved in CAROUSEL from the
beginning, he would have liked to see it done as in the
original play, not with him already dead and the story told
in flashbacks.

When MacRae went to have surgery on a castoid artery
in the fall of 1985, he was diagnosed as having cancer. He
had long been a heavy smoker. Gordon and Elizabeth were
flown to UCLA Medical Center, where Gordon stayed for three
days, undergoing a series of tests. By then the cancer had
spread throughout his body. Long-time friend, comedian
Larry Storch and his wife Norma phoned Sheila, who flew

from New York to be with Gordon. His illness prevented him
from performing, and he was forced to officially announce
his retirement in 1985. He had plans to write his own
autobiography, but his illness prevented this. On November
27, 1985, his condition worsened, causing his hospital-
ization for treatment of cancer of the mouth and jaw as well
as pneumonia.

"He is very sick," said Elizabeth MacRae. "They are
doing what they can. He is fighting hard. Gordon is tough.
He has a tough constitution."[46]

He received well wishes from former President Gerald
R. Ford and former First Lady Betty Ford, editor Norman
Cousins, and singers Frank Sinatra and Robert Goulet.

Spokesman for the Bryan Memorial Hospital, Edwin
Shafer announced that MacRae died at 2:15 a.m., on Friday
January 24, 1986.

"His last days were really spent trying to overcome
this," Mrs. MacRae reported. "Gordon was a very religious
man, and spent most of his time in prayer."[47] "He died
very peacefully in his sleep," said Mrs. MacRae.[48]

On Monday, January 27, 1986, memorial services were
held at 11:30 a.m. at the Sheridan Lutheran Church in
Lincoln, Nebraska. A private burial had been planned.
Because of MacRae's work publicizing the problems and
needs of alcoholics, the family requested that any
memorials be given to the National Council on Alcoholism.

MacRae had been Shirley Jones's idol, before they
worked together, and Gordon had been godfather to Shaun
Cassidy (Shirley's son). They kept in touch over the years
and had remained friends. Shirley had spoken with Gordon
the month before his death.

Doris Day remembered him as having a "magnetic,
joyous, and loving personality. Gordon was really my
favorite singer. His voice was magnificent, and no one
sang like him. We had so much fun when we made films
together, and our favorites were ON MOONLIGHT BAY and BY
THE LIGHT OF THE SILVERY MOON. I am going to miss him
so."[49]

As can readily be seen in this partial overview of a
seasoned performer's life and career, Gordon MacRae was a
man for all media!

NOTES

1. Starr, Maxine. "He's Riding High." <u>TV Stage</u>.
    August 1956. Page 14.
2. MacRae, Sheila. "The Day He Proposed." <u>Motion
    Picture & TV Magazine</u>. June 1953.
3. Mr. Godfrey's response to author's letter, 1980.
4. <u>Downbeat</u>. March 24, 1954.
5. Mr. Vallee's response to author's letter, 1980.
6. Lee, Marilyn. "MacRae Tops In 5 Media." <u>Los
    Angeles Examiner</u>. October 18, 1953.
7. Mr. Simeon's response to author's letter, 1980.
8. Mr. Jackson's response to author's letter, 1980.
9. Mr. Kinkle's response to author's letter, 1980.
10. <u>Downbeat</u>. March 24, 1954.
11. Miss Truman's response to author's letter, 1980.
12. Miss Zimmer's response to author's letter, 1980.
13. Miss Whiting's response to author's letter, 1980.
14. Mr. Hope's response to author's letter, 1980.
    Further quotes from Mr. Hope are from this source.
15. Whitburn, Joel. <u>Pop Memories 1890-1954</u>.
16. Miss Stafford's and Mr. Weston's response to
    author's letter, 1980.
17. Miss Haver's response to author's letter, 1980.
    Other quotes by Miss Haver are from this source.
18. Mr. Cagney's response to author's letter, 1980.
19. Miss Diller's response to author's letter, 1980.
    Other quotes by Miss Diller are from this source.
20. Miss Marie's response to author's letter, 1980.
21. Parsons, Louella. <u>Los Angeles Examiner</u>. June
    1, 1952.
22. Mr. Thomas's response to author's letter, 1980.
23. Miss Grayson's response to author's letter, 1980.
24. Miss Adam's response to author's phone call, 1980.
25. Mr. Levene's response to author's letter, 1980.
26. Miss Powell's response to author's letter, 1980.
27. Miss Holm's response to author's letter, 1980.
28. Miss Martin's response to author's letter, 1980.
    Other quotes by Miss Martin are from this source.
29. Esterow, Milton. "On a Baritone's Score." <u>New
    York Times</u>. December 11, 1955.
30. Miss Jones's response to author's letter, 1980.
    Other quotes by Miss Jones are from this source.
31. <u>New York Times</u>. December 11, 1955.
32. Mr. Weaver's response to author's letter, 1980.
    Other quotes by Mr. Weaver are from this source.
33. Whitburn, Joel. <u>Top Pop Albums 1955-1985</u>. The
    charting of CAROUSEL is also from this source.
34. Mr. Borgnine's response to author's letter, 1980.
35. Mr. Pitts's response to author's letter, 1980.
36. Mr. Harris's response to author's letter, 1980.
37. Mr. Clark's response to author's letter, 1980.
38. Mr. Gleason's response to author's letter, 1980.
39. Mr. Douglas's response to author's letter, 1980.
40. Mr. Newhart's response to author's letter, 1980.
41. Mr. Kelly's response to author's letter, 1980.

42. Miss Winter's response to author's letter, 1980.
43. President Ford's response to author's letter,
     1980.
44. Associated Press. _Philadelphia Inquirer_.
     January 25, 1986.
45. O'Connor, Bill. "Mornings Are Beautiful Again."
     Philadelphia Inquirer. November 27, 1981.
46. Speers, W. "MacRae in Hospital and is Very
     Sick." _Philadelphia Inquirer_. 1985.
47. Associated Press. "Cancer Kills Actor Gordon
     MacRae, 64." _Delaware County Sunday Times_.
     January 26, 1986.
48. Associated Press. _Chicago Tribune_. January
     25, 1986.
49. _Delaware County Sunday Times_. January 26, 1986.

2

Stage Appearances

S 1. TROJAN HORSE

Stock. October 30, 1940. Millpond Playhouse, Roslyn, Long Island, New York.

CREDITS: Three act play by Christopher Morley. Settings: Edward Colin Dawson. Producer and Director: David Lowe.

CAST: Edward Thompson(King Priam), Ira Gossel (Hector), Peter Johnston (Paris), Gordon MacRae (Deiphobus), Brian Gilbert (Antenor), Edward McVitty (Aeneas), Richard Graham (Troilus), Fred Colecord (Cleon), Dwitt Spencer (Fuscus), David Lowe (Illum), John Viebrock (Pandarus), Kerry Stuart (Cressida), Mary Jane Morrow (Antigone), Dorothy Eaton (Hecuba), Sheila Stephens (Helen of Troy), Barbara Winslow (Cassandra), Genevieve Townsend (Andromache), Mary Esherich (Creuss), Andrea Duncan (Lyde), Betram Wood (Dr. Calchas), Gaylord Mason (Rev. Laocoon, Dares, Nestor), Melba Rae (Miss Dictes), Jess Kruger (Agamemnon), Dennis King (Menelaus), Jack Chakrin (Achilles), Charles Kreith (Ajax), Lewis Sisk (Ulysses), Leon Smith (Diomedes), Otto Klemperer (Sarpedoni), Julia Herrick (Chryseis), Marjorie Hastings (Bryseis), Mona Francis (A. Chippendale).

SYNOPSIS: Chaucer was the source of Christopher Morley's story about the Greek and Trojan War and the horse the Greeks built in order to get them inside Troy's walls.

COMMENT: Mr. Morley delivered a speech about Chaucer and the Trojan Horse to the Adelphi College students who attended the premiere.

S 2. JUNIOR MISS

Broadway. November 18, 1941. Lyceum Theatre, New York. 710 performances.

CREDITS: Adapted from Sally Benson's stories by Jerome Chodorov and Joseph Fields. Producer: Max Gordon. Director: Moss Hart. Settings: Frederick Fox.

CAST: Patricia Peardon (Judy Graves), Barbara Robbins (Grace Graves), Philip Ober (Harry Graves), Lenore Lonergan (Fluffy Adams), Alexander Kirkland (Willis Reynolds), Francesca Bruning (Ellen Curtis), Paula Laurence (Hilda),

Billy Redfield (Hashell Cummings), Joan Newton (Lois Graves), Matt Briggs (J.B. Curtis), John Cushman (Barlow Adams), Kenneth Forbes (Joe), James Elliott (Western Union Boy), Peter Scott (Merrill Feuerbach), Robert Willey (Sterling Brown), Jack Manning (Albert Kunody), Walter Collins (Tommy Arbuckle), Jack Greer (Charles), John Hundson (Henry)

SYNOPSIS: JUNIOR MISS is a comedy about adolescence and life in a middle-class family. It concerns food, clothes, makeup and boys, which supposedly are what most teenage girls think about. Adolescent Judy Graves mistakenly thinks her father is having an affair with his boss's daughter, Ellen Curtis. So with the help of her friend Fluffy Adams, Judy tries to get Ellen together with her Uncle Willis. Ellen's father is initially against the match. Things are resolved, and Judy happily goes on her first date.

COMMENT: MacRae assumed the Tommy Arbuckle role in 1943.

REVIEW: Time (December 1, 1941) considered JUNIOR MISS "gay, bright and fairly authentic." The plot was cluttered up with too many adults.

S 3. THREE TO MAKE READY

Broadway. March 7, 1946. Adelphi Theatre, New York. 327 performances. The show also played in Boston (February 7, 1946); the Shubert Theatre, Philadelphia (February 19, 1946); the Broadhurst Theatre, New York (September 16, 1946); the Forrest Theatre, Philadelphia (May 19, 1947); the Colonial Theatre, Boston (June 2, 1947).

CREDITS: Revue by Nancy Hamilton. Producers: Stanley Gilky and Barbara Payne. Music: Morgan Lewis. Orchestra: Russell Bennett, Charles L. Cooke, Elliott Jacoby, Ted Royal, Hans Spialek. Staged by John Murray Anderson. Sketches directed by Margaret Webster. Dances and Musical numbers directed by Robert Sidney. Music Director: Ray M. Kavanaugh. Scenery Designer: Donald Oenslager. Costumes: Audre.

CAST: Ray Bolger, Brenda Forbes, Rose Inghram, Gordon MacRae, Harold Lang, Bibi Osterwald, Jane Deering, Arthur Godfrey, Althea Elder, Joe Jonson, Meg Mundy, Mary Alice Bingham, Mary McDonnell, Edythia Turnell, Candace Montgomery, Iris Linde, Garry Davis, Carleton Carpenter, Martin Kraft, Jack Purcell, Irwin Charles, Jimmy Venable, Jim Elsewood.

SONGS: "It's a Nice Night For It"-MacRae and Cast; "After You"-Bolger, Inghram; "Oh You're a Wonderful Person"-Inghram, MacRae, danced by Bolger, Elder; "Desert Isle"-Forbes; "That Old Soft Shoe"-sung and danced by Bolger; "Furnished Bed"-Osterwald, danced by Deering; "Barnaby Beach"-MacRae, danced by Deering, Lang; "Tell Me the Story"-Inghram, MacRae; "Kenosha Canoe Ballet"-danced by Lang and Cowboys; "New Clothes"-danced by Lang; "Lovely Lazy Kind of Day"-Godfrey, danced by Bolger; And Why Not I"-Forbes; "If It's Love"-Deering, Lang, Montgomery, Charles.

COMMENT: THREE TO MAKE READY is a revue in two acts and twenty-four scenes. Gordon MacRae played Mr. Snow in the "Kenoha Canoe Scene," an MP in "Why Not I Scene," and

Tsai-Young in the "Lute Song Scene."
     REVIEW: <u>New York Times</u> (March 8, 1946) felt that Ray
Bolger was "at the top of his form," but that the show was
"very sadly a disappointment." The other cast members were
"mainly attractive and willing."

S 4. CAROUSEL
     Stock. July 13, 1955. Dallas State Fair Music Hall.
     CREDITS: Music and Lyrics: Rodgers and Hammerstein.
     CAST: Gordon MacRae (Billy), Rosemary Kuhlmann
(Nettie), Paula Stewart (Julie), Andrew Gainey (Jigger),
Susan Johnson (Carrie), Reid Shelton (Snow).
     SYNOPSIS: Billy (MacRae), a carnival barker, meets
Julie (Stewart), a factory worker, at the carnival. They
fall in love and are married. Billy, who was fired from the
carnival, is in desperate need of money to support his
forthcoming child.   He attempts a robbery with his pal
Jigger (Gainey) and is killed in the process. Years later,
he is allowed to return to earth for a day to help his
unhappy daughter.
     SONGS: "Carousel Waltz;" "Mr. Snow"-Johnson; "If I
Loved You"-MacRae, Stewart; "June Is Busting Out All Over"-
Kuhlmann, Johnson; "When the Children Are Asleep"-Shelton,
Johnson; "Soliloquy"-MacRae; "A Real Nice Clambake"-Johnson,
Kuhlmann, Shelton, Gainey; "What's the Use of Wondering"-
Stewart; "Highest Judge of All"-MacRae.
     COMMENT: John Raitt and Jan Clayton played the
Broadway Billy and Julie. Gordon played Billy Bigelow, in
this three week engagement, before landing the film version,
after Frank Sinatra withdrew from the film. (See entry F19
in the Filmography).

S 5. KISMET
     Stock. 1955.
     CREDITS: Music and Lyrics: Robert Wright and George
Forrest. Book: Charles Lederer and Luther Davis.
     CAST: Gordon MacRae, Carlo Alberghetti, Marthe
Errolle.
     SYNOPSIS: Gordon MacRae, who plays Hajj a poet from
ancient Bagdad, arrives in town with his daughter, Marsinah,
and plans to marry her off to a young Caliph. The police
wazir abducts Marsinah and takes her to his harem. Caliph,
who has fallen in love with Marsinah, rescues her and they
are married. Hajj elopes with the policeman's widow,
Lalume, and writes poetry in competition with Omar the tent
maker.
     SONGS: "Sands of Time;" "Rhymes Have I"-MacRae; "Not
Since Nineveh;" "Baubles, Bangles and Beads;" "Stranger in
Paradise;" "Night of My Nights;" "And This Is My Beloved"-
MacRae; "The Olive Tree"-MacRae; "Gesticulate"-MacRae;
"Fate"-MacRae; "He's in Love;" "Bored"-MacRae; "Was I
Wazir;" "Rahadlakum"-MacRae; "Zubbediya."
     COMMENT: Alfred Drake created the role of Hajj on
Broadway.

S 6. BELLS ARE RINGING
     Stock. August 3, 1959. Starlight Theatre, Kansas
City.

CREDITS: Score: Jules Styne. Book: Betty Comden and Adolph Green.

CAST: Sheila MacRae (Ella Peterson), Gordon MacRae (Jeff Moss).

COMMENT: The MacRaes drew the biggest crowd of the season (76,210 persons) and set a five year box office record grossing over $139,000. A member of the Official Gordon MacRae Fan Club went back stage after the show and during a conversation with the MacRaes learned that Gordon had been Mayor of North Hollywood the previous year. Gordon had been under consideration for the Broadway production, but couldn't come to terms. For synopsis and songs refer to entry S10.

S 7. REDHEAD

Stock. Summer of 1959. Warwick, Rhode Island. The show also played in Massachusetts and Ohio.

CREDITS: Music: Albert Hague. Lyrics: Dorothy Fields. Book: Herbert and Dorothy Fields, Sidney Sheldon, David Shaw.

CAST: Gordon MacRae (Tom Baxter), Sheila MacRae (Essie Whimple).

SYNOPSIS: Essie (Sheila) works in her aunt's wax museum. She meets Tom (Gordon) a strong-man performer. While helping catch the murderer of his partner, they fall in love.

SONGS: "The Simpson Sisters' Door;" "The Right Finger of My Left Hand"-Sheila; "Just For Once"-Gordon, Sheila; "Merely Marvelous"-Sheila; "The Uncle Sam Rag;" "Erbie Fitch's Twitch"-Sheila; "She's Just Not Enough Woman For Me"-Gordon; "Behave Yourself"-Sheila; "Look Who's in Love"-Gordon, Sheila; "My Girl is Just Enough Woman For Me"-Gordon; "Essie's Vision;" "Two Faces in the Dark;" "I'm Back in Circulation"-Gordon; "We Loves Ya, Jimmy;" "Pick-Pocket Tango;" "I'll Try"-Sheila, Gordon.

COMMENT: Richard Kiley and Gwen Verdon played Tom and Essie on Broadway.

S 8. ANNIE GET YOUR GUN

Stock. 1960. Starlight Theatre, Kansas City.

Stock. 1980. Sacramento Music Circus, Sacramento, California. (This new production is without Sheila)

CREDITS: Music and Lyrics: Irving Berlin. Book: Herbert and Dorothy Fields.

CAST: Gordon MacRae (Frank Butler), Sheila MacRae (Annie Oakley), the entire MacRae family.

SYNOPSIS: Annie Oakley (Sheila), the star of Buffalo Bill's Wild West Show, meets Frank Butler (Gordon), the star of the competing Pawnee Bill Show. They fall in love but being with rival shows, they are kept apart until the shows merge.

SONGS: "Colonel Buffalo Bill;" "I'm a Bad Bad Man"-Gordon; "Doing What Comes Naturally"-Sheila; "The Girl That I Marry"-Gordon; "You Can't Get a Man With a Gun"-Sheila; "They Say It's Wonderful"-Gordon; "My Defenses Are Down"-Gordon; "Moonshine Lullaby"-Sheila; "I'm an Indian Too"-Sheila; "I Got Lost in His Arms"-Sheila; "Who Do You Love I Hope;" "I Got the Sun in the Morning"-Sheila;

"Anything You Can Do"-Gordon, Sheila; "There's No Business Like Show Business.
COMMENT: Ethel Merman and Ray Middleton created the roles of Annie and Frank on Broadway.

S 9. GUYS AND DOLLS
Stock. January 27, 1964 to February 8, 1964. Phoenix Theatre, Phoenix.
CREDITS: Music and Lyrics: Frank Loesser. Book: Jo Swerling and Abe Burrows. Presented by: Buster Bonoff. Director: James Hammerstein. Musical Director: René Weigert. Choreographer: Zac Solov. Scenic Designer: Hal Shafer. Lighting Designer: Robert Bowd. Associate Conductor: Ronald Stein. Production Stage Manager: John Trelfall. Wardrobe: Murill Furr.
CAST: Gordon MacRae (Sky Masterson), Sheila MacRae (Miss Adelaide), Cliff Norton (Nathan Detroit), Beverly Allison (Sarah Brown), Robert Miller Driscoll (Nicely-Nicely Johnson), Slapsy Maxie Rosenbloon (Big Julie), Ben Bryant (Benny Southstreet), Kirk Norman (Rusty Charlie), Lindsey Workman (Arvide Abernathy), Miriam Birch, Elfie Furst, William D. Gibben, Brian Mitchell, Maralynne York (Mission Band), Anthony Weber (Drunk), Eddie Hanley (Harry the Horse), Tom Gleason (Lt. Brannigan), Tom Gleason (Joey Biltmore), Ginger Warner (Mimi), Maryesther Denver (General Matilda Cartwright), Stephen Potter (Waiter), Kirk Norman, Robert Webb (Havana waiters), Rudy Rajkovich, Robert Webb (Policemen).
SYNOPSIS: Nathan Detroit (Norton), who runs a floating crap game, bets gambler Sky Masterson (Gordon) that he can't get the next girl he sees to fall in love with him. The next girl he sees is Sarah Brown (Allison) from the Save-a-Soul Mission, who is there to save the souls of the local riffraff. The two do fall in love. The other romance centers around Nathan, who has been engaged for 14 years to Miss Adelaide (Sheila), the major attraction at the Hot Box Night Club.
SONGS: "Fugue for Tinhorns"-Driscoll, Bryant, Norman; "Follow the Fold"-Allison, Workman; "The Oldest Established"-Norton, Driscoll, Bryant; "I'll Know"-Allison, G. MacRae; "A Bushel and a Peck"-S. MacRae, Hot Box Girls; "Adelaide's Lament"-S. MacRae; "Guys and Dolls"-Driscoll, Bryant; "Havana"-Onna White, Ensemble; "If I Were a Bell"-Allison; "My Time of Day"-G. MacRae; "I've Never Been in Love Before"-G. MacRae, Allison; "Take Back Your Mink"-S. MacRae, Hot Box Girls; Reprise-"Adelaide's Lament"-S. MacRae; "More I Cannot Wish You"-Workman; "The Crap Game Dance"-Ensemble; "Luck Be a Lady"-G. MacRae, Crap Shooters; "Sue Me"-Norton, S. MacRae; "Sit Down You're Rockin' the Boat"-Driscoll, Company; Reprise-"Follow the Fold"-Mission Meeting Group; "Marry the Man Today"-S. MacRae, Allison; Reprise-"Guys and Dolls"-Entire Company.
COMMENT: Robert Alda and Vivian Blaine created the roles of Sky and Miss Adelaide on Broadway.

S10. BELLS ARE RINGING
Stock. July 21, 1964. Melodyland Theatre, Anaheim.
Stock. November 1964. Valley Music Theatre.

CREDITS: Score: Jules Styne. Book: Betty Comden and Adolph Green. Staged by David Tihman. Ernest Sarravini VMT). Dances: Calvin Von Reinhold(VMT). Producers: Lewis and Dare.

CAST: Sheila MacRae (Ella Peterson), Gordon MacRae (Jeff Moss), Ben Lessy (Bookie), Dorothy Greener (Owner of Answering Service), Roy Stuart (Dentist), Bart Howard (Brando type actor), Others: Henry Hunter, Eddie Hanley, Larry Barthelot, Richard Venture, Melodyland dancers and singers.

CAST: (Valley Music Theatre) included Kathleen Freeman, Werner Klemperer, Dort Clark.

SYNOPSIS: BELLS ARE RINGING is centered around an answering service in Manhattan, where Ella (Sheila) is an operator who gets involved in her clients' problems. One of her clients is Jeff (Gordon), a playwright with writers block. Ella helps him overcome the problem and in doing so falls in love with him. In a subplot, Sandor (Lessy), a bookie posing as a head of a record company, uses the service's office for book making. The police catch on and close him down.

SONGS: "It's a Perfect Relationship"-Sheila; "On My Own"-Gordon; "You've Got to Do It"-Gordon; "It's a Simple Little System;" "Is It a Crime?"-Sheila; "Hello, Hello There!"-Sheila, Gordon; "I Met a Girl"-Gordon; "Long Before I Knew You"-Gordon, Sheila; "Mu Cha Cha"-Sheila; "Just in Time"-Gordon, Sheila; "Drop That Name"-Sheila; "The Party's Over"-Sheila; "Salzburg;" "The Midas Touch;" "Long Before I Knew You" (Reprise); "I'm Going Back"-Sheila.

COMMENT: The roles of Jeff and Ella were played on Broadway by Sydney Chaplin and Judy Holliday. The MacRaes did an excerpt from their night club act after the show. Imitations by the couple included Sheila's Elizabeth Taylor, and Carol Channing, and Gordon's Dean Martin and Frank Fontaine's Crazy Guggenheim.

S11. OKLAHOMA

Stock. August 21, 1967 to August 26, 1967. Valley Forge Music Fair, Devon, Pennsylvania.

Stock. August 28, 1967 to September 2, 1967. Camden County Music Fair, Camden, New Jersey. The show also toured in Indianapolis, where MacRae broke Jack Benny's attendance record.

CREDITS: Director: Bob Herget. Musical Director: Milton Stetzer. Sets: Milton Duke. Costumes: Sara Brook. Musical Staging and Choreography: Wakefield Poole. Lighting: Lester Tapper. Music and Lyrics: Rodgers and Hammerstein.

CAST: Jean Sincere (Aunt Eller), Gordon MacRae (Curly), Joleen Foder (Laurey), Peter Conlow (Will Parker), Daniel P. Hannafin (Jud Fry), Carolyn Kemp (Ado Annie), Arnold Soboloff (Ali Hakim), Richard Miller (Andrew Carnes), Janet Sumner (Dancing Laurey), Dennis Cole (Dancing Curly).

SYNOPSIS: OKLAHOMA concerns the love story between Curly and Laurey and the complications that result when Laurey decides to go to the box social with hired hand Jud Fry.

SONGS: "Oh What a Beautiful Morning"-MacRae; "The

Surrey With the Fringe on Top"-MacRae, Fodor, Sincere;
"Kansas City"-Conlow, Sincere, Boys; "I Can't Say
No"-Kemp; "Many a New Day"-Fodor, Girls; "It's a Scandal,
It's an Outrage"-Soboloff; "People Will Say We're in
Love"-MacRae, Fodor; "Poor Jud"-MacRae, Hannafin; "Lonely
Room"- Hannafin; "Out of My Dreams"-Fodor; "Farmer and the
Cowman"-Miller, Sincere, MacRae, Conlow, Kemp; "All Or
Nothing"-Conlow, Kemp; "People Will Say"-reprise, MacRae
and Fodor; "Oklahoma"-MacRae, Fodor, Sincere; "Oh What a
Beautiful Morning" (Reprise)-MacRae, Fodor.
    COMMENT: The roles of Curly and Laurey were played on
Broadway by Alfred Drake and Joan Roberts. Gordon received
a standing ovation at curtain call. He also did a short
excerpt from his night club routine.
    REVIEW: Critic Holly Webster felt that the show "kept
all its appeal" and that it seemed "newly minted" because
of MacRae, who was in "fine voice," the director, and the
others connected with the show.

S12. I DO! I DO!
    Broadway. December 5, 1966 to June 15, 1968. 46th
Street Theatre, New York. 560 performances.
    CREDITS: Book and Lyrics: Tom Jones. Based on the
play: THE FOUR POSTER by Jande Hartog. Music: Harvey
Schmidt. Scene Production: Oliver Smith. Costumes: Freddy
Witthop. Lighting: Jean Rosenthal. Director: Gower Champion.
Musical Director: John Lesko. Orchestration: Philip J.
Lang. Production Supervisor: Lucia Victor. Staff
Associates: Sylvia Swartz, Lynn Middleton, Juliet Taylor.
Hairstylist: Vincent J. Nasso. At the pianos: Woody Kessler
and Jack Holmes. A David Merrick and Champion Six Inc.
Production. Original Cast Album: RCA Victor. General Manager:
Jack Schilissel. Company Manager: Richard Highley. Press:
Harvey B. Sabinson, Lee Solters, Jay Russell. Stage
Managers: Wade Miller, Henry Sutton, Robert Vangergriff.
    CAST: Gordon MacRae (Michael), Carol Lawrence
(Agnes).
    SYNOPSIS: I DO! I DO! deals with fifty years of a
marriage and the problems and love that ensues.
    SONGS: (M-Michael, A-Agnes, B-Both)
"All the Dearly Beloved," "Together Forever," "I Do, I Do,"
"Goodnight"-B; "I Love My Wife"-M; "Something Has
Happened"-A; "My Cup Runneth Over," "Love Isn't
Everything," "Nobody's Perfect"-B; "A Well Known Fact"-M;
"Flaming Agnes"-A; "The Honeymoon is Over," "Where Are the
Snows?" "When the Kids Get Married"-B; "The Father of the
Bride"-M; "What is a Woman?" "Someone Needs Me"-A; "Roll Up
the Ribbons," "This House"-B.
    COMMENT: Robert Preston and Mary Martin were the
original cast. MacRae and Lawrence worked their way into
the show in matinee performances, beginning October 18,
1967, and took over on December 4, 1967, when Preston and
Martin took the show on tour.
    REVIEW: New York Times, Clive Barnes, (November 28,
1967) Clive Barnes thought very highly of Mary Martin's
performance in I DO! I DO! but felt that Carol Lawrence was
"more than her equal." He said that Carol handled the
younger scenes with "less cuteness," and that her acting

"had a depth" that you usually didn't find in a musical.
He felt that Robert Preston was a better actor than MacRae
but that MacRae had "a better if more conventional voice,"
and that his "grizzled amiability" was just fine.

S13. GOLDEN RAINBOW
Stock. July 7, 1969 to July 12, 1969. Valley Forge
Music Fair, Devon, Pennsylvania.
CREDITS: Director: Jay Harnick. Choreography: Martin
Allen. Sets: Gordon Micunis. Costumes: Sara Brooks.
Lighting: Lester Tapper. Music and Lyrics: Walter Marks.
Book: Ernest Kinoy. Musical Director: Oscar Kosarian. Based
on A HOLE IN THE HEAD.
CAST: Gordon MacRae (Larry Davis), Alisha Kashi (Judy
Harris), Scott Jacoby (Ally), William Mooney (Lou Garrity),
Sid Raymond (Mr. Diamond), Jerome Collamore (Prospector),
Sam Swartz (Mr. Novotney), John Anania (Mr. Hauskracht),
Sally DeMay (Mrs. Magruder), Jacqueline Britt (Rosemary),
Larry Meritt (Jerome Stone), Richard Foomer (Korngold).
SYNOPSIS: Larry (MacRae), a widower, runs a seedy
hotel in Vegas with the help of his son, Ally (Jacoby).
Being in need of money, he gambles at the Vegas casinos.
Judy (Kashi), Larry's sister-in-law, is trustee of the
money left her nephew by his grandfather. She is also in
love with Larry.
SONGS: "24 Hours a Day"-Las Vegans; "We Got
Us"-MacRae, Jacoby; "He Needs Me Now"-Kashi; "I've Gotta
Be Me"-MacRae; "Fall of Babylon"-Babylonians; "Taste"-Lou,
friends; "Desert Moon"-MacRae, Kashi; "All in Fun"-MacRae,
Kashi; "I've Gotta Be Me"(Reprise)-MacRae; "It's You
Again"-Kashi; "How Could I Be So Wrong"-Kashi; Finale-"We
Got Us"-Kashi, MacRae, Jacoby.
COMMENT: On Broadway, Larry, Judy, and Ally were
played by Steve Lawrence, Edie Gorme, and Scott Jacoby.

S14. MILK AND HONEY
Stock. 1973. Warren, Pennsylvania.
CREDITS: Music and Lyrics: Jerry Herman. Book: Don
Appell.
CAST: Gordon MacRae (Phil), Molly Picon (Clara).
SYNOPSIS: Phil (MacRae), an American tourist in
Jerusalem, meets Ruth Stein who is also a tourist. They
keep meeting and their relationship grows.
Phil's daughter invites them to visit a Kibbutz in
Negev where she and her husband live. Phil is considering
staying in Israel and building a home for Ruth and him.
Barbara wants her father to tell Ruth he is married,
although separated for years, which he does.
At first Ruth accepts his explanation but reconsiders
and returns to Tel Aviv. Phil goes there to find her. He
finds Clara Weiss (Picon) who is a tourist searching for a
husband. Clara refuses to help Phil find Ruth.
Clara, meanwhile, meets an American widower, Mr.
Horowitz, and gets him to propose.
Ruth returns to Phil who now wants to wait for his
divorce before they get together. He says good bye at the
airport, promising to get the divorce as soon as possible.
Ruth leaves hoping that someday they will be reunited.

SONGS: "Shepherd's Song"-MacRae; "Shalom"-MacRae;
"Independence Day Hora;" "Milk and Honey," "There's No
Reason in the World"-MacRae; "Chin Up Ladies"-Picon; "That
Was Yesterday"-MacRae; "Let's Not Waste a Moment"-MacRae;
"The Wedding"-MacRae; "Like a Young Man"-MacRae; "I Will
Follow You;" "Hymn to Hymie"-Picon; "There's No Reason in
the World" (Reprise); "Milk and Honey" (Reprise); "As
Simple as That"-MacRae; "Shalom" (Reprise)-MacRae.
    COMMENT: The roles of Phil and Clara were created on
Broadway by Robert Weede and Molly Picon.

S15. UNSINKABLE MOLLY BROWN
    Stock. 1977. Sacramento Music Circus, Sacramento,
California.
    CREDITS: Music and Lyrics: Meredith Wilson. Book:
Richard Morris.
    SYNOPSIS: MacRae stars as prospector "Leadville
Johnny" Brown and marries Molly, who rose from poverty to
wealth via the Colorado silver mines. Not accepted by
Denver society, they go to Europe where Molly becomes Monte
Carlo's social leader. After nearly losing Johnny, she
wins him back after her heroism during the sinking of the
Titanic, and they are finally accepted by Denver society.
    SONGS: "I Ain't Down Yet;" "Belly Up to the Bar
Boys;" "I've A'Ready Started In"-MacRae; "I'll Never Say
No"-MacRae; "My Own Brass Bed;" "The Denver Police;" "Bea-
u-ti-ful People of Denver;" "Are You Sure?" "I Ain't Down
Yet"-MacRae & Molly; "Happy Birthday Mrs. J. J. Brown;"
"Bon Jour;" "If I Knew-MacRae; "Chick-A-Pen"-MacRae &
Molly; "Keep--Hoppin'"-MacRae; "Leadville Johnny Brown"-
MacRae; "Up There Where the People Are;" "Dolce Far
Niente;" "I May Never Fall In Love With You."
    COMMENT: Harve Presnell created the role of Johnny on
Broadway.

S16. PAINT YOUR WAGON
    Stock. August 12, 1978. Star Theatre, Flint,
Michigan.
    Stock. 1978. Sacramento Music Circus, Sacramento
California.
    Stock. August 3-9, 1981. Sacramento Music Circus,
Sacramento, California. With Grant Goodeve (Julio) & Cathy
Rigby (Jennifer).
    CREDITS: Music: Frederick Loewe. Lyrics and Book:
Alan J. Lerner.
    SYNOPSIS: Gordon MacRae stars as Ben Rumson, a
grizzled prospector, who with his daughter, Jennifer, lives
in Rumson, California, a town named for its founder.
    While drawing water from a stream, Jennifer finds
gold. When word of this gets around, prospectors from all
around come to town. Jennifer, the only girl in town,
draws attention. Ben sends her back East to school.
However, she has already fallen for Mexican prospector,
Julio Valveras.
    The gold find in Rumson begins to dwindle. Jennifer
returns home in time to be with Ben before his death. Her
romance with Julio starts up again. Irrigation and
agriculture give Rumson a chance for survival.

SONGS: "I'm On My Way;" "Rumson;" "What's Going On
Here?" "I Talk to the Trees;" "They Call the Wind Maria;"
"I Still See Elisa"-MacRae; "How Can I Wait?" "In Between"-
MacRae; "Whoop-Ti-Ay!" "Carino Mio;" "There's A Coach
Comin' In;" "Hand Me Down That Can O' Beans;" "Another
Autumn," "All For Him;" "Wand'rin Star"-MacRae; "Take the
Wheels Off the Wagon"-MacRae.
COMMENT: The role of Ben was created on Broadway by
James Barton.

S17. SHENANDOAH
Stock. February 16, 1979. San Berdoo, California.
Stock. 1979. Sacramento Music Circus, Sacramento,
California.
CREDITS: Music: Gary Geld. Lyrics: Peter Udell. Book:
James Lee Barett, Gloria and Louis Sher.
SYNOPSIS: MacRae stars as Charles Anderson, a widower,
who owns a farm in the Shenandoah Valley in Virginia, and is
determined to keep his six sons out of the Civil War. His
younger son is kidnapped by Union Soldiers. While Charles
and his family are out looking for him, his eldest son and
his family are killed. The remaining family are reunited at
church.
SONGS: "Raise the Flag of Dixie," "I've Heard it all
Before"-MacRae, "Why Am I Me," "Next to Lovin' I Like
Fightin'," "Over the Hill," "The Pickers Are
Comin'"-MacRae, "Meditation"-MacRae, "We Make a Beautiful
Pair," "Violets and Silverbells," "It's a Boy"-MacRae,
"Papa's Gonna Make It Alright"-MacRae, "Freedom," "Violets
and Silverbells" (reprise), "The Only Home I Know,"
"Meditation"-MacRae, "Pass the Cross to Me."
COMMENT: The role of Charlie Anderson was created on
Broadway by John Cullum.

S18. THE BIG BROADCAST OF 1944
Stock. March 25, 1980 to April 6, 1980. Fox Theatre,
San Diego, California.
Stock. April 8, 1980 to May 4, 1980. Pantages
Theatre, Los Angeles.
Stock. May 6, 1980 to June 1, 1980. San Francisco.
CREDITS: Producers: Lee Guber and Shelly Gross.
CAST: Gordon MacRae, Don Wilson, Dennis Day, Harry
James, Hidegarde, Fran Warren, Warren Covington, Pied
Pipers, Ink Spots.
COMMENT: MacRae was part of the West Coast cast.
The show included songs from 1944 or before.

3

Radio Appearances

R 1. 1947 ACADEMY AWARDS (ABC, March 20, 1948)
Broadcast 8:15 p.m. from the Shrine Auditorium, Los
Angeles.
<u>Hosts</u>: Dick Powell, Agnes Moorehead. <u>Presenters</u>:
George Murphy, Robert Montgomery, Shirley Temple, Larry
Parks, Donald Crisp, Olivia de Havilland, Dinah Shore, Dick
Powell, Jean Hersholt, Ingrid Bergman, Agnes Moorehead,
Anne Baxter, Fredric March. <u>Nominated Songs</u>: "A Gal in
Calico"-Gordon MacRae; "I Wish I Didn't Love You So"-Dennis
Day; "Pass That Peace Pipe"-Dinah Shore; "You Do"-Frances
Langford; "Zip-a-Dee-Doo-Dah"*-Johnny Mercer and the Pied
Pipers. (* indicates winning song)

R 2. 1948 ACADEMY AWARDS (March 24, 1949)
Broadcast 8:00 p.m. at the Academy Theatre, Hollywood.
<u>Host</u>: Robert Montgomery. <u>Presenters</u>: George Murphy,
Ava Gardner, Louis Jourdan, Deborah Kerr, Glen Ford, Ann
Blyth, Jeannie Crain, Wendell Cory, Arlene Dahl, Elizabeth
Taylor, Robert Ryan, Kathryn Grayson, Celeste Holm, Edmund
Gwen, Jean Hersholt, Frank Borzago, Loretta Young, Ronald
Colman, Ethel Barrymore. <u>Nominated Songs</u>: "Buttons and
Bows"*-Jane Russell; "For Every Man There's a Woman"-Gordon
MacRae; "It's Magic"-Doris Day; "This is the Moment"-Jo
Stafford; "The Woody Woodpecker Song"-Gloria Wood and Harry
Babbitt. (* indicates winning song)

R 3. ALL STAR REVUE (1949)
<u>Host</u>: Gordon MacRae. <u>Sponsor</u>: American Cancer Society
with the cooperation of the Hollywood Coordinating
Committee. <u>Announcer</u>: Toby Reed. <u>Orchestra</u>: Carmen Dragon.
<u>Writer</u>: Dick Conway. <u>Producer and Director</u>: Bob Forward.
<u>Guests</u>: Jerry Colonna, George Burns and Gracie Allen, Peggy
Lee, Jane Wyman. <u>Songs</u>: "Blue Skies;" "Can't Help Loving
That Man"-Lee; "It's Magic"-MacRae; "Carolina"-Colonna;
"Through the Years"-MacRae.

R 4. ARTHUR GODFREY (WCAU-CBS affiliate in Philadelphia)
<u>Host</u>: Arthur Godfrey. <u>Guests</u>: Gordon MacRae, June Valli.

R 5. BIG SHOW (NBC, February 11, 1950)

Hostess: Tallulah Bankhead. Guests: Gordon MacRae,
Dean Martin, Jerry Lewis, Joan Davis, Judy Garland, Groucho
Marx, Andrews Sisters. Orchestra: Meredith Wilson.
Writer: Goodman Ace. Announcers: Ed Herliky, Jimmy
Wallington. Songs: "You & I"-Garland; "Sweet
Sixteen"-MacRae; "Here Comes the Springtime," "There Goes
My Heart," "Let Me Call You Sweetheart," "May the Good Lord
Bless and Keep You"-All.

R 6. BIG SHOW (NBC, April 29, 1951)
Hostess: Tallulah Bankhead. Guests: Gordon MacRae,
Milton Berle, Rosemary Clooney, Jimmy Durante, Ethel Merman,
Frank Lovejoy. Orchestra: Meredith Wilson. Writer: Goodman
Ace. Announcers: Ed Herliky, Jimmy Wallington.

R 7. BOB HOPE SHOW (NBC, December 19, 1950)
Host: Bob Hope. Guests: Gordon MacRae, Tallulah
Bankhead.

R 8. CHARLIE McCARTHY SHOW (NBC, 1954?)
Hosts: Edgar Bergan, Charlie McCarthy, Mortimer Snerd.
Orchestra: Ray Noble. Guests: Gordon MacRae, Nelson Eddy.
Song: "Face to Face"-MacRae; Skit: "Bush Pilot Story."
Cast: Wild Blue Yonder MacRae-MacRae; Pilot Noble-Noble;
Mounty-Eddy.

R 9. CHESTERFIELD SUPPER CLUB (NBC, September 25, 1947)
Hostess: Jo Stafford. Orchestra: Paul Weston. Singers:
Starlighters. Sponsor: Chesterfields. Guest: Gordon MacRae.
Songs: "Tallahassee"-Stafford; "Dixieland"-Orchestra; "Body
and Soul"-MacRae; "I've Been So Wrong"-Stafford.

R10. CHESTERFIELD SUPPER CLUB (NBC, 1950?)
Host: Perry Como. Orchestra: Mitchell Ayres. Sponsor:
Chesterfields. Guests: Margaret Whiting, Ella Fitzgerald,
Gordon MacRae, Andy and Della Russell, Gordon Jenkins, Guy
Lombardo, Fontaine Sisters, Mindy Carson, Johnny Johnston,
Art Mooney, Kitty Kallen. Songs: "Bye Bye Baby"-Como,
Fontaine Sisters; "Mrs Murphy"-Como; "Fairy Tales"-Fontaine
Sisters; "Tisket-a-Tasket"-Fitzgerald; "Happy Anniversary"-
Johnston, MacRae; "Auld Lang Syne"-Lombardo; "Bibbidi,
Bobbidi, Boo"-Como, Fontaine Sisters. Skit: Dramatization
of "Martin Block Story" in celebration of the 15th
Anniversary of Martin Block's Make Believe Ballroom. Cast:
Pa Block-MacRae; Ma Block-Carson; Coach-Lombardo; Boyhood
Pal-Jenkins; Boyhood Pal's Pal- Mooney; Teacher-Kallen;
Announcer-Johnston; Girlfriend-Whiting; Themselves-Andy and
Della Russell.

R11. 1948 CHRISTMAS SEAL PARTY (1948)
Host: Bob Hope. Orchestra: Benny Goodman. Announcer:
Don Wilson. Writer-Producer: Carl Slickman, Allan Sands,
Allen Livingston, Glen Clauson. Guests: Margaret Whiting,
Jo Stafford, Paul Weston, Andy Russell, Peggy Lee, Jack
Smith, Johnny Mercer, Pied Pipers, King Cole Trio, Frank
DeVol, Gordon MacRae. Songs: "It's Magic"-MacRae; "Tree in
the Meadow"-Whiting; "Barbara Allen"-Stafford, Weston;
"Silent Night"-Russell; "Carnival in Venice"-Smith, DeVol;

"For Every Man There's a Woman"-Lee.

R12. COMMAND PERFORMANCE (1948?)
The show was done in cooperation with the Hollywood coordinating committee.
Host: Gordon MacRae. Announcer: Jimmy Wallington. Theme: "Over There." Guests: Eve Arden, Andrews Sisters. Songs: "Feudin' and Fightin'"-Andrews Sisters; "It's Magic"-MacRae; "Pussy Cat Song"-MacRae, Patty Andrews; "You Call Everybody Darling"-Andrews Sisters. Skit: "Carmen" Cast: Don Jose-MacRae; Carmen-Arden; Cigarette Factory Workers/Smugglers-Andrews Sisters.

R13. DORIS DAY SHOW (CBS, July 15, 1952)
Hostess: Doris Day. Announcer: Johnny Jacobs, Ray Rowan. Guest: Gordon MacRae.

R14. DORIS DAY SHOW (CBS, August 10, 1952)
Hostess: Doris Day. Announcer: Johnny Jacobs, Ray Rowan. Guest: Gordon MacRae.

R15. GENERAL ELECTRIC SHOW (CBS, November 6, 1952)
Guest Host: James Stewart. Announcer: Ken Carpenter. Orchestra: John Scott Trotter. Sponsor: General Electric. Guests: Gordon MacRae, Rosemary Clooney, Joe Venuti. Songs: "Jazz Violin," "Autumn Leaves"-Venuti; "Who Kissed Me Last Night," "This Can't Be Love," "Half As Much"-Clooney; "A Cock-Eyed Optimist," "Somewhere Along the Way," "Begin the Beguine"-MacRae; "Walking My Baby Back Home"-MacRae, Clooney.

R16. GORDON MacRAE-SONGS (CBS, 1945)
The show aired for 15 minutes, 5 days a week, at 4:30. Host: Gordon MacRae. Regulars: Sheila MacRae, Marian Bell. Sponsor: Club Aluminum.

R17. GUEST STAR (Syndicated, April 1951)
Host: Gordon MacRae. Announcer: Del Sharbutt. Orchestra: Carmen Dragon. Sponsor: U.S. Treasury and Savings Bonds. Songs: "If I Loved You," "Sylvia," "Ich Liebe Dich"-MacRae; "Danny Boy"-Dragon.

R18. GUEST STAR (Syndicated, October 1951)
Host: Gordon MacRae. Announcer: Del Sharbutt. Orchestra: Paul Weston. Songs: "Lullaby of Broadway," "We Kiss in a Shadow," "Old Man River"-MacRae; "When Your Love Has Gone"-Weston.

R19. GULF SPRAY (Summer, 1947)
The show was a summer replacement for Fannie Brice. Host: Gordon MacRae. Announcer: Dan Seymour. Sponsor: Gulf Bug Spray. Theme: "Life is a Song."
1 Songs: "Let's Go Back and Kiss the Girls Goodnight Again," "Tavern in the Town," "April Showers," "Anniversary Waltz," "Oh But I Do"-all by MacRae.
2 Songs: "I'll Remember April," "Begin the Beguine," "I've Got the Sun in the Morning"-MacRae; "Lady Be

Good"-Tony Matola, Johnny Gwenary, Triger Albert.
19.3   Songs: "Cecelia," "It's Only a Paper Moon," "My
Moonlight Madonna," "Of Thee I Sing," "Smoke Gets
in Your Eyes"-MacRae.
4   Songs: "Smoke Gets in Your Eyes," "She's Funny That
Way," "Blue Moon"-MacRae; "Girl of My Dreams"-Tony
Matola, John Gwenary, Triger Elbert.
5   Songs: "Nice Work If You Can Get It," "The Very
Thought of You," "Sigh By Night," "Sunday Kind of
Love"-MacRae.

R20. HERE'S TO VETERANS (Syndicated, 1958)
Host: Gordon MacRae. Sponsor: Veteran's Administration
with the cooperation of the American Federation of
Musicians. Songs: "When You Kiss Me," "Secret," "If I Forget
You," "Sayonara"-MacRae.

R21. HERE'S TO VETERANS (Syndicated, 1962)
Host: Gordon MacRae. Sponsor: Veteran's Administration
with the cooperation of the American Federation of
Musicians. Guest: Jo Stafford. Songs: "Sweetest Sounds"-
MacRae; "Whispering Hope"-MacRae, Stafford; "Nobody Told
Me"-MacRae; "Beyond the Sunset"-MacRae, Stafford.

R22. HORACE HEIDT (1941)
Two shows were broadcast each week on network radio.

R23. JOHNSON'S WAX SUMMER PROGRAM (NBC, July 12, 1949)
Host: Ken Darby & Kingsmen. Orchestra: Elliot Daniel.
Announcer: Ken Niles. Guest: Gordon MacRae. Songs: "Skyball
Paint," "Over the Rainbow"-Darby and Kingsmen; "Younger Than
Springtime," "So in Love"-MacRae; "Picalo, Harp, Six
Typewriters, a Slither, and a Leaky Balloon"-Darby and
Kingsmen; "Tea For Two"-Buddy Coleman (piano), Daniel's
Orchestra; "Evelyn"-Darby and Kingsmen; "Do You Ever Think
of Me?"-MacRae, Darby and Kingsmen.

R24. MINIATURE MINSTRELS
Gordon was featured weekly on station WFBL.
Writer, Producer: Bill Lundigan. Song: "If I Had a
Million Dollars"-MacRae.

R25. NAVY STAR TIME (1953, 30 minutes)

R26. NBC HOLLYWOOD CALLING (September 30, 1949)

R27. RAILROAD HOUR (NBC, 1952)
This 15-minute broadcast was for the Red Cross.

R28. RAILROAD HOUR (1948-1954)
The show was first broadcast on ABC in a 45-minute
format, then moved to NBC and trimmed to 30 minutes. It
was aired Monday nights at 8:00.
Star: Gordon MacRae. Orchestra: John Rairg, Carmen
Dragon. Announcer: Marvin Miller. Director: Ken Burton,
Fran Van Hartesfeld, Murray Bolen. Writers: Jean Holloway,
Jerry Lawrence, Bob Lee. Choral Director: Norman Luboff.
Theme: "I've Been Working on the Railroad." Sponsor:

Association of American Railroads. <u>Opening</u>: Marvin
Miller-"Ladies and Gentlemen, the RAILROAD HOUR."
The following is a log of RAILROAD HOURS provided by Ray
Stanich.

RAILROAD HOUR LOG

<u>1948 WJZ (ABC) 8:00-8:45 p.m.</u>

28.1 GOOD NEWS-October 4, 1948. (Premier) (Dinah
     Shore/Jane Powell)
   2 ANYTHING GOES-October 11, 1948. (Victor Moore/
     Margaret Whiting)
   3 CAT & THE FIDDLE-October 18, 1948. (Rise Stevens)
   4 STUDENT PRINCE-October 25, 1948. (Dorothy
     Kirsten)
   5 ROBERTA-November 1, 1948. (Eddie Bracken/Jan
     Clayton)
   6 RIO RITA-November 8, 1948. (Margo and Leo
     Carillo)
   7 VAGABOND KING-November 15, 1948. (Dorothy
     Kirsten)
   8 HIT THE DECK-November 22, 1948. (Frances
     Langford)
   9 NEW MOON-November 29, 1948. (Nadine Connor/Rudy
     Vallee)
  10 GIRL CRAZY-December 6, 1948. (Doris Day)
  11 SALLY-December 13, 1948. (Dinah Shore/Leon Errol)
  12 HOLIDAY INN-December 20, 1948. (George Murphy/
     Martha Tilton)
  13 DESERT SONG-December 27, 1948. (Nadine Connor)

<u>1949</u>

  14 WHOOPEE-January 3, 1949. (Eddie Cantor/Eileen
     Wilson)
  15 RED MILL-January 10, 1949. (Lucille Norman/Gene
     Kelly)
  16 NAUGHTY MARIETTA-January 17, 1949. (Jeanette
     MacDonald)
  17 BLOSSOM TIME-January 24, 1949. (Patrice Munsel)
  18 BITTER SWEET-January 31, 1949. (Jeanette
     MacDonald)
  19 ROSE MARIE-February 7, 1949. (Patrice Munsel)
  20 SWEETHEARTS-February 14, 1949. (Jane Powell)
  21 LADY BE GOOD-February 21, 1949. (Groucho Marx)
  22 SONG OF NORWAY-February 28, 1949. (M. Koshetz)
  23 MERRY WIDOW-March 7, 1949. (Jeanette MacDonald)
  24 EILEEN-March 14, 1949. (Irene Manning)
  25 STATE FAIR-March 21, 1949. (Jo Stafford)
  26 BEST FOOT FORWARD-March 28, 1949. (Betty Garrett)
  27 MLLE. MODISTE-April 4, 1949. (Dorothy Kirsten)
  28 FIREFLY-April 11, 1949. (Nadine Connor)
  29 APPLE BLOSSOMS-April 18, 1949. (Jeanette
     MacDonald)
  30 FORTUNE TELLER-April 25, 1949. (Patrice Munsel)

<u>WJZ (ABC) 8:00-8:30 p.m.</u>

(RAILROAD HOUR LOG continued)

28.31   SHOWBOAT-May 2, 1949. (Lucille Norman)
   32   KISS ME KATE-May 9, 1949. (Lucille Norman)
   33   ROBIN HOOD-May 16, 1949. (Lucille Norman)
   34   PORGY and BESS-May 23, 1949. (Lucille Norman)
   35   LIFE OF CJ BOND-May 30, 1949. (Lucille Norman)
   36   OKLAHOMA-June 6, 1949. (Lucille Norman)
   37   S. FOSTER STORY-June 13, 1949. (Lucille Norman)
   38   BURKE/VAN HEUSEN SALUTE-June 20, 1949. (Lucille Norman)
   39   CHICAGO RR FAIR SALUTE-June 27, 1949. (Lucille Norman)
   40   MISS LIBERTY-July 4, 1949. (Lucille Norman)
   41   J. McHUGH STORY-July 11, 1949. (Lucille Norman)
   42   BANDWAGON-July 18, 1949. (Lucille Norman)
   43   TIN PAN ALLEY SALUTE-July 25, 1949. (Lucille Norman)
   44   E. NEVIN SALUTE-August 1, 1949. (Lucille Norman)
   45   BRIGADOON-August 8, 1949. (Lucille Norman)
   46   GORDON/WARREN SALUTE-August 15, 1949. (Lucille Norman)
   47   CALL ME MISTER-August 22, 1949. (Lucille Norman)
   48   J. GREEN SALUTE-August 29, 1949. (Lucille Norman)
   49   WIZARD OF OZ-September 5, 1949. (Lucille Norman)
   50   H. CARMICHAEL SALUTE-September 12, 1949. (Lucille Norman)
   51   N.H. BROWN SALUTE-September 19, 1949. (Lucille Norman)
   52   RODGERS & HAMMERSTEIN SALUTE-September 26, 1949. (Lucille Norman)

WNBC (NBC) 8:00-8:30 p.m.

   53   SHOWBOAT-October 3, 1949. (Lucille Norman/Dorothy Kirsten)
   54   NEW MOON-October 10, 1949. (Lucille Norman)
   55   CHOCOLATE SOLDIER-October 17, 1949. (Nadine Connor)
   56   MUSIC IN THE AIR-October 24, 1949. (Jane Powell)
   57   BLOSSOM TIME-October 31, 1949. (Lucille Norman)
   58   GREAT WALTZ-November 7, 1949. (Jarmilla Novotna)
   59   VAGABOND KING-November 14, 1949. (Lucille Norman)
   60   NO NO NANETTE-November 21, 1949. (Doris Day)
   61   STUDENT PRINCE-November 28, 1949. (Jane Powell)
   62   MIKADO-December 5, 1949. (Kenny Baker/E. Case)
   63   DESERT SONG-December 12, 1949. (Dorothy Sarnoff)
   64   ROSE MARIE-December 19, 1949. (Patrice Munsell)
   65   SNOW WHITE-December 26, 1949. (Jane Powell)

1950

   66   RED MILL-January 2, 1950. (Lucille Norman)
   67   BITTERSWEET-January 9, 1950. (Dorothy Kirsten)
   68   LA. PURCHASE-January 16, 1950. (Lucille Norman)
   69   MERRY WIDOW-January 23, 1950. (Dorothy Kirsten)
   70   BRIGADOON-January 30, 1950. (Jane Powell)
   71   APPLE BLOSSOMS-February 6, 1950. (Dorothy

(RAILROAD HOUR LOG continued)

Kirsten)
28.72   SWEETHEARTS-February 13, 1950. (Jane Powell)
   73   COUNT OF LUXEMBURG-February 20, 1950. (Nadine
        Connor)
   74   MLLE. MODISTE-February 27, 1950. (Jane Powell)
   75   HMS PINAFORE-March 6, 1950. (Lucille Norman)
   76   LITTLE NELLIE KELLY-March 13, 1950. (Jane Powell)
   77   THE ONLY GIRL-March 20, 1950. (Dorothy
        Warenskjold)
   78   SUNNY-March 27, 1950. (Jo Stafford)
   79   SONG OF NORWAY-April 3, 1950. (D. Coulter/I.
        Petina)
   80   NAUGHTY MARIETTA-April 10, 1950. (Nadine Connor)
   81   MADAME SHERRY-April 17, 1950. (M. Bell)
   82   PRINCE OF PILSEN-April 24, 1950. (Nadine Connor)
   83   SALLY-May 1, 1950. (M. Bell)
   84   PINK LADY-May 8, 1950. (Lucille Norman)
   85   ROBIN HOOD-May 15, 1950. (Dorothy Kirsten)
   86   PRINCESS PAT-May 22, 1950. (Lucille Norman)
   87   REVIEW OF 1927-May 29, 1950. (Lucille Norman)
   88   REVIEW OF 1937-June 5, 1950. (Lucille Norman)
   89   REVIEW OF 1931-June 12, 1950. (Lucille Norman)
   90   REVIEW OF GAY 90s-June 19, 1950. (Lucille Norman)
   91   REVIEW 1900-1905-July 3, 1950. (Lucille Norman)
   92   REVIEW 1934-July 10, 1950. (Lucille Norman)
   93   REVIEW 1905-1910-July 17, 1950. (Lucille Norman)
   94   REVIEW OF 1938-July 24, 1950. (Lucille Norman)
   95   REVIEW 1915-1920-July 31, 1950. (Lucille Norman)
   96   REVIEW 1932-August 7, 1950. (Lucille Norman)
   97   REVIEW 1926-August 14, 1950. (Lucille Norman)
   98   REVIEW 1935-August 21, 1950. (Lucille Norman)
   99   REVIEW 1929-August 28, 1950. (Lucille Norman)
  100   REVIEW 1922-September 4, 1950. (Lucille Norman)
  101   REVIEW 1933-September 11, 1950. (Lucille Norman)
  102   REVIEW 1910-1915-September 18, 1950. (Lucille
        Norman)
  103   REVIEW 1924-September 25, 1950. (Lucille Norman)
  104   ALLEGRO-October 2, 1950. (Nadine Connor)
  105   ROBERTA-October 9, 1950. (Ginny Simms)
  106   COUNTESS MARITZA-October 16, 1950. (Dorothy
        Warenskjold)
  107   REVENGE WITH MUSIC-October 23, 1950. (Nadine
        Connor)
  108   SHOW BOAT-October 30, 1950. (Dorothy Kirsten)
  109   IRENE-November 6, 1950. (Eileen Wilson)
  110   ORANGE BLOSSOMS-November 13, 1950. (Dorothy
        Warenskjold)
  111   SNOW WHITE-November 20, 1950. (Ilene Woods)
  112   A CONNECTICUT YANKEE-November 27, 1950. (Ginny
        Simms)
  113   FIREFLY-December 4, 1950. (Dorothy Sarnoff)
  114   PIRATES OF PENSANCE-December 11, 1950. (Lucille
        Norman)
  115   BRIGADOON-December 18, 1950. (M. Bell)
  116   CHRISTMAS SONGS-December 25, 1950. (Lucille
        Norman)

(RAILROAD HOUR LOG continued)

1951

28.117	REVIEW 1950-January 1, 1951. (Lucille Norman)
118	CAROUSEL-January 8, 1951. (Patricia Morrison)
119	STUDENT PRINCE-January 15, 1951. (E. Case)
120	DEAREST ENEMY-January 22, 1951. (Nadine Connor)
121	NEW MOON-January 29, 1951. (Dorothy Kirsten)
122	CAT AND THE FIDDLE-February 5, 1951. (F. Yeend)
123	SARI-February 12, 1951. (Vivien Della Chiesa)
124	SONG OF NORWAY-February 19, 1951. (Ira Petina)
125	2 HEARTS IN 3/4 TIME-February 26, 1951. (M. Bell)
126	VAGABOND KING-March 5, 1951. (Ira Petina)
127	ROSALINDA-March 12, 1951. (A. Dickey)
128	APPLE BLOSSOMS-March 19, 1951. (Dorothy Kirsten)
129	FORTUNE TELLER-March 26, 1951. (Nadine Connor)
130	ANNIE LAURIE-April 2, 1951. (Dorothy Warenskjold)
131	GREAT WALTZ-April 9, 1951. (Dorothy Kirsten)
132	ONE TOUCH OF VENUS-April 16, 1951. (Ginny Simms)
133	MDE. BUTTERFLY-April 23, 1951. (Nadine Connor)
134	MUSIC IN THE AIR-April 30, 1951. (Jo Stafford)
135	HIGH BUTTON SHOES-May 7, 1951. (Margaret Whiting)
136	NINA ROSA-May 14, 1951. (Mimi Benzell)
137	CHOCOLATE SOLDIER-May 21, 1951. (M. Bell)
138	KATINKA-May 28, 1951. (A. Dickey)
139	VERY WARM FOR MAY-June 4, 1951. (A. Dickey)
140	GYPSY PRINCESS-June 11, 1951. (Jarilma Novotna)
141	BOYS FROM SYRACUSE-June 18, 1951. (E. Case)
142	MERRY WIDOW-June 25, 1951. (Nadine Connor)
143	BEAUTIFUL DREAMER-July 2, 1951. (Dorothy Warenskjold)
	PRE-EMPTED-July 9, 1951.
144	CASEY AT THE BAT-July 16, 1951. (Dorothy Warenskjold)
145	ROARING CAMP-July 23, 1951. (Dorothy Warenskjold)
146	PIRATES OF PICADILLY-July 30, 1951. (Dorothy Warenskjold)
147	THE BIG TOP-August 6, 1951. (Dorothy Warenskjold)
148	1001 NIGHTS-August 13, 1951. (Dorothy Warenskjold)
149	LONG AGO-August 20, 1951. (Dorothy Warenskjold)
150	DANNY FREEL-August 27, 1951. (Dorothy Warenskjold)
151	INNOCENTS ABROAD-September 3, 1951. (Dorothy Warenskjold)
152	JOURNEY INTO THE SUN-September 10, 1951. (Dorothy Warenskjold)
153	RIP VAN WINKLE-September 17, 1951. (Dorothy Warenskjold)
154	EMPEROR OF SAN FRANCISCO-September 24, 1951. (Dorothy Warenskjold)
155	STATE FAIR-October 1, 1951. (Dorothy Kirsten)
156	MADAME SHERRY-October 8, 1951. (Nadine Connor)
157	MARTHA-October 15, 1951. (Dorothy Kirsten)
158	SWEETHEARTS-October 22, 1951. (Mimi Benzell)
159	HOLIDAY INN-October 29, 1951. (Dorothy Kirsten)
160	ROSE MARIE-November 5, 1951. (Dorothy Kirsten)

(RAILROAD HOUR LOG continued)

28.161   BOHEMIAN GIRL-November 12, 1951. (Dorothy
         Kirsten)
   162   JUBILEE-November 19, 1951. (Dorothy Kirsten)
   163   MLLE. MODISTE-November 26, 1951. (Dorothy
         Kirsten)
   164   MARINKA-December 3, 1951. (Gladys Swarthout)
   165   RED MILL-December 10, 1951. (Rise Stevens)
   166   ROSALIE-December 17, 1951. (Nadine Connor)
   167   HAPPY PRINCE-December 24, 1951. (Lucille Norman)
   168   REVIEW 1951-December 31, 1951. (Lucille Norman)

   1952

   169   BLOSSOM TIME-January 7, 1952. (Nadine Connor)
   170   I MARRIED AN ANGEL-January 14, 1952. (Nadine
         Connor)
   171   DESERT SONG-January 21, 1952. (Mimi Benzell)
   172   3 MUSKETEERS-January 28, 1952. (Dorothy
         Warenskjold)
   173   EAST WIND-February 4, 1952. (Mimi Benzell)
   174   ORANGE BLOSSOMS-February 11, 1952. (E. Case)
   175   FREDERIKA-February 18, 1952. (Patricia Morrison)
   176   FIREFLY-February 25, 1952. (Dorothy Kirsten)
   177   WHITE EAGLE-March 3, 1952. (Lucille Norman)
   178   CAT AND THE FIDDLE-March 10, 1952. (Dorothy
         Kirsten)
   179   SARI-March 17, 1952. (Margaret Truman)
   180   KISS ME KATE-March 24, 1952. (Patrice Munsel)
   181   COUNTESS MARITZA-March 31, 1952. (Blanche Thebom)
   182   ROBERTA-April 7, 1952. (Nadine Connor)
   183   ROSALINDA-April 14, 1952. (Dorothy Warenskjold)
   184   ERMINIE-April 21, 1952. (N. Tangeman)
   185   PINK LADY-April 28, 1952. (Nadine Connor)
   186   SUNNY-May 5, 1952. (V. Haskins)
   187   SPRING IS HERE-May 12, 1952. (A. Dickey)
   188   GREAT WALTZ-May 19, 1952. (Lucille Norman)
   189   MY MARYLAND-May 26, 1952. (Dorothy Kirsten)
   190   MINSTREL BOY-June 2, 1952. (Dorothy Warenskjold)
   191   SWEDISH NIGHTINGALE-June 9, 1952. (Dorothy
         Warenskjold)
   192   RIGHT DRESS-June 16, 1952. (Dorothy Warenskjold)
   193   LITTLE MINISTER-June 23, 1952. (Dorothy
         Warenskjold)
   194   SPRINGTIME IN PARIS-June 30, 1952. (Dorothy
         Warenskjold)
   195   SCHEHEREZADE-July 7, 1952. (Lucille Norman)
   196   THE NECKLACE-July 14, 1952. (Dorothy Warenskjold)
   197   LOVE SONG-July 21, 1952. (Dorothy Warenskjold)
   198   PIRATE OF NEW ORLEANS-July 28, 1952. (Dorothy
         Warenskjold)
   199   STARLIGHT-August 4, 1952. (Lucille Norman)
   200   THE BROWNINGS-August 11, 1952. (Dorothy
         Warenskjold)
   201   MISS CINDERELLA-August 18, 1952. (Dorothy
         Warenskjold)
   202   FANTASIE-August 25, 1952. (Dorothy Warenskjold)

(RAILROAD HOUR LOG continued)

28.203   PIRATES OF PICADILLY-September 1, 1952. (Dorothy
         Warenskjold)
   204   SWAN LAKE-September 8, 1952. (Dorothy
         Warenskjold)
   205   MAESTRO-September 15, 1952. (Dorothy Warenskjold)
   206   GOLDEN CURTAIN-September 22, 1952. (Lucille Norman)
   207   ANNIE LAURIE-September 29, 1952. (Lucille Norman)
   208   MAYTIME-October 6, 1952. (Dorothy Kirsten)
   209   A WALTZ DREAM-October 13, 1952. (Dorothy Kirsten)
   210   NAUGHTY MARIETTA-October 20, 1952. (Dorothy
         Kirsten)
   211   GYPSY PRINCESS-October 27, 1952. (Blanche Thebom)
   212   SEVENTH HEAVEN-November 3, 1952. (Ann Ayers)
   213   DEAREST ENEMY-November 10, 1952. (Eileen Farrell)
   214   ON YOUR TOES-November 17, 1952. (M. Bell)
   215   VAGABOND KING-November 24, 1952. (Mimi Benzell)
   216   BABES IN TOYLAND-December 1, 1952. (Lucille Norman)
   217   GYPSY BARON-December 8, 1952. (Mimi Benzell)
   218   HOLIDAY INN-December 15, 1952. (Dorothy
         Warenskjold)
   219   CHRISTMAS PARTY-December 22, 1952. (Dorothy
         Kirsten)
   220   REVIEW OF YEAR-December 29, 1952. (Dorothy
         Warenskjold)

   <u>1953</u>

   221   MY ROMANCE-January 5, 1953. (Nadine Connor)
   222   2 HEARTS IN 3/4 TIME-January 12, 1953. (M. Bell)
   223   SHOW BOAT-January 19, 1953. (Dorothy Kirsten)
   224   MERRY WIDOW-January 26, 1953. (Dorothy Kirsten)
   225   CAROUSEL-February 2, 1953. (Nadine Connor)
   226   MISS LIBERTY-February 9, 1953. (Nadine Connor)
   227   BLUE PARADISE-February 16, 1953. (Nadine Connor)
   228   BITTERSWEET-February 23, 1953. (Dorothy
         Warenskjold)
   229   ROSE OF ALGERIA-March 2, 1953. (Lucille Norman)
   230   UP IN CENTRAL PARK-March 9, 1953. (Mimi Benzell)
   231   EILEEN-March 16, 1953. (Lucille Norman)
   232   LUTE SONG-March 23, 1953. (Mimi Benzell)
   233   PRINCESS PAT-March 30, 1953. (Elaine Malbin)
   234   SALLY-April 6, 1953. (Lucille Norman)
   235   FORTUNE TELLER-April 13, 1953. (Dorothy
         Warenskjold)
   236   EL CAPITAN-April 20, 1953. (Ann Ayers)
   237   PINK LADY-April 27, 1953. (Nadine Connor)
   238   MARY-May 4, 1953. (Dorothy Kirsten)
   239   ROSALINDA-May 11, 1953. (Dorothy Kirsten)
   240   CIRCUS PRINCESS-May 18, 1953. (Dorothy Kirsten)
   241   IRENE-May 25, 1953. (Dorothy Warenskjold)
   242   QUALITY STREET-June 1, 1953. (Dorothy
         Warenskjold)
   243   DEAR YESTERDAY-June 8, 1953. (Dorothy
         Warenskjold)
   244   LOVE STORY-June 15, 1953. (Dorothy Warenskjold)
   245   NEW WINE-June 22, 1953. (Dorothy Warenskjold)

(RAILROAD HOUR LOG continued)

28.246 MAN WITHOUT A COUNTRY-June 29, 1953. (Dorothy
        Warenskjold)
   247 PENNY WHISTLE-July 6, 1953. (Dorothy Warenskjold)
   248 FRIMIL STORY-July 13, 1953. (Dorothy Warenskjold)
   249 STARLIGHT-July 20, 1953. (Dorothy Warenskjold)
   250 GOLDEN EXPRESS-July 27, 1953. (Dorothy
        Warenskjold)
   251 ON THE WINGS OF A SONG-August 3, 1953. (Dorothy
        Warenskjold)
   252 TRILBY-August 10, 1953. (Dorothy Warenskjold)
   253 ROARING CAMP-August 17, 1953. (Dorothy
        Warenskjold)
   254 HOPE IS A WOMAN-August 24, 1953. (Dorothy
        Warenskjold)
   255 LORNA DOONE-August 31, 1953. (Dorothy
        Warenskjold)
   256 NIGHT MUSIC-September 7, 1953. (Dorothy
        Warenskjold)
   257 MILLION DOLLAR BANK NOTE-September 14, 1953.
        (Dorothy Warenskjold)
   258 MINSTREL BOY-September 21, 1953. (Dorothy
        Warenskjold)
   259 FAMILIAR STRANGER-September 28, 1953. (Dorothy
        Warenskjold)
   260 STUDENT PRINCE-October 5, 1953. (Dorothy
        Warenskjold)
   261 SHOW BOAT-October 12, 1953. (Dorothy Warenskjold)
   262 SUNNY-October 19, 1953. (Lucille Norman)
   263 FIREFLY-October 26, 1953. (Dorothy Warenskjold)
   264 ROSALINDA-November 2, 1953. (Elaine Malbin)
   265 ROBERTA-November 9, 1953. (Dorothy Kirsten)
   266 MERRY WIDOW-November 16, 1953. (Dorothy Kirsten)
   267 CHOCOLATE SOLDIER-November 23, 1953. (V. Haskins)
   268 STATE FAIR-November 30, 1953. (Lucille Norman)
   269 SWEETHEARTS-December 7, 1953. (Elaine Malbin)
   270 CAT AND THE FIDDLE-December 14, 1953. (Dorothy
        Kirsten)
   271 SNOW WHITE-December 21, 1953. (Dorothy
        Warenskjold)
   272 REVIEW OF THE YEAR-December 28, 1953. (Dorothy
        Kirsten)

   1954

   273 VAGABOND KING-January 4, 1954. (J.S. Smith)
   274 GYPSY BARON-January 11, 1954. (Mimi Benzell)
   275 GIRL FROM UTAH-January 18, 1954. (Ann Ayers)
   276 MUSIC IN THE AIR-January 25, 1954. (Mimi Benzell)
   277 MAYTIME-February 1, 1954. (Nadine Connor)
   278 SHUMANN STORY-February 8, 1954. (Dorothy
        Warenskjold)
   279 THROUGH THE YEARS-February 15, 1954. (Dorothy
        Kirsten)
   280 MARTHA-February 22, 1954. (Gladys Swarthout)
   281 THE GREAT WALTZ-March 1, 1954. (Elaine Malbin)
   282 THE RED MILL-March 8, 1954. (Eileen Farrell)

(RAILROAD HOUR LOG continued)

28.283   MINSTREL BOY-March 15, 1954. (Lucille Norman)
   284   IRENE-March 22, 1954. (Elaine Malbin)
   285   THREE MUSKETEERS-March 29, 1954. (Dorothy
          Warenskjold)
   286   GREAT DAY-April 5, 1954. (Mimi Benzell)
   287   BABES IN TOYLAND-April 12, 1954. (Lucille Norman)
   288   SMILES-April 19, 1954. (Elaine Malbin)
   289   ROSE MARIE-April 26, 1954. (V. Haskins)
   290   BIRTHDAY-May 3, 1954. (Lucille Norman)
   291   WONDERFUL ONE HORSE SHAY-May 10, 1954. (Lucille
          Norman)
   292   AROUND THE WORLD IN 80 DAYS-May 17, 1954. (Lucille
          Norman)
   293   PENNY WHISTLE-May 24, 1954. (Lucille Norman)
   294   HOMING-May 31, 1954. (Nadine Connor)
   295   ROSALIE-June 7, 1954. (Nadine Connor)
   296   PINK LADY-June 14, 1954. (Lucille Norman)
   297   NEW MOON-June 21, 1954. (Lucille Norman) LAST
          SHOW

R29. SARDI'S RADIO SHOW (February, 1953. Bill Slater's
Luncheon)

R30. SHOWTIME
   1   "Whoopee." (January 3, 1949)
        Music: Walter Donaldson. Lyrics: Gus Kahn. Host:
        Gordon MacRae. Guests: Eddie Cantor, Eileen
        Wilson. Characters: Henry Williams-Cantor;
        Wynennas-MacRae; Sally- Wilson.
   2   "Bittersweet." (January 31, 1949)
        By Noel Coward. Adapted by Jean Holloway. Host:
        Gordon MacRae. Orchestra: Carmen Dragon. Choir:
        Norman Luboff. Guest: Jeanette MacDonald.
   3   "Rose Marie." (February 7, 1949)
        By Rudolf Frimil. Story: Otto Harback. Adapted by
        Bill Deling. Host: Gordon MacRae. Orchestra:
        Carmen Dragon. Choir: Norman Luboff. Guests: Pinky
        Lee, Patrice Munsel. Characters: Hardboiled
        Herman-Lee; Jim Kent-MacRae; Rosemarie-Munsel.
   4   "Sweethearts." (February 14, 1949)
        By Victor Herbert. Host: Gordon MacRae. Guests:
        Jane Powell, Walter O'Keefe, Verna Felton.
        Characters: Sylvia-Powell; Fran-MacRae; McKell-
        O'Keefe; Dame Paula owner of Laundry White Geese-
        Felton.
   5   "Lady Be Good." (February 21, 1949)
        By Ira and George Gershwin. Host: Gordon MacRae.
        Guest: Groucho Marx. Characters: Tee Watas and
        Watkins-Marx; Dick Trevor-MacRae.
   6   "Chocolate Soldier." (October 17, 1949)
        By Oscar Strauss. Adapted by Lawrence and Lee.
        Host: Gordon MacRae. Guests: Nadine Connor, Beau
        Benederet, Ed Begley. Characters: Lt. Bomer-
        MacRae; Nadina-Connor.
   7   "Music in the Air." (October 24, 1949)
        By Jerome Kern and Oscar Hammerstein. Host:

Gordon MacRae. Guest: Jane Powell.
30.8   "Jubilee." (November 19, 1951)
By Cole Porter. Host: Gordon MacRae. Guest:
Dorothy Kirsten. Characters: Prince-MacRae;
Princess-Kirsten.
   9   "Count of Luxenbourg." (February 20, 1950)
By Franz Lehar. Host: Gordon MacRae. Guests:
Nadine Connor, Jack Kirkwood.
  10   "HMS Pinafore." (March 6, 1950)
By Gilbert and Sullivan. Host: Gordon MacRae.
Guests: Lucille Norman, Kenny Baker.

R31. SKYLINE ROOF (CBS, 1946)
Host: Gordon MacRae. Announcer: Harry Clark.
Orchestra: Archie Bleyer.

R32. STARS FOR DEFENSE (1959)
Star: Gordon MacRae. Orchestra: Van Alexander.
Announcer: Marvin Miller. Guest: Director Leo A. Hoygt from
the Civil Defense Mobilization. Songs: "Secret," "A Man
Once Said," "If I Forget You"-MacRae; "Blue Rhythm Jam"-
Alexander.

R33. TEENTIMERS CLUB (NBC, March 15, 1947)
The show was broadcast for 30 minutes on Saturday at
11:00 a.m.   Gordon was host for the 1946-1947 season.
Host: Gordon MacRae. Announcer: Fred Robis. Guest:
Lionel Hampton. Sponsor: Teentimer Clothes. Songs: "Rainy
Night in Rio," "Bless You," "Linda," "Life Can Be
Beautiful"-MacRae; "Flying Home," "How High the Moon," "The
Pencil Broke"-Hampton.

R34. TEXACO STAR THEATRE (CBS, March 24, 1947)
The show aired Monday at 9:30 p.m.   Gordon was host
for the 1947-1948 season.   By 1948, the show had moved to
ABC.   Milton Berle replaced MacRae in the 1948-1949 season.
Host: Gordon MacRae. Chorus: Jeff Alexander. Orchestra:
Victor Young. Regulars: Evelyn Knight, Alan Young.

R35. THIS IS OUR MUSIC (April 12, 1957)
Host: Gordon MacRae. Chorus: Roger Wagner. Guest: Dr.
Kenneth Clark (from the American Cancer Society). Sponsor:
American Cancer Society. Songs: "Cindy"-Wagner Chorale; "Oh
What a Beautiful Morning," "Oklahoma"-MacRae.

R36. USN RESERVE SHOW (1950)
Host: Gordon MacRae. Orchestra: Paul Weston. Vocals:
Starlighters. Announcer: Tom Reddy. Songs: "Ragtime Cowboy
Joe"-Weston & Starlighters; "I Surrender Dear." "Body and
Soul"-MacRae.

R37. YOURS FOR A SONG (1949)
This was the premiere show from Hollywood.
Host: Bernard Dudley. Orchestra: Harry Zimmerman.
Sponsor: Conti Castile Shampoo. Regulars: Betty Rose
(Vocalist), Sheila Graham (Columnist). Guest: Gordon
MacRae. Sheila's guest: Victor Mature. Walk-on: Betty
Hutton. Songs: "How Do You Face the Sunshine"-MacRae; "My

Dream is Yours," "Always True to You"-Rose; "So in Love"-MacRae, Rose.

R38. YOURS FOR A SONG (1949)
      Host: Bernard Dudley. Orchestra: Harry Zimmerman.
Guest: Gordon MacRae. Sponsor: Conti Castile Shampoo.
Regulars: Betty Rose, Sheila Graham.

NOTE: Shows listed below are available on tape from private dealers: "All Star Revue;" "Big Show" (February 11, 1950); "Charlie McCarthy Show;" "Chesterfield Supper Club"-both; "1948 Christmas Seal Party;" "Command Performance;" "General Electric Show;" "Gulf Spray"-all; "Guest Star"-both; "Here's to Veterans"-both; "Johnson's Wax Summer Show;" "Railroad Hour"-many segments; "Showtime"-all; "Stars For Defense;" "Teentimers Club;" "This is Our Music;" "USN Reserve Show;" "Yours For a Song"-Premiere show, & all below but R41 & R44.

ADDENDA

R39. CALLING ALL HEARTS
      with Gordon MacRae & Shirley Jones. Song: "Many a New Face."

R40. GORDON MacRAE-TROUBADOR (CBS, August 1, 1947)
      with Gordon MacRae, & Marion Bell. Announcer: Dan Seymour. Song: "Tallahassee." Sponsor: Jello.

R41. LUX RADIO THEATRE (CBS, 1950s)
      This 60 minute anthology aired Monday nights at 8:00.
      Host: William Keighley. Announcer: Ken Carpenter.
Sponsor: Lux Soap. Guests: Jane Wyman, Gordon MacRae.

R42. SALUTE TO RESERVISTS
      with Gordon MacRae, Ellen Sutton, Marvin Ash. Song: "Nobody's Sweetheart Now." Orchestra: Eddie Scrivanik.
Producer: C.P. MacGregor. Announcer: Charles Arlington.

R43. STAND BY FOR MUSIC
      with Gordon MacRae. Orchestra: Jerry Gray. Announcer: Hy Averback.

R44. STEVE ALLEN SHOW (CBS, November, 1950)
      Host: Steve Allen. Guest: Gordon MacRae.

R45. STEVE LAWRENCE SHOW
      Host: Steve Lawrence. Guest: Gordon MacRae.

R46. TREASURY SONG PARADE
      with Gordon MacRae, David Broekman & the Treasury Ensemble. Sponsor: US War Bonds.

R47. YOUR RHYTHM REVUE
      with Gordon & Sheila MacRae. Song: "By the Light of the Silvery Moon." Sponsor: Sister Elizabeth Kenny Foundation.

4

Filmography

F 1. THE BIG PUNCH (Warner Brothers, June 1948) 80 minutes
BW
  CREDITS: Producer: Saul Elkins. Director: Sherry
Shrouds. Story: George C. Brown (<u>The Holy Terror</u>).
Screenplay: Bernard Girard. Photography: Carl Gutherie.
Film Editor: Frank Magee. Music: William Lava. Sound:
Charles Lang. Dialogue Director: John Maxwell. Set
Decorator: William Wallace. Technical Adviser: Clair
Gahagen. Special Effects: William McGann. Cameraman: H. F.
Koenekamp. Orchestral Arrangements: Charles Maxwell.
Assistant Director: Elma Decker. Makeup: Perc Westmore.
Unit Manager: Don Page.
  CAST: Wayne Morris (Chris Thorzenson), Lois Maxwell
(Karen Long), Gordon MacRae (Johnny Grant), Mary Stuart,
Anthony Warde, Jimmy Ames, Marc Logan, Eddie Dunne, Charles
Marsh.
  SYNOPSIS: Boxer Johnny Grant (MacRae) is framed for
murder and takes refuge at the home of acquaintance Chris
Thorzenson (Morris), who has given up boxing for the
ministry. Johnny does not say anything about his past until
he is exposed by blackmailers.
  Instead of turning Johnny over to the police, Chris
goes to New York to help clear Johnny by exposing the
gamblers as murders. Johnny is cleared and leaves town to
resume his boxing career.
  REVIEW: <u>Daily Variety</u> (May 19, 1948) felt that THE BIG
PUNCH was a "tightly knit, fast-moving melodrama." Wayne
Morris did an "excellent job," and MacRae gave a "convincing
'first-out' performance." The picture profited from the
"above average production values" given it by Producer Saul
Elkins.

F 2. LOOK FOR THE SILVER LINING (Warner Brothers, July 1949)
106 minutes
  CREDITS: Producer: William Jacobs. Director: David
Butler. Story: Harry Ruby (<u>Life of Marilyn Miller</u>).
Screenplay: Phoebe and Henry Ephron, Marian Spitzer.
Photography: Peverell Marley. Film Editor: Irene Morra.
Music Adapted: David Buttolph. Art: John Hughes. Sound:
David Forrest. Dances: LeRoy Prinz. Music: Ray Heindorf.

Sound: Francis J. Scheid, David Forrest. Dialog director:
Herschel Daughterty. Technical Advisor: Mecca Graham. Set
Decorator: Fred M. MacLean. Men's Costumes: Marjorie Best.
Makeup: Perc Westmore. Orchestrations: Frank Perkins.
Songs: Jerome Kern, Buddy DeSylva, Vincent Youmans, Harold
Adamson, Mack Gordon, Otto Harbach, Oscar Hammerstein,II,
Victor Herbert. Assistant Director: Phil Quinn.
    CAST: June Haver (Marilyn Miller), Ray Bolger (Jack
Donahue), Gordon MacRae (Frank Carter), Charles Ruggles
(Pop Miller), Rosemary DeCamp (Mom Miller), Lee Wilde
(Claire Miller), Lyne Wilde (Ruth Miller), Dick Simmons
(Henry Doran), SZ Sakall (Shandorff), Walter Catlett
(Himself), George Zoritch, Oleg Tupine (Ballet Specialty),
Lillian Yarbo (Violet), Paul E. Burns (Mr. Beenan), Douglas
Kennedy (Doctor).
    SYNOPSIS: In flashbacks, the career of Broadway star
Marilyn Miller is told from her vaudeville beginnings with
her family, Mom Miller (DeCamp) and Pop Miller (Ruggles),
through her climb to fame with the help of friend Jack
Donahue (Bolger).
    While on Broadway, she meets Frank Carter (MacRae), and
after his release from the service, they are married. Frank
continues to guide Marilyn's career, while persuing a less
successful career of his own. It was customary that Frank
would send her a China elephant before each opening, for
good luck. When one arrives broken, Marilyn views it as a
bad omen. The omen comes true, when Frank is killed in an
auto crash while on his way to one of her openings.
    After getting over Frank's death, Marilyn remarries,
knowing Frank would have wanted her to. Later Marilyn
becomes ill but continues performing, knowing she will die.
    SONGS: Main Title-WB Studio Orchestra; "Shine on
Harvest Moon," "Back to Baltimore"-Wilde Twins, Ruggles,
DeCamp; "Can't You Hear Me Callin' Carolina?"-Bolger; Dance
Number-WB Studio Orchestra, Bolger, Haver; "Pirouette"-
Wilde Twins; "Yama Man"-Haver; Dance Number-WB Studio
Orchestra, Bolger, Haver; "Time on My Hands"-MacRae,Haver;
"A Kiss in the Dark"-MacRae; "Look For the Silver Lining"-
MacRae; "Look For the Silver Lining"-Haver; Russian Dance
Number-WB Studio Orchestra; "Sunny"-Chorus; "Who"-Bolger,
Chorus; "Wild Rose," "Look For the Silver Lining"-Haver.
    REVIEW: Daily Variety (June 21, 1949) rated LOOK FOR
THE SILVER LINING as one of the year's top musicals because
of "an elegant production framework and socko direction."
MacRae's acting and singing of the period songs were "potent
parts of the entertainment."
    MORE REVIEWS: New York Times (June 24, 1949); New
Yorker (July 2, 1949); Photoplay (July 1949); Time (July 4,
1949).

F 3. BACKFIRE (Warner Brothers, February 11, 1950)
    91 minutes BW
    CREDITS: Producer: Anthony Veillin. Director: Vincent
Sherman. Story: Larry Marcus (Until the Day I Die).
Screenplay: Larry Marcus, Ivan Goff, Ben Roberts.
Photography: Carl Gutherie. Film Editor: Thomas Reilly.
Music: Daniels Amfitheatrof. Musical Director: Ray
Heindorf. Assistant Director: James McMahon. Art Director:

Anton Grot. Sound: Stanley Jones. Dialog Director: Maurice
Murphy. Set Director: William Wallace. Orchestrations: Sid
Cutner, Leo Shuken. Unit Manager: Don Page. Makeup: Perc
Westmore.
   CAST: Virginia Mayo (Julie Benson), Gordon MacRae
(Bob Cory), Edmond O'Brien (Steve Connolly), Dane Clark
(Ben Arno), Viveca Linfors (Lysa Randolph), Ed Begley
(Captain Garcia), Frances Robinson (Mrs. Blane), Richard
Rober (Solly Blane), Sheila Stephens (Bonnie), David
Hoffman (Burns), Monty Blue (Detective Sgt. Pluthner), Ida
Moore (Sybil), Leonard Strong (Quong), John Ridgely (Plain
Clothesman).
   SYNOPSIS: Veterans Bob Cory (MacRae) and Steve
Connolly (O'Brien) plan to buy a ranch together, but plans
are put on hold while Cory recovers in the hospital from
injuries.
   Connolly disappears after allegedly murdering a gambler.
Cory and nurse Benson (Mayo) set out to prove his innocence.
They learn that Ben Arno (Clark), a mortuary proprietor and
former member of Connolly's outfit, was jealous over the
love affair between Lysa Randolph (Linfors) and Connolly and
framed Connolly for the gamblers murder and has been holding
Connolly captive. Arno tries to escape, and is killed by
police.
   REVIEW: Daily Variety (January 10, 1950) considered
BACKFIRE a "suspenseful mystery melodrama," built suspense
and "held interest to end." MacRae "performed competently."
   MORE REVIEWS: Film Daily (January 19, 1950); New York
Times (January 27, 1950)

F 4. THE DAUGHTER OF ROSIE O'GRADY (Warner Brothers,
   April 29, 1950) 104 minutes
   CREDITS: Producer: William Jacobs. Director: David
Butler. Story: Jack Rose, Mel Shavelson. Screenplay: Jack
Rose, Mel Shavelson, Peter Milne. Photography: Wilfred M.
Cline. Film Editor: Irene Morra. Music Adapted: David
Buttolph. Music: M.K. Jerome, Jack Scholl. Dances: LeRoy
Prinz. Art Director: Douglas Bacon.
   CAST: June Haver (Patricia O'Grady), Gordon MacRae
(Tony Pastor), James Barton (Dennis O'Grady), Gene Nelson
(Doug Martin), Debbie Reynolds (Maureen O'Grady), Cuddles
Sakall (Miklos Toretsy), Sean McClory (James Moore), Marsha
Jones (Katie O'Grady), Jane Darwell (Mrs. Murphy).
   SYNOPSIS: Patricia O'Grady (Haver) wants a career
like her parents. Against her father, Dennis O'Grady's
(Barton), wishes, she meets Tony Pastor (MacRae), who owns
a theatre. With his help and that of dancer Doug Martin
(Nelson), she gets her break.
   Tony and Patricia fall in love. When Dennis O'Grady
becomes ill, Tony belittles Patricia's talent to force her
to go back to her father. Dennis realizes he is being
selfish and convinces her to return to the stage and to
Pastor.
   SONGS: "My Own True Love and I," "As We Are Today,"
"My Blushin' Rose," "The Rose of Tralee," "A Farm Off Old
Broadway," "A Picture Turned to the Wall," "Winter,
Winter," "Winter Serenade," "The Daughter of Rosie O'Grady."
   REVIEW: Variety (March 29, 1950) considered THE

DAUGHTER OF ROSIE O'GRADY a "familiarly patterned musical" whose plot dealt with the happenings back stage. The film had "charm, some wit, nice music," and a "good pace." MacRae and Haver "ably delivered" their several good songs.
MORE REVIEWS: Film Daily (April 3, 1950); Newsweek (April 10, 1950); New York Times (March 31, 1950, April 9, 1950); Time (April 17, 1950).

F 5. RETURN OF THE FRONTIERSMAN (Warner Brothers, June 24, 1950) 74 minutes
CREDITS: Producer: Saul Elkins. Director: Richard Bare. Story: Edna Anhalt. Screenplay: Edna Anhalt. Photography: Peverell Marley. Music: David Buttolph. Art Director: Charles H. Clarke. Film Editor: Frank Magee. Sound: Stanley Jones. Set Decorator: G.W. Bernsten. Makeup: Perc Westmore. Orchestration: Maurice de Packh. Technicolor Consultant: Morgan Padelford. Assistant Director: Frank Mattison.
CAST: Gordon MacRae (Logan Partett), Julie London (Janie Martin), Rory Calhoun (Larrabee), Jack Holt (Sam Barrett), Fred Clark (Ryan), Edwin Rand (Kearney), Raymond Bond (Dr. Martin), Matt McHugh (Harvey), Britt Wood (Barney).
SYNOPSIS: After a brawl with a local rancher, the sheriff's son, Logan Barrett (MacRae), is arrested for murder when the rancher turns up dead. Logan escapes from jail with the help of the local editor, Larrabee (Calhoun). The bank is robbed, allegedly by Barrett, who takes the doctor's daughter, Janie Martin (London), hostage and leaves town. When Janie sees Barrett's masquerador robbing the stage, she believes his claim of innocence.
At Larrabee's cabin, Logan learns the editor is the masquerador. After a fight, Logan takes him into custody.
SONGS: "Underneath A Western Sky," "Cowboy."
REVIEW: Variety (May 17, 1953) felt that RETURN OF THE FRONTIERSMAN was a "spotty western." MacRae played the part "acceptably." The film was "basically an okay action yarn," but the script was "inept" both in dialog and development.
MORE REVIEWS: Film Daily (May 19, 1950); New York Times (June 10, 1950).

F 6. TEA FOR TWO (Warner Brothers, September 2, 1950) 98 minutes
CREDITS: Producer: William Jacobs. Director: David Butler. From the Play by: Otto Harbach, Frank Mandel (No No Nanette). Screenplay: Harry Clork. Photography: Wilfred M. Cline. Film Editor: Irene Morra. Songs: Vincent Youmens, Irving Caesar, Otto Harbach, Harry Warren, Al Durbin, George Gershwin, Richard Rodgers, Lorenz Hart, Sammy Fain, Irving Fahal. Art: Douglas Bacon. Sets: Lyle B. Reifsnider. Sound: Dolphim Thomas, David Forrest. Dances: LeRoy Prinz, Eddie Prinz. Music Director: Ray Heindorf. Technicolor Consultant: Mitchell Kovaleski.
CAST: Doris Day (Nan), Gordon MacRae (Jimmy), Gene Nelson (Tommy), Patrice Wymore (Beatrice), Eve Arden (Pauline), Billy DeWolfe (Larry), S.Z. Sakall (Max), Bill Goodwin (Early), Virginia Gibson (Mabel), Crawford Kent (Stevens).

SYNOPSIS: Larry (DeWolfe) needs to raise money to put on a Broadway show scored by Jimmy (MacRae). He asks Nan (Day) to invest $25000. Jimmy asks her to star in the show.

Nan is unaware her Uncle Max (Sakall) invested her money unwisely and has temporarily lost her fortune. He gets Nan to say no to every question for twenty-four hours. Trying to see Nan lose the bet, he gets the housekeeper, Pauline (Eve Arden) to keep tabs on her. During the twenty-four hours, Jimmy proposes, to which Nan must say no.

Jimmy's friend and dancer in the show, Tommy (Nelson), forces Larry out of the show. Nan wins the bet only to learn of her financial condition. Pauline helps raise the finances and the show goes on successfully. Nan and Jimmy are married.

SONGS: Main Title-WB Studio Orchestra and Chorus; "I Know That You Know"-Day, MacRae/Dance by Day, Nelson; "Crazy Rhythm"-Wymore, Chorus/Dance by Wymore, Nelson; "I Only Have Eyes For You"-MacRae; "Tea For Two"-MacRae, Day; "Tea For Two"-Day; "Charleston"-Ernie Felice Quartet; "I Want To Be Happy"-Day, MacRae; "Do Do Do"-Day, MacRae; "Oh Me Oh My"-Nelson/Dance by Nelson, Day, and Group; "No No Nanette," "The Call of the Sea," "I Want To Be Happy," "Tea For Two"-MacRae, Day, Nelson, Chorus; "Tea For Two"-MacRae, Day.

REVIEW: Hollywood Reporter (August 15, 1950) felt that the music and actors helped "lift creaky yarn." Doris Day's performance wasn't far behind her "usual exceptional vocal work," and Gordon MacRae "charmed" and "registered impressively" when he sang his songs.

MORE REVIEWS: Film Daily (August 15, 1950); Newsweek (September 18, 1950); New York Times (September 2, 1950); Time (September 11, 1950).

F 7. WEST POINT STORY [FINE AND DANDY] (Warner Brothers, November 25, 1950) 170 minutes BW

CREDITS: Producer: Lois F. Edelman. Director: Roy Del Ruth. Story: Irving Wallace (Classmates). Screenplay: John Monks, Jr., Charles Hoffman, Irving Wallace. Photography: Sid Hickox. Film Editor: Owen Marks. Songs: Jule Styne, Sammy Cahn. Art Director: Charles H. Clarke. Sets: Armor E. Marlowe. Sound: Francis J. Scheid. Dances: LeRoy Prinz, Eddie Prinz, Al White, Johnny Boyle, Jr. Music: Ray Heindorf. Production Manager: Al Alleborn. Operating Cameraman: Mike Joyce. Hair Stylist: Gertrude Wheeler. Mr. Cagney's Dances created by: Johnny Boyle, Jr. Orchestration: Frank Perkins. Costumes: Milo Anderson, Marjorie Best. Makeup: Otis Malcolm. Special Effects: Edwin Dupar. Assistant Director: Mel Deller. Still Man: Mac Julian.

CAST: James Cagney (Elwin Bixby), Virginia Mayo (Eve Dillon), Doris Day (Jan Wilson), Gordon MacRae (Tom Fletcher), Gene Nelson (Hal Courtland), Alan Hale, Jr. (Bull Gilbert), Roland Winters (Harry Eberhart), Wilton Graff (Lt. Col. Martin), Jerome Cowan (Jocelyn), Frank Ferguson (Commandant), Raymond Rowe (Bixby's Wife).

SYNOPSIS: Broadway Producer, Harry Eberhart (Winters) hires Elwin Bixby (Cagney), a musical director down on his luck, to go to West Point to put on the "100th Night," a

show written by Eberhart's nephew, Tom Fletcher (MacRae).
He wants Bixby to get the show and Fletcher out of West
Point and on Broadway. To help him, Bixby gets his
assistant Eve Dillon (Mayo) and movie star Jan Wilson
(Day). Fletcher doesn't want to leave until he falls in
love with Jan and goes AWOL to marry her.
     When the show is cancelled, Bixby and Tom's friend Hal
(Nelson) go AWOL to bring him back.
     To get immunity so the show can go on, Bixby shows the
French Ambassador his French Medal of Honor. The show goes
on but Bixby, not Eberhart, gets the show for Broadway.
     SONGS: Main Title-WB Studio Orchestra, Chorus; "It's
Raining Sundrops"-vocal group/Dance by Cagney; "100 Days
Till June"-MacRae, Chorus; "By the Kissing Rock"-Cagney,
Mayo; "Long Before I Knew You"-MacRae/Dance by Nelson;
"Ten Thousand Four Hundred and Thirty-two Sheep"-Day;
"Military Polka"-Day, MacRae, Chorus; "You Love Me"-MacRae;
"By the Kissing Rock"-Day, MacRae; "The Corp"-MacRae,
Chorus; "Parade of Wooden Soldiers"-WB Studio Orchestra/
Dance by Nelson; "You Love Me"-MacRae, Day, Chorus;
"Brooklyn"-Cagney, Chorus; Finale-Cagney, Day, MacRae,
Chorus.
     REVIEW: Variety (November 15, 1950) felt that the WEST
POINT STORY gave the musical formula a "fresh treatment and
new twists." The story was long but "engagingly presented"
and that the songs "listened well." The seven new songs
benefited greatly from Doris Day and Gordon MacRae's "class
vocal treatment."
     MORE REVIEWS: Film Daily (November 16, 1950);
Newsweek (December 25, 1950); New York Times (December 23,
1950); Time (December 4, 1950).

F 8. THE SCREEN DIRECTOR (Vita, 1951) Film Short

F 9. ON MOONLIGHT BAY (Warner Brothers, July 28, 1951) 95
     minutes
     CREDITS: Producer: William Jacobs. Director: Roy Del
Ruth. Screenplay: Jack Rose, Melville Shavelson. From the
stories by Booth Tarkington (Penrod & Penrod & Sam).
Photography: Ernest Haller. Art Director: Douglas Bacon.
Film Editor: Thomas Reilly. Sound: Francis J. Scheid, David
Forrest. Dialog Director: Herschel Daugherty. Musical
Numbers Directed and Staged by LeRoy Prinz. Musical
Director: Ray Heindorf. Music Adapted by Max Steiner.
Special Effects: William McGann. Set Decorator: William
Wallace. Wardrobe: Milo Anderson, Marjorie Best. Makeup:
Gordon Bau. Technicolor Consultant: Mitchell Kovaleski.
Assistant Director: Mel Dellar.
     CAST: Doris Day (Marjorie Winfield), Gordon MacRae
(William Sherman), Jack Smith (Hubert Wakely), Leon Ames
(Mr. Winfield), Rosemary DeCamp (Mrs. Winfield), Mary
Wickes (Stella), Ellen Corby (Miss Stevens), Billy Gray
(Wesley), Henry East (Dogman), Jeffrey Stevens (Jim
Sherman), Eddie Marr (The Baker).
     SYNOPSIS: Tomboy, Marjorie Winfield (Day), who loves
baseball and music, enters a barn to take a gun away from
her brother, Wesley (Gray), and Jim Sherman (Stevens). It
accidentally fires blowing the barn door on-top of William

Sherman (MacRae), Jim's older brother.

Marjorie and William begin dating. He is an Indiana College student who doesn't believe in baseball, music, or marriage. Mr. Winfield (Ames) forbids Marjorie to see him until he comes to his senses. William patches things up before returning to college.

Returning from dance lessons, Marjorie breaks her leg in a snow ball fight. Wesley tells his teacher, Miss Stevens (Corby) his father drinks and beats his family. At the train station, Miss Stevens tells William.

He goes to the Winfield's, smells rubbing alcohol used on Marjorie's leg, and assumes the worst. He is asked to leave, until they realize Wesley is responsible for the tall tale.

At William's graduation, the Winfield's learn he is in ROTC and must serve in the Army. When Mr. Winfield learns William doesn't believe in marriage, he forces Marjorie to leave. She runs off to meet William on the troop train, in hopes of getting married. William believes in marriage, but they decide to wait until his return from the Army.

SONGS: "On Moonlight Bay"-MacRae, Male Quartet; "Cuddle Up A Little Closer"-MacRae; "Tell Me"-Day; "I'm Forever Blowing Bubbles"-Smith; "Love Ya"-Day, Smith; "Love Ya"-Day; Silent Movie Music-Piano; "Christmas Story"-Day, MacRae, Children's Chorus; "Pack Up Your Troubles"-MacRae, Chorus; "Every Little Movement"-Smith; "Till We Meet Again"-MacRae, Day; "On Moonlight Bay"-Smith, Chorus.

REVIEW: Daily Variety (July 9, 1951) considered ON MOONLIGHT BAY "a light frothy production" that had a nice blend of romance, comedy and nostalgic tunes. Doris Day and Gordon MacRae "very capably" performed their songs and "tandem neatly" as the romantic leads.

MORE REVIEWS: Film Daily (July 16, 1951); Newsweek (August 6, 1951); New York Times (July 27, 1951); Time (August 20, 1951).

F10. STARLIFT (Warner Brothers, December 1, 1951)
    103 minutes BW
    CREDITS: Producer: Robert Arthur. Director: Roy Del Ruth. Screenplay: John Klorer, Karl Kamb. Based on the Story by: John Klorer (Operation Starlift). Photography: Ted McCord. Art Director: Charles H. Clarke. Set Decorator: G.W. Bersten. Editor: William Ziegler. Sound Recorder: Francis J. Scheid. Musical Director: Ray Heindorf. Costumes: Leah Rhodes. Makeup: Gordon Bau. Hair Stylist: Gertrude Wheeler. Choreographer: LeRoy Prinz. Assistant Director: Mel Dellar. Technical Advisors: Major James G. Smith, USAF, M. A. T. S., Major George E. Andrews, USAF, S. A. C.
    CAST: Themselves: Doris Day, Gordon MacRae, Virginia Mayo, Gene Nelson, Ruth Roman; Janice Rule (Neil Wayne); Dick Wesson (Sergeant Mike Nolan); Ron Haggerty (Rick Williams); Richard Webb (Colonel Callan); Hayden Rorke (Chaplin); Howard St. John (Steve Rogers); Ann Doran (Mrs. Callan); Tommy Farrell (Turner); John Maxwell (George Norris); Don Beddoe (Bob Wayne); Mary Adams (Sue Wayne); Bigelowe Sayre (Dr. Williams); Eleanor Audley (Mrs. Williams); Pat Henry (Theatre Manager); Gordon Polk (Chief

Usher); Robert Hammack (Piano Player); Ray Montgomery
(Captain Nelson); Bill Neff (Co-Pilot); Stan Holbrook
(Ground Officer); Jill Richards (Flight Nurse); Joe Turkel
(Litter Case); Rush Williams (Virginia Boy); Brian McKay
(Pete); Jack Larson (Will); Lyle Clark (Nebraska Boy);
Dorothy Kennedy, Jean Dean, Dolores Castle (Nurses);
William Hunt (Boy With Cane); Elizabeth Flournoy (Army
Nurse); Walter Brennan, Jr. (Driver); Robert Karnes, John
Hedloe (Lieutenants); Steve Gregory (Boy With Camera);
Richard Monohan (Morgan); Joe Recht, Herb Latimer (Soldiers
in Bed); Dick Ryan (Doctor); Bill Hudson (Crew Chief);
Sarah Spencer (Miss Parson's Assistant); James Brown
(Non-Com); Ezelle Poule (Waitress); Guest Stars: James
Cagney, Gary Cooper, Virginia Gibson, Phil Harris, Frank
Lovejoy, Lucille Norman, Louella Parsons, Randolph Scott,
Jayne Wyman, Patrice Wymore.
    SYNOPSIS: STARLIFT concerns the romance between a GI
and a Hollywood star. Warners celebrities provide
entertainment for wounded veterans and for replacement
soldiers headed for Korea.
    SONGS: Main Title-WB Studio Orchestra; "You're Gonna
Lose Your Gal"-Day, MacRae; "'S Wonderful"-Day; "You
Oughta Be in Pictures"-Day; "You Do Something to Me"-Day;
"What is This Thing Called Love?"-MacRae, Norman; "Liza"-
Wymore; "God's Green Acres"-MacRae, Chorus; "It's Magic"-
Nelson (dubbed by Hal Derwin); "I May Be Wrong"-Wyman;
"Noche Caribe"-WB Studio Orchestra; "I'm a Texas Ranger"-
Harris, Cooper.
    REVIEW: Variety (November 7, 1951) considered STARLIFT
a "pleasant tunefilm" about an all-star cast providing
entertainment for soldiers either returning from or leaving
for Korea. It was felt that the film would have "okay box
office."
    MORE REVIEWS: Film Daily (November 5, 1951); Newsweek
(December 10, 1951); New York Times (December 15, 1951);
Time (December 3, 1951).

F11. SCREEN SNAPSHOTS NO. 205 (Columbia, 1952) Film Short

F12. ABOUT FACE (Warner Brothers, May 31, 1952) 94 minutes
    CREDITS: Producer: William Jacobs. Director: Roy Del
Ruth. From the Play by: John Monks, Jr., Fred Finklehoffe
(Brother Rat). Screenplay: Peter Milne. Photography: Bert
Glennon. Film Editor: Thomas Reilly. Songs: Charles Tobias,
Peter De Rose. Musical Director: Ray Heindorf. Vocal
Arrangements: Norman Luboff. Orchestration: Frank Perkins.
Art Director: Charles H. Clarke.
    CAST: Gordon MacRae (Tony Williams), Eddie Bracken
(Boff Roberts), Dick Wesson (Dave Crouse), Virginia Gibson
(Betty Long), Phyllis Kirk (Alice Wheatley), Aileen
Stanley, Jr. (Lorna Carter), Joel Grey (Bender), Larry
Keating (Colonel Long), Cliff Ferre (Lieutenant Jones),
John Baer (Hal Carlton).
    SYNOPSIS: Three friends, Tony Williams (MacRae), Boff
Roberts (Bracken), and Dave Crouse (Wesson), attend a
military academy. Boff is secretly married and about to
become a father, which if discovered would mean his
dismissal from school before graduation.

SONGS: Main Title-WB Studio Orchestra; "Reveille"-
MacRae, Bracken, Wesson, Grey, Chorus; "SMI March"-Chorus
"Tar Heels"-Chorus; "If Someone Had Told Me"-MacRae,
Bracken, Kirk; "Wooden Indian"-MacRae, Wesson, Chorus;
"Spring Has Sprung"-Wesson, Gibson; "They Haven't Lost a
Father Yet"-MacRae, Wesson, Bracken; "I'm Nobody"-Grey;
"Piano, Bass and Drums"-MacRae, Wesson, Stanley, Jr.; "SMI
March"-Chorus; "No Other Girl For Me"-MacRae, Stanley, Jr.,
Chorus; Medley: "Piano, Bass and Drums," "SMI March"-WB
Studio Orchestra and Chorus/Dance by Cliffe Ferre.
    REVIEW: Variety (April 16, 1952) felt that ABOUT FACE
was a "refurbished BROTHER RAT with music." MacRae's "good
voice" didn't get enough use on ballad songs.
    MORE REVIEWS: Film Daily (April 17, 1952); Newsweek
(June 2, 1952); New York Times (May 24, 1952); Time (June
2, 1952).

F13. SO YOU WANT A TELEVISION SET (Vita, 1953) Film Short

F14. BY THE LIGHT OF THE SILVERY MOON (Warner Brothers, May
2, 1953) 102 minutes
    CREDITS: Producer: William Jacobs. Director: David
Butler. From Stories by Booth Tarkington (Penrod & Penrod &
Sam). Screenplay: Robert O'Brien, Irving Elison.
Photography: Wilfred M. Cline. Film Editor: Irene Morra.
Music Adaptation: Max Steiner. Art Director: John Beckman.
Sound: Stanley Jones, David Forrest. Set Director: William
L. Kuehl. Musical Direction: Ray Heindorf. Assistant
Director: Philip Quinn. Vocal Arrangements: Norman Luboff.
Numbers Staged by Donald Saddler. Wardrobe: Leah Rhodes.
Makeup: Gordon Bau. Technicolor Consultant: Mitchell G.
Kovaleski.
    CAST: Doris Day (Marjorie Winfield), Gordon MacRae
(William Sherman), Leon Ames (George Winfield), Rosemary
DeCamp (Mrs. Winfield), Billy Gray (Wesley), Mary Wickes
(Stella), Russell Arms (Chester Finley), Maria Palmer (Miss
LaRue), Walter Flannery (Pee Wee), Geraldine Wall (Mrs.
Harris), John Maxwell (Ike Hickey), Carol Forman (Dangerous
Dora).
    SYNOPSIS: When William Sherman (MacRae) returns home
from World War I, he and Marjorie Winfield (Day) go to a
dance. Everyone awaits the couple's announcement of a
wedding date. William, to Marjorie's surprise, announces
plans to wait until he gets a job, and builds a little nest
egg. After Marjorie calms down, she agrees. Wesley's
(Gray) piano teacher, Chester Finley (Arms), secretly hopes
the couple will break up so he can have Marjorie.
    Mr. Winfield (Ames) goes to actress, Miss LaRue's
(Palmer) hotel room to discuss plans to rent the town
theatre. Mr. Winfield makes a note of an objectionable
portion of the script. Marjorie discovers the note and
assumes her father is being unfaithful to Mrs. Winfield
(DeCamp).
    William takes out a loan at the bank where he works,
so he and Marjorie won't have to wait to get married.
Marjorie, too upset about her parents, turns him down.
William cancells the loan, quits his job, and leaves town.
Wesley wires William to explain things. William returns,

and disquised as Ike Hickey, takes the Winfields on a sleigh
ride to Miller's Pond for their anniversary. The note is
explained and all ends well.
    SONGS: Main Title-WB Studio Orchestra, Chorus; "My
Home Town"-MacRae, Chorus; "Your Eyes Have Told Me So"-Day,
MacRae; "Be My Little Bumble Bee"- Day, Arms; "By the Light
of the Silvery Moon"-Day, MacRae; "If You Were the Only
Girl"- MacRae; "King Chanticleer"-Day; "I'll Forget You"-
Day; "By the Light of the Silvery Moon"-Day, MacRae, Ames,
DeCamp, Chorus; "Ain't We Got Fun"-Day, MacRae.
    REVIEW: <u>Hollywood Reporter</u> (March 25, 1953) considered
BY THE LIGHT OF THE SILVERY MOON a "nostalgic comedy,
tuneful and funny." Miss Day's performance was "charming"
and she sang "better than ever." It was stated that MacRae
was "excellent" in his role and sang his songs in "fine
voice."
    MORE REVIEWS: <u>Film Daily</u> (March 25, 1953); <u>Newsweek</u>
(March 25, 1953); <u>New York Times</u> (March 27, 1953); <u>Time</u>
(April 13, 1953).
    COMMENT: BY THE LIGHT OF THE SILVERY MOON is the
sequel to the 1951 Day-MacRae film ON MOONLIGHT BAY.

F15. DESERT SONG (Warner Brothers, May 30, 1953) 110 minutes
    CREDITS: Producer: Rudi Fehr. Director: Bruce
Humberstone. From the Play by Laurence Schwab, Otto
Horbach, Frank Mandel, Sigmund Romberg, Oscar Hammerstein
II. Screenplay: Roland Kibbee. Photography: Robert Burks.
Film Editor: William Ziegler. Music Adaptation: Max
Steiner. Art Director: Stanley Fleischer. Sound: C.A.
Riggs, David Forrest. Musical Numbers Staged and Directed
by LeRoy Prinz. Musical Director: Ray Heindorf.
Orchestration: Murray Cutter. Song "Gay Parisienne" by Jack
Scholl and Serge Walter. Wardrobe: Leah Rhodes, Marjorie
Best; Set Decorator: William Kuehl. Makeup: Gordon Bau.
Assistant Director: Russell Saunders. Vocal Arrangements:
Norman Luboff.
    CAST: Kathryn Grayson (Margot), Gordon MacRae (Paul
Bonnard/El Kobar), Steve Cochran (Captain Fontaine),
Raymond Massey (Yousseff), Dick Wesson (Benjy Kidd), Allyn
McLerie (Azuri), Ray Collins (General Birabeau), Paul
Picerni (Hassan), Frank Dekova (Mindar), William Conrad
(Lachmed), Trevor Bardette (Neri), Mark Dana (Lt. Duvalle).
    SYNOPSIS: Sheik Yousseff's (Massey) men rob the
villagers and puts the blame on the Riffs. Paul Bonnard
(MacRae), an anthropologist, and secret Riff leader, El
Khobar, sets out to stop the bad Arabs.
    When Margot (Grayson) and her father General
Birabeau (Ray Collins) arrive at Foreign Legion headquarters
to investigate the Arab troubles, Bonnard is hired as
Margot's tutor. Bored with Bonnard, she is attracted to
Captain Fontaine (Cochran).
    While Birabeau, Fontaine, and Margot are talking peace
at Yousseff's palace, Kobar meets Margot in the garden and
tries to convince her Yousseff is her father's enemy. When
a phony attack is made on the palace, framing the riffs,
Kobar takes Margot, until he talks sense to her father.
Margot is kidnapped from Kobar's camp by Yousseff's men.
The Riffs storm the palace and capture Yousseff and his

men, thus rescuing Margot. Bonnard announces Kobar's death, crushing Margot, who loved him. Bonnard sings "One Alone," as he had done in Yousseff's garden, and Margot realizes both men were really one.

SONGS: Main Title-WB Studio Orchestra, Chorus; "Riff Song"-MacRae, Chorus; "Romance"-Grayson; "Desert Song"-MacRae; "Gay Parisienne"-Grayson, Chorus; "One Flower Grows Alone in Your Garden"-Grayson; "One Alone"-MacRae, Grayson; "Riff Song"-Chorus.

REVIEW: Variety (April 29, 1953) felt that the story and songs in DESERT SONG were "well-worn" although the songs "aged with charm." Miss Grayson and Mr. MacRae "nicely delivered" their songs, but the songs wouldn't "create much of a stir" in that day and age.

MORE REVIEWS: Film Daily (April 30, 1953); New York Times (May 21, 1953); Time (May 25, 1953).

F16. THREE SAILORS AND A GIRL (Warner Brothers, December 26, 1953) 98 minutes

CREDITS: Producer: Sammy Cahn. Director: Roy Del Ruth. From Play by George S. Kaufman (The Butter and Egg Man). Screenplay: Roland Kibbee, Devery Freeman. Photography: Carl Gutherie. Film Editor: Owen Marks. Music: Sammy Fain, Sammy Cahn. Art Director: Leo K. Kuter. Sound: Leslie G. Hewitt, David Forrest. Set Decorator: G.W. Bernsten. Wardrobe: Moss Mabry. Musical Numbers Staged and Directed by LeRoy Prinz. Musical Director: Ray Heindorf. Orchestrations: Frank Comstock, Gus Levene. Vocal Arrangements: Norman Luboff. Technicolor Consultant: Mitchell G. Kovaleski. Makeup: Gordon Bau. Assistant Director: Mel Dellar.

CAST: Jane Powell (Penny Weston), Gordon MacRae (Jones), Gene Nelson (Twitch), Sam Levene (Joe Woods), Jack E. Leonard (Porky), George Givot (Rossi), Veda Ann Borg (Faye Foss), Archer MacDonald (Webster), Raymond Greenleaf (Morrow), Henry Slate (a sailor). Also with: Mickey Simpson, Elizabeth Flournoy, Claire Mead, Dick Simmons, John Parrish, Everett Glass, Bob Carson, Phil Van Zandt, Wayne Taylor, Al Hill, Guy E. Hearn, Cliff Ferre, Paul Burke, Grandon Rhodes, David Bond, Alex Gerry, Frank Scannell, Roh Engel, Murray Alper, Ed Hinton, Joe Forte, John Crawford, Dennis Dengate, Merv Griffin, Arthur Walsh, Jack Larson, Michael Pierce, Bess Flowers, Harold Miller, and a cameo by Burt Lancaster.

SYNOPSIS: Returning from eight months duty overseas, three sailors, Jones (MacRae), Twitch (Nelson), and Porky (Leonard), collect $50,000 from their crew mates to invest on Wall Street. Instead, they invest in a Broadway show produced by Joe Woods (Levene) and starring singer Penny Weston (Powell). When the show flops, the trio buy out Woods with Marine funds. Some top Broadway musical writers help the show succeed in New York. Woods buys out the sailors and they head back to the ship where Jones and Penny declare their mutual love.

SONGS: Main Title-Powell, MacRae, WB Studio Orchestra; "You're But Oh So Right"-Nelson, MacRae, Leonard, Chorus; "Kiss Me Or I'll Scream"-Powell; "Face to Face"-Powell; "Lately Song"-Powell, MacRae, Nelson, Leonard; "There Must Be a Reason"-MacRae, Powell; "When It's Love"-Powell,

MacRae; "My Heart Is a Singing Heart"-Powell, MacRae; "Show
Me a Happy Woman"-Powell, Leonard; "Kiss Me Or I'll Scream"-
Powell; "Now Hear This"-Chorus; "Home Is Where the Heart
Is"-Powell, MacRae, Nelson, Leonard; "Lately Song"-Powell,
MacRae, Nelson, Leonard.

REVIEW: <u>Variety</u> (November 25, 1953) considered THREE
SAILORS AND A GIRL a "light breezy musical." The songs and
performances were "sprightly." The laughs were "well
spotted" and the dances, costumes and technicolor tints had
"plenty of flash." The "chief exponents" of the songs and
dances were its stars Jane Powell, Gordon MacRae and Gene
Nelson.

MORE REVIEWS: <u>Film Daily</u> (December 4, 1953); <u>New York
Times</u> (November 23, 1953).

COMMENT: To enhance MacRae's dances, he wore
lead-souled shoes (weighing 5 pounds each) during
rehearsal, then during filming, he wore especially made
pumps (weighing 17 ounces each).

F17. THE LAST COMMAND (Republic, August 3, 1955)
Gordon MacRae sang the theme song, "Jim Bowie."

F18. OKLAHOMA (Magna Production, October 11, 1955) 145
minutes.
CREDITS: Producer: Arthur Hornblow, Jr. Director:
Fred Zinnemann. Music: Richard Rodgers. Book and Lyrics:
Oscar Hammerstein II. Dances: Agnes DeMille. Screenplay:
Sonya Levien, William Ludwig. Production Design: Oliver
Smith. Art Direction: Joseph Wright. Costumes: Orry-Kelly
and Motley. Originally Produced for Stage by the Theatre
Guild. Music Conducted and Supervised by Jay Blackstone.
Based on Dramatic Play by Lyn Riggs (<u>Green Grow the
Lilacs</u>). Director of Photography: Robert Surtees.
Assistant Director: Arthur Black, Jr. Recording
Supervisor: Fred S. Hynes. Set Decorator: Keough Gleason.
Hair Styles: Annabell. Makeup: Ben Lane.
CAST: Gordon MacRae (Curly McLain), Gloria Grahame
(Ado Annie), Gene Nelson (Will Parker), Charlotte
Greenwood (Aunt Eller), Shirley Jones (Laurey Williams),
Eddie Albert (Ali Hakim), James Whitmore (Carnes), Rod
Steiger (Jud Fry), Barbara Lawrence (Gertie), J.C. Flippin
(Skidmore), Roy Barcroft (Marshall), James Mitchell (Dream
Curly), Bambi Linn (Dream Laurey), Dancers: James Mitchell,
Bambi Linn, Jennie Workman, Kelly Brown, Marc Platt,
Lizanne Truex, Virginia Bosler, Evelyn Taylor, Jane Fischer.
SYNOPSIS: Laurey (Jones) is upset when Curly (MacRae)
asks her, at the last minute, to the box social, so she
agrees to go with hired hand, Jud Fry (Steiger). She
regrets the act but is too afraid of him to go back on her
decision.

While on the way to the box social, Jud tries to force
his intentions on Laurey. During a struggle, the horses and
buggy race off, nearly colliding with a train. The horses
are brought under control just in time. Laurey manages to
push Jud out of the buggy and takes off, leaving him
stranded. Arriving at the box social on foot, Jud finds the
folks bidding on the hamper baskets of their favorite girl.
Curly and Jud compete for Laurey's, but Curly eventually

out bids Jud.

Jud threatens Laurey, and she fires him. Newlyweds, Curly and Laurey are on top of a hay stack as part of a shivaree, when Jud sets fire to it. In a fight with Curly, Jud falls on his knife and is killed. Curly, tried for murder, is found not guilty, and the couple embark on their honeymoon.

SONGS: "Oh What a Beautiful Morning"-MacRae; "Surrey With the Fringe On Top"-MacRae, Jones, Greenwood; "Kansas City"-Nelson, Greenwood, Chorus; "I Can't Say No"-Grahame; "Many a New Day"-Jones; "People Will Say We're in Love"-Jones, MacRae; "Poor Jud"-MacRae, Steiger; "Out of My Dreams"-Jones; "Ballet Sequence"-Linn, Mitchell; "Farmer and the Cowman"-MacRae, Grahame, Nelson, Greenwood, Whitemore, Flippin; "All or Nothing"-Grahame, Nelson; "Oklahoma"-MacRae, Jones, Nelson, Greenwood, Whitemore, Flippin.

REVIEW: _Variety_ (October 12, 1955) felt that aside from some technical problems, OKLAHOMA was "fresh, crispy acted and beautifully sung," and its box office appeal was "outstanding." MacRae and Jones shined as the romantic leads, were in "top vocal form" and would surely capture America's heart. MacRae looked and acted the part of Curly with a "modicum of theatrics" and his songs were performed in "grand style." OKLAHOMA was dubbed one of the "industries best."

MORE REVIEWS: _Film Daily_ (October 11, 1955); _Newsweek_ (October 24, 1955); _New York Times_ (October 11, 1954); _Saturday Review_ (November 5, 1955); _Time_ (October 24, 1955).

COMMENT: The _New York Times_ selected OKLAHOMA as one of the top ten films of 1955. OKLAHOMA marked Shirley Jones's film debut. Meredith's sequence in the film was cut. Edward Clark grew the 2100, 16 foot corn stalks at a cost of $8.95 an ear and the farm, designed by Oliver Smith, was built for $100,000. The "Kansas City" sequence was filmed at Elgin (about 30 miles from Nogales). American artist Mort Kunstler created a limited-edition, four-plate series, for Edwin M. Knowles China Company. RKO Radio Pictures released the film in 35mm. Twentieth Century Fox re-released it in both Todd-AO and Cinemascope on November 1, 1956. The Samuel Goldwyn Company reissued it in Todd-AO and 70mm Cinemascope. OKLAHOMA is available on CBS/FOX Video and MGM/CBS Video as well as CED (RCA Disc) on MGM/CBS.

F19. CAROUSEL (Twentieth Century Fox, February 16, 1956) 128 minutes

CREDITS: Producer: Henry Ephron. Director: Henry King. Screenplay: Phoebe and Henry Ephron. Music: Richard Rodgers. Book and Lyrics: Oscar Hammerstein II. Based on Play by Ferenc Molnar (_Liliom_). Adapted by Benjamin Glazer. Produced on Stage by Theatre Guild. Choreography: Rod Alexander. Louise's Ballet Derived from Original by Agnes DeMille. Music Supervised and Conducted by Alfred Newman. Associate: Ken Darby. Orchestration: Edward B. Powell, Herbert Spencer, Earle Hagen, Nelson Riddle, Bernard Mayers, Gus Levene. Director of Photography: Charles G. Clarke. Art Director: Lyle R. Wheeler, Jack Martin Smith. Set Decorator: Walter M. Scott, Chester Bayhi. Special

Effects: Ray Kellog. Film Editor: William Reynolds. Wardrobe:
Charles Le Maire. Costume Design: Mary Wills. Assistant
Director: Stanley Hough. Makeup: Ben Nye. Hair Stylist:
Helen Turpin. Sound: Bernard Freericks, Harry M. Leonard.
Color Consultant: Leinard Doss. Cinemascope Lenses: Bausch
and Lomb.

CAST: Gordon MacRae (Billy Bigelow), Shirley Jones
(Julie Jordan), Cameron Mitchell (Jigger), Barbara Ruick
(Carrie), Claramae Turner (Cousin Nettie), Robert
Rounseville (Mr. Snow), Gene Lockhart (Starkeeper), Audrey
Christie (Mrs. Mullin), Susan Luckey (Louise), William Le
Massena (Heavenly Friend), John Dehner (Mr. Bascombe),
Jacques D'Amboise (Louise's Dancing Partner), Frank Tweddell
(Captain Watson), Sylvia Stanton (Contortionist), Mary
Orozio (Fat Woman), Tor Johnson (Strong Man), Harry Duke
Johnson (Juggler), Marion Dempsey (Sword Swallower), Ed
Mundy (Fire Eater), Angelo Rossito (Midget), Dee Pollock
(Enoch Snow, Jr.).

SYNOPSIS: In flashbacks from heaven, we learn that
carousel barker Billy Bigelow (MacRae) met Julie Jordan
(Jones) at an amusement park. Billy is fired for paying
attention to Julie. Despite warnings against Billy, Julie
marries him. They stay with Cousin Nettie (Turner), as
Billy is out of work.

When Billy learns he's to be a father, he feels
desparate for money. He and his unsavory friend Jigger
(Mitchell) decide to rob the mill, where Julie once worked,
of its payroll. During the robbery attempt, Billy falls on
his knife and is killed.

From heaven, Billy watches his unhappy daughter,
Louise (Luckey). He is permitted to return to earth to try
and help her. At Louise's graduation, he convinces her to
listen to the speaker's advice not to live by the success or
failure of their parents. Billy returns to heaven, knowing
he has finally done some good.

SONGS: "Carousel Waltz"-20th Century Fox Studio
Orchestra; "Mister Snow"-Ruick; "If I Loved You"-MacRae,
Jones; "June is Bustin' Out All Over"-Turner, Ruick,
Chorus; "Soliloquy"-MacRae; "When the Children Are Asleep"-
Ruick, Rouseville; "Real Nice Clambake"-Mitchell, Ruick,
Turner, Rouseville, Chorus; "Stone Cutters Cut It On
Stone"-Mitchell, Chorus; "What's the Use of Wonderin'-Jones,
Chorus; "You'll Never Walk Alone"-Turner; Ballet-20th
Century Fox Studio Orchestra; "If I Loved You"-MacRae;
"You'll Never Walk Alone"-Jones, Chorus.

REVIEW: Daily Variety (February 17, 1956) felt that
CAROUSEL's transfer to film was handled "beautifully"
resulting in a "sock" musical drama that would gross well
all over. The critic viewed CAROUSEL's success as due
largely to Jones and MacRae's "winning way with a song" as
well as a book and script that fit their acting abilities
like a "glove." Credit was also given to Henry King's "fine
direction" that used both talent and material to
advantage.

MORE REVIEWS: Film Daily (February 17, 1956); Life
(February 6, 1956); Newsweek (March 19, 1956); New York
Times (February 17, 1956); Saturday Review (March 15, 1956);
Time (March 19, 1956).

COMMENT: Meredith was in the crowd scene at the amusement park. Heather declined her film debut in the film. CAROUSEL was the first motion picture to be filmed in the new Cinemascope 55 process. William LeMassena (Heavenly Friend) played the same role with MacRae in the Dallas production. Oscar Gunnarson was to sculpture portraits of Jones and MacRae for the forecourt of Grauman's Chinese Theatre. King made an aerial survey of the Boothbay area in 1947 for the film DEEP WATERS. The company included 126 and during filming as many as 25 yachts (of on-lookers) were moored in the harbor and on shore crowds surpassed one thousand. The schooner Blue Dolphin was rented and re-named the Nancy-B. Of the films he made, CAROUSEL was MacRae's favorite. CAROUSEL is available on CBS/FOX Video.

F20. BEST THINGS IN LIFE ARE FREE (Twentieth Century Fox, September, 1956) 104 minutes
CREDITS: Producer: Henry Ephron. Director: Michael Curtiz. Screenplay: William Bowers, Phoebe Ephron. Story: John O'Hara. Music Supervised and Conducted by Lionel Newman. Vocal Supervision: Charles Henderson. Orchestration: Herbert Spencer, Earle Hagen, Bernard Mayers. Director of Photography: Leon Shamroy. Art Director: Lyle Wheeler, Maurice Ransford. Musical Settings: John DeCuir. Set Decorations: Walter M. Scott, Paul S. Fox. Special Photographic Effects: Ray Kellog. Film Editor: Dorothy Spencer. Wardrobe Designer: Charles LeMaire. Additional Choreography: Bill Foster. Assistant Director: Davis Silver. Makeup: Ben Nye. Hair Styles: Helen Tarpin. Sound: E. Clayton Ward, Harry M. Leonard. Cinemascope Lenses: Bausch and Lomb. Color by Deluxe. Color Consultant: Leonard Doss.
CAST: Gordon MacRae (Buddy DeSylva), Dan Dailey (Ray Henderson), Ernest Borgnine (Lew Brown), Sheree North (Kitty Kane), Tommy Noonan (Carl), Murvyn Vye (Manny Costair), Phyllis Avery (Maggie Henderson), Larry Keating (Winfield Sheehan), Tony Galento (Fingers), Norman Brooks (Al Jolson), Jacques D' Amboise (Specialty Dancer), Roxanne Arlen (Perky Nicholas), Byron Palmer (Hollywood Star), Linda Brace (Jeannie Henderson), Patty Lou Hudson (Susie Henderson), Julie Van Zandt (Miss Van Seckland), Larry Kerr (Brewer), Charles Victor (Andrews), Eugene Borden (Louis), Harold Miller (Percy a Reporter), Emily Belser (Photographer), Paul Glass (Piano Player), Bill Foster (Dance Director).
SYNOPSIS: After their show GEORGE WHITE SCANDALS closes, Buddy DeSylva (MacRae) and Lew Brown (Borgnine) meet Ray Henderson (Dailey). They like his songs and offer him an equal partnership. To get backing for their show FLYING HIGH, the trio allow gangster Manny Costair (Vye), Lew's pal, to invest in the show. Manny insists his girl friend, Perky Nichols (Arlen), play the lead. Perky is bad in the part and Buddy wants to replace her with Kitty Kane (North). Manny gets mad, but Lew saves the day.
The trio does well and Fox's studio head, Winfield Sheehan (Keating), gets the trio to come to Hollywood to score films. A quarrel follows when Buddy makes deals

without consulting his partners. The partnership breaks
up and Lew and Ray join Kitty in New York to try and make
it on their own. Buddy realizes he loves Kitty, and hearing
about Lew and Ray's hard luck, he quits Hollywood and is
reunited with his partners and with Kitty.

SONGS: Main Title-MacRae, Dailey, Borgnine, North
(Dubbed by Eileen Wilson); "Just a Memory"-North; "Here I
Am Broken Hearted"-MacRae, Borgnine; "Button Up Your
Overcoat"-MacRae, Dailey, Borgnine, North; "This Is the
Mrs."-North, Borgnine; "This is My Lucky Day"-Dailey;
"Lucky in Love," "Good News," "It All Depends On You,"
"Don't Hold Anything"-MacRae, Dailey, Borgnine, North;
"Black Bottom"-North, Chorus; "One More Time"-MacRae; "You
Try Somebody Else"-Arlen; "Birth of the Blues"-MacRae,
Chorus; "You Try Somebody Else"-North; "Together"-Dailey,
Avery; "Sonny Boy"-Brooks; "If I Had a Talking Picture of
You"-Palmer, Chorus; "Sunny Side Up"-North, Vocal Group;
"Without Love"-North; "The Best Things in Life are Free"-
North, Chorus.

REVIEW: Daily Variety (September 24, 1956) felt that
BEST THINGS IN LIFE ARE FREE was "an entertaining swing down
memory lane" and would especially interest older people.
The names Gordon MacRae, Dan Dailey, Ernest Borgnine, and
Sheree North would help sell the picture and most viewers
would find the film a "likeable musical entry." MacRae
played DeSylva "cheerfully and with a pleasant air."

MORE REVIEWS: Film Daily (September 25, 1956); Life
(September 10, 1956); Newsweek (October 8, 1956); New York
Times (September 29, 1956); Time (October 29, 1956).

F21. THE PILOT (Summit, 1979) 98 minutes PG
CREDITS: Producer: C. Gregory Earls. Director: Cliff
Robertson. Screenplay: Robert P. Davis. Based on the novel
by Robert P. Davis (The Pilot). Photography: Walter
Lassally. Editor: Evan Lottman. Score: John Addison.

CAST: Cliff Robertson (Mike Hagen), Frank Converse
(Jim Cochran), Diane Baker (Pat Simpson), Gordon MacRae
(Joe Barnes), Dana Andrews (Mr. Evers), Milo O' Shea
(Dr. O'Brien), Ed Binns (Larry Zanoff).

SYNOPSIS: A senior airline pilot, Mike Hagen
(Robertson) is unhappy with his career and failing marriage,
and prefers crop dusting to flying for a major airline. His
girl friend, Pat Simpson (Baker), and his daughter are the
only things in his life that matter. He starts drinking
while flying, thus endangering his passengers and crew.
The stewardess suspects Mike's drinking problem and
reports her suspicions to Chief Pilot Joe Barnes (MacRae).
Barnes gets pilot Larry Zanoff (Binns) to fly with Mike to
check out the suspicions.

Meanwhile, Mike goes to Dr. O'Brien (O' Shea) for
medical treatment, due to a near accident and because his
co-pilot, Jim Cochran (Converse), won't fly with him. Mike
decreases his amount of booze and goes through withdrawal
but still carries a flask for security.

On a take off, an engine malfunctions and the plane
catches fire. Mike's flask is found by Larry. Mike quits
the airlines to return to crop dusting and to Pat and his
daughter.

REVIEW: Leonard Maltin's Tv Movies & Video Guide
(1988 Edition) THE PILOT was a "predictable drama" that
was enhanced by Walter Lassally's "spectacular aerial
photography" and John Addison's "soaring (and seemingly
misplaced) score."
COMMENT: THE PILOT is available from Paragon Video.

OVER EASY host Hugh Downs and Gordon applauding Bruce MacRae who sang "Forever Young," a song he had written for his father. PBS, October 23, 1979. OVER EASY is a production of KQED-TV and Power/Rector Productions.

5

Television Appearances

T 1. TUNE TIME (May 20, 1953)
<u>Host</u>: Don Ameche. MacRae subbed for Eddie Fisher for four shows, this being the last one. <u>Guest</u>: Sheila MacRae. <u>Song</u>: "I Still Get Jealous"-Gordon, Sheila.

T 2. JACKIE GLEASON SHOW (CBS, 1954?)
MacRae subbed for Jackie Gleason.

T 3. PERRY COMO SHOW (CBS, 1954?)
MacRae subbed for Perry Como.

T 4. PREMIERE OF A STAR IS BORN (September 29, 1954)
The show was telecast from the lobby of the Pantages Theatre in Hollywood. 30 minutes
<u>MC'S</u>: George Fisher, Jack Carson, George Jessel, Larry Finley. <u>Among the stars appearing</u>: (most were interviewed) Louella Parsons, Jimmy McHugh, Mamie Van Doren, Dean Martin, Gloria Grahame, Cy Howard, Edward Arnold, Jon Hall, Hedda Hopper, Raymond Burr, Jean Hersholt, Edward G. Robinson, Donald Crisp, Virginia Mayo, Marilyn Maxwell, Elizabeth Taylor and Michael Wilding, Liberace and his mother, Dennis Morgan, Debbie Reynolds, Kim Novak, Richard Long, Gordon and Sheila MacRae, Dorothy Lamour, Andy Devine, Clark Gable, Peggy Lee, Ray Bolger, Gordon Scott, Mitzi Gaynor, Danny Thomas, William Bendix, Sophie Tucker, James Dean, Joan Crawford, Cesar Romero, Marie Wilson, Jack Palance, Doris Day, Vera-Ellen, Fred MacMurray, Judy Garland and Sid Luft, Jack L. Warner, Van Heflin, Pat O'Brien, Ben Alexander, Shelly Winters, Sonja Henie, Ann Sheridan, Lauren Bacall, Janet Leigh and Tony Curtis, Alan Ladd, Lucille Ball and Desi Arnaz, Claire Trevor, Greer Garson, Sheila Graham, Earl Wilson, Amanda Blake. <u>Comment</u>: Available on video from Video Yesteryear.

T 5. TOAST OF THE TOWN (CBS, 1954?)
MacRae was substitute host for Ed Sullivan.

T 6. GENERAL FOODS 25th ANNIVERSARY SHOW (CBS, March 28, 1954)
The show was a salute to Rodgers & Hammerstein and

was carried on all four networks.
    Performers included: Yul Brynner, Patricia Morrison,
Mary Martin, Enzio Pinza, Celeste Holm, Gordon MacRae,
Tony Martin, Rosemary Clooney, Groucho Marx, Jack Benny
Ed Sullivan, Jan Clayton, John Raitt, Florence Henderson.
Producer: Jess Oppenheimer. Director: Charles Dubin.
Musical Director: Bernard Green. Writer: Helen Deutsch.

T 7. COLGATE COMEDY HOUR (NBC, November 14, 1954 to
    November 27, 1955.)
    The show aired on Sunday 8:00-9:00.
    Host: Gordon MacRae. Sponsor: Colgate Company.

    1 November 14, 1954
       This was MacRae's premiere appearance.
       Host: Gordon MacRae. Guests: Larry Storch, Sammy
       Davis, Dorothy Kirsten. Song: "Cara Mia."
    2 November 28, 1954
       Host: Gordon MacRae. Guests: Jack Carter, Gene
       Sheldon, Gale Storm, Debra Paget. Orchestra:
       Carmen Dragon.
    3 December 12, 1954
       Host: Gordon MacRae. Guests: Gene Sheldon, Terry
       Brennan, Jeff Chandler, Rock Hudson, Queen of
       Tournament of Roses, and a preview of Universal
       International's SO THIS IS PARIS.
    4 January 16, 1955
       This show was broadcast from the Fontainebleau in
       Miami.
       Host: Gordon MacRae. Orchestra: Carmen Dragon.
       Guests: Patti Page, Jack Carter.
    5 January 23, 1955
       Host: Gordon MacRae. Orchestra: Carmen Dragon.
       Guests: Paul Winchell, Jerry Mahoney.
    6 February 20, 1955
       The show aired from New Orleans during Madi Gras.
       Host: Gordon MacRae. Guests: Peggy Lee, Louis
       Armstrong.
    7 March 6, 1955
       The show aired aboard the SS. United States on
       the Hudson River.
       Host: Gordon MacRae. Guests: Zsa Zsa, Eva, and
       Julie Gabor, J.P. Morgan.
    8 March 13, 1955
       Host: Gordon MacRae. Guests: Abbott and Costello,
       Debra Paget.
    9 March 20, 1955
       Host: Gordon MacRae. Guests: Katherine Valente,
       Kay Ballard. Preview of film BIG COMBO.
   10 April 10, 1955
       Performance of the play ROBERTA.
       Gordon MacRae (John Kent), Nina Foch (Sophie
       Teale), Lucille Norman (Stephanie), Agnes
       Moorehead (Aunt Minnie), Jack Carter (Huckleberry
       Haines), Reginald Denny (Lord Henry Delves), Luba
       Malina (Madame Nunez/Countess Schawenja), Fritz
       Feld (Ladislaco). Songs by MacRae: "You're
       Devastating," "The Touch of Your Hand"-MacRae,

Norman; "Don't Ask Me Not to Sing"-MacRae, Norman,
Carter.
7.11   May 15, 1955
       This show saluted Armed Forces Week from March
       Field in Riverside, California.
       Host: Gordon MacRae. Hostess: Rhonda Fleming.
       Guests: Abbott and Costello. Special Appearance:
       President Dwight Eisenhower. Comment: Available on
       Video from Skoku Video.
    12 October 16, 1955
       This show was aired from the Hollywood Bowl in a
       salute to Rodgers and Hammerstein. Those saluting
       Rodgers and Hammerstein: Gordon MacRae, Shirley
       Jones, Gene Nelson, Yul Brynner. Other Guests:
       Martin and Lewis, Bambi Linn, Rod Alexander, Will
       Rogers, Jr. Songs by MacRae: "People Will Say,"
       "Oh What a Beautiful Morning," "If I Loved You"-
       MacRae, Jones.
    13 November 20, 1955
       Host: Gordon MacRae, who sings songs for Thanks-
       giving.
    14 November 27, 1955
       Guests: Gordon MacRae, John Wayne, Rock Hudson,
       Debbie Reynolds, Bob Hope, Anna Maria Alberghetti,
       Claudette Colbert, Louella Parsons, Jimmy McHugh,
       Lana Turner.

T 8. STAGE SHOW (CBS, 1955)
    Hosts: Tommy and Jimmy Dorsey. MC: Gordon MacRae.
Guests: Kim Novak, Connie Francis. Song by MacRae: "If I
Loved You." Comment: This show is available on video from
Video Yesteryear.

T 9. JIMMY DURANTE SHOW (NBC, 1956)
    Host: Jimmy Durante. Guest: Gordon MacRae

T 10. DINAH SHORE SHOW (NBC, 1956)
    Hostess: Dinah Shore. Guest: Gordon MacRae

T 11. GORDON MacRAE SHOW (NBC, March 5, 1956 to August 27,
    1956)
    The 15-minute show aired on Monday 7:30-7:45 and
began the half hour ended by network news. Gordon and
Sheila produced the show for their company Kintail
Enterprises. Sheila helped write and produce the show. The
setting was a replica of the MacRaes' livingroom. The scene
from the window corresponded with that evenings songs.
    Host: Gordon MacRae. Vocalists: Cheerleaders.
Orchestra: Van Alexander. REVIEW: TV Guide (April
21, 1956) felt that MacRae combined his voice with a "warm
exuberant personality" that made the show "easy to take."

    1 March 5, 1956
       This was the premiere show.
       Guest: Phil Harris.
    2 March 12, 1956
       The MacRae family joined Gordon for his birthday,
       by singing "Happy Birthday." Songs: "Little

Child"-Gordon and Meredith, "Cockeyed Optimist,"
"You Made Me Feel So Young"-Gordon.

11.3 March 19, 1956
      Songs by MacRae: "Steppin' Out With My Baby,"
      "Fine Romance," "It's Almost Tomorrow."

4   March 26, 1956
      Songs by MacRae: "So In Love," "Hallelujah," "Who
      Are We."

5   April 2, 1956

6   April 9, 1956
      Songs by MacRae: "Love Thy Neighbor," "Glory of
      Love," "Love is Sweeping the Country."

7   April 16, 1956
      Songs by MacRae: "It's De-Lovely," "One For My
      Baby," "Jingle, Jangle, Jingle."

8   April 23, 1956
      Songs by MacRae: from the movies BEST THINGS IN
      LIFE ARE FREE and SERENADE.

9   April 30, 1956
      Songs by MacRae: "With a Little Bit of Luck," "On
      the Street Where You Live," "Get Me to the Church
      on Time," "I Could Have Danced All Night," "I've
      Grown Accustomed to Her Face."

10   May 7, 1956
      Songs by MacRae: "Blue Skies," "Without a Song,"
      "Surrey With the Fringe on Top."

11   May 14, 1956
      Songs by MacRae: "Falling in Love With Love," "One
      For My Baby," "Where's My Bess."

12   May 21, 1956
      Sheila appeared to mark their 15th Anniversary.

13   May 28, 1956
      Song by MacRae: "Blues of the Night."

14   June 4, 1956
      Songs by MacRae: "How About You," "On the Street
      Where You Live," "I Asked the Lord."

15   June 11, 1956
      Songs by MacRae: "Hot Diggity," "Where or When,"
      "One Misty Morning."

16   June 18, 1956

17   June 25, 1956
      Salute to Eddie Duchin.
      Songs by MacRae: "Manhattan," "I'll Take Romance,"
      "Body and Soul," "Exactly Like You."

18   July 2, 1956
      Guest: June Hutton.

19   July 9, 1956
      Guest: Jan Clayton.

20   July 16, 1956

21   July 23, 1956
      Salute to Sammy Cahn.
      Guest: Sammy Cahn. Songs: "Face to Face."

22   July 30, 1956
      Songs by MacRae: "Things We Did Last Summer,"
      "Where or When," "Wait Til the Sun Shines Nellie,"
      "By the Light of the Silvery Moon," "Moonlight
      and Roses," "If I Loved You."

23   August 6, 1956

Review of MacRae's life.
Songs by MacRae: "Where the Mountain Meets the
Sky" (1941, first record), "I Don't Want to Walk
Without You," "Desert Song."

11.24 August 13, 1956
Songs by MacRae: "I Didn't Know What Time it Was,"
"As Time Goes By," "From This Moment On," "Till
the End of Time."

25 August 27, 1956
This was the last show of the series.
Songs: "Blue Skies," "On the Street Where You
Live," "Summertime."

T 12. FORD STAR JUBILEE-"You're the Top." (CBS, October 6,
1956)
The show was a 90 minute salute to Cole Porter.
Guests: Gordon MacRae, Sally Forest, Shirley Jones,
Dolores Gray, Louis Armstrong, Dorothy Dandridge, George
Sanders, Peter Lind Hayes, Mary Healy, the Toppers, George
Chakiris, David Rose and his orchestra, with special
appearances by Bing Crosby and Cole Porter. Songs by MacRae:
"In the Still of the Night"-MacRae, Jones; "So In Love"-
MacRae; "Wunderbar"-MacRae, Jones; "I Love You" and
impressions by MacRae; "Begin the Beguine"-MacRae. Comment:
Available on video from Video Classics.

T 13. LUX VIDEO THEATRE (NBC, October 18, 1956 to June 20,
1957)
The show aired on Thursday 10:00-11:00. Gordon hosted
all of the following shows and starred in those where noted.

1 FLAMINGO ROAD-October 18, 1956. **Guests:** Joanne
Dru, Raymond Burr, Robert Middleton
2 BECAUSE OF YOU-October 25, 1956. **Guests:** Vera
Miles, John Benteley, Irene Hervey, Sandy
Descher
3 YOU CAN'T ESCAPE FOREVER-November 1, 1956.
Guests: Virginia Gregg, Don DeFore
4 JEZEBEL-November 8, 1956. **Guest:** Martha Heyer
5 GLASS WEBB-November 15, 1956. **Guests:** George
Nader, Kathy Hayes
6 THE GAY SISTERS-November 22, 1956. Guests: Alexis
Smith, Helen Wescott, Tim Hovey, Karen Steele
7 OLD ACQUAINTANCES-November 29, 1956. Guests: Ruth
Hussey, Lynn Bari, Joan Evans
8 CHRISTMAS IN CONNECTICUT-December 13, 1956. Guest:
Mona Freeman
9 HOLLYWOOD'S MUSICAL HOLIDAY REVUE-December 20,
1956.
Guests: Gordon MacRae, Shirley Jones, Jack
Cassidy, Phil Harris, Jeannette MacDonald, Nelson
Eddy. Songs by MacRae: Blue Skies," "Rock Around
the Clock," "Anything But Love"-MacRae, Harris;
"Love is a Many Splendored Thing," "Tender Trap,"
"Love Me Tender," "Best Things in Life Are Free,"
"Laura," "Sonny Boy."
10 MICHAEL AND MARY-December 27, 1956. Guest: Maureen
O' Sullivan

13.11   IT HAPPENED ON FIFTH AVENUE–January 3, 1957.
        Guests: Ernest Truex, Gene Lockhart, Leon Ames,
        Diane Jergens, William Campbell
   12   JUST ACROSS THE STREET–January 10, 1957. Guests:
        Julie Adams, Jack Kelly, Cecile Kellaway
   13   TO HAVE AND HAVE NOT–January 17, 1957. Guests:
        Edmond O' Brien. This show is available on video
        from Video Yesteryear.
   14   VICE SQUAD–January 24, 1957. Guest: Pat O'Brien
   15   ONE SUNDAY AFTERNOON–January 31, 1957. Guests:
        Gordon MacRae (Biff Grimes), Sheila MacRae
        (Virginia Brush), Mary Healy (Amy), Peter Lind
        Hayes (Hugo Barnstead).
   16   THE UNDESIRABLE–February 7, 1957. Guests: Richard
        Denning, Vivian Blaine
   17   DARK VICTORY–February 14, 1957. Guests: Shirley
        Jones, Jack Cassidy
   18   ONE WAY STREET–February 21, 1957. Guest: George
        Nader, Nancy Gates
   19   POSSESSED–February 28, 1957. Guests: Laraine Day,
        Brian Keith
   20   ONE WAY PASSAGE–March 7, 1957. Guest: Barry
        Sullivan, Bonita Granville, Barton MacLane
   21   EILEEN–March 14, 1957. Guests: Gordon MacRae,
        Wendy Martin, Patricia Morrison
   22   THE GREAT LIE–March 21, 1957. Guests: Jan
        Sterling, Catherine McLeod, Glenn Langan
   23   BLACK ANGEL–March 28, 1957. Guests: John Ireland,
        Marilyn Erskine, Anne Bancroft
   24   ADAM HAD FOUR SONS–April 4, 1957. Guest: Leon
        Ames, Valentina Cortesa
   25   THE TAGGART LIGHT–April 18, 1957. Guests: Roger
        Moore, John McIntire, Vera Miles
   26   THE MAN WHO PLAYED GOD–April 25, 1957. Guests:
        Mary Astor, June Lockhart, Boris Karloff
   27   THE HARD WAY–May 2, 1957. Guest: Ann Sheridan,
        Nancy Gates
   28   STAND-IN FOR MURDER–May 9, 1957. Guest: Dewey
        Martin
   29   DEATH DO US PART–May 16, 1957. Guests: Alexis
        Smith, Kent Smith
   30   ARMED VENUS–May 23, 1957. Guests: Esther Williams,
        Steve Forrest, Peter Graves
   31   PARIS CALLING–May 30, 1957. Guest: Joanne Dru,
        Grant Williams
   32   PAYMENT IN KIND–June 6, 1957. Guest: Ruth Hussey
   33   EDGE OF DOUBT–June 20, 1957. Guest: Kathleen
        Crowley, Philip Carey

T 14. FIVE STARS IN SPRINGTIME (NBC, June 1, 1957)
     This show was a salute to the Spring of 1957.
     Host: Bud Collyer. Guests: Patti Page, Gordon MacRae,
Nat King Cole, June Valli, Andy Williams, Ricky Nelson.
Producer/Director: Joe Cates. Musical Director: Harry
Sosnik.

T 15. ED SULLIVAN SHOW (CBS, July 27, 1958)

T 16. I AM AN AMERICAN DAY (September 1958)
This 30 minute program was sponsored by the <u>Los Angeles Examiner</u> as a tribute to persons becoming U.S. Citizens within the past twelve months. The show was hosted by Ralph Edwards and featured many civic dignitaries and show business personalities including Gordon MacRae and Danny Thomas. Four new citizens were sworn in by Leon R. Yankwich, Chief Judge of the U.S. District Court.

T 17. DICK CLARK SATURDAY NIGHT BEECHNUT SHOW (1958)
<u>Host</u>: Dick Clark. <u>Guest</u>: Gordon MacRae. <u>Song</u>: "The Secret"-MacRae.

T 18. WHAT'S MY LINE? (CBS, October 19, 1958)
<u>Host</u>: John Daly. <u>Mystery Guest</u>: Gordon MacRae.

T 19. VOICE OF FIRESTONE (ABC, October 20, 1958)
<u>Narrator</u>: John Daly. <u>Guests</u>: Jo Stafford, Gordon MacRae. <u>Songs by MacRae</u>: "Autumn in New York," "Oh What a Beautiful Morning," "If I Loved You"-MacRae; Medley: "Embraceable You," "The Girl That I Marry," "Come Rain or Come Shine," "Some Enchanted Evening," "Tea For Two"-Daly, Stafford, MacRae; "With a Song in My Heart"-Stafford, MacRae.

T 20. WHAT'S MY LINE? (CBS, November 2, 1958)
<u>Host</u>: John Daly. <u>Guest Panelist</u>: Gordon MacRae.

T 21. DINAH SHORE CHEVY SHOW (NBC, November 23, 1958)
The show aired at 9:00 p.m. and was a salute to Thanksgiving.
<u>Hostess</u>: Dinah Shore. <u>Guests</u>: Roy Rogers, Dale Evans, George Montgomery, Gordon and Sheila MacRae.

T 22. THE GIFT OF THE MAGI (CBS, December 9, 1958)
This special was the musical version of the O'Henry story. <u>Cast</u>: Gordon MacRae (James Dillingham Young), Sally Ann Howes (Della), Howard St. John (Mr. Spiegel), Bibi Osterwald (Madame Safronie), Tammy Grimes (Hazel), Mildred Trares (Clara), Bea Arthur. <u>Songs by MacRae</u>: "The Name's the Same"-Howes, MacRae, "A Better Word Than Love"-MacRae. <u>Executive Producer</u>: Albert Selden. <u>Producer</u>: George Schaefer. <u>Associate Producer</u>: Murray Susskind. <u>Music Director</u>: Hal Hastings. <u>Orchestra</u>: Don Walker. <u>Music & Lyrics</u>: Richard Adler. <u>Writer</u>: Wilson Lehr.

T 23. THE TENNESSEE ERNIE FORD SHOW (NBC, December 18, 1958)
<u>Host</u>: Tennessee Ernie Ford. <u>Guest</u>: Gordon MacRae. <u>Skit</u>: There was a skit about unwanted Christmas gifts.

T 24. RUTH LYONS 50-50 CLUB (NBC, September 29, 1959)
The show was broadcast from Cincinatti, Ohio.
<u>Hostess</u>: Ruth Lyons. <u>Guests</u>: Gordon and Sheila MacRae. <u>Songs</u>: "If I Loved You," "Oh What a Beautiful Morning."

T 25. RUTH LYONS 50-50 CLUB (NBC, October 1, 1959)
The show was broadcast from Cincinatti, Ohio. Gordon appeared alone, as Sheila was ill.

T 26. ED SULLIVAN SHOW (CBS, October 11, 1959)
Gordon and Sheila gave a 15 minute excerpt from their
Kansas City appearance in BELLS ARE RINGING.

T 27. TO TELL THE TRUTH (CBS, October 15, 1959)
<u>Host</u>: Bud Collyer. <u>Guest Panelist</u>: Gordon MacRae.

T 28. MASQUERADE PARTY (CBS, November 2, 1959)
<u>Host</u>: Bert Parks. <u>Guest Panelist</u>: Gordon MacRae.

T 29. MASQUERADE PARTY (CBS, November 9, 1959)
<u>Host</u>: Bert Parks. <u>Guest Panelist</u>: Gordon MacRae.

T 30. BUDDY DEANNE SHOW (late 1950s/early 1960s)
WJZ-TV Channel 13

T 31. NO PLACE LIKE HOME (NBC, April 1960) 30 minutes
<u>Stars</u>: Gordon and Sheila MacRae. <u>Director</u>: William
Asher. <u>Producer/Writer</u>: Ed James. <u>Cast</u>: Children-Kelly
Smith (Laurie), Stephen Talbot (Brad), Maid-Louise Lorimer
(Minnie). <u>Guest Stars</u>: Andy Devine and William Frawley.
This was an unsold TV pilot featuring Gordon and Sheila
in a domestic comedy about a show business couple.

T 32. REVLON REVUE (CBS, 1960)
Gordon and Sheila were guests.

T 33. VOICE OF FIRESTONE (ABC, 1960)

T 34. BELL TELEPHONE HOUR "We Two" (NBC, January 15, 1960)
<u>Guests</u>: Mr. and Mrs. Raymond Scott (Dorothy Collins),
Jose and Ampari Iturbi (Piano Team), Gordon and Sheila
MacRae. <u>Songs by Gordon and Sheila</u>: "We're in Love With New
York;" Title Song (from TAKE ME ALONG); "Till Tomorrow"
(from FIORELLO); "I Once Knew a Fella" (from DESTRY RIDES
AGAIN); "Gypsy;" "Sound of Music" (Gordon's solo); "Small
World" (Gordon serenaded Sheila); "Everything's Coming Up
Roses" (Sheila's solo); "Together Wherever We Go," "We're in
Love With New York."

T 35. ED SULLIVAN SHOW (CBS, May 1960)
<u>Host</u>: Ed Sullivan. <u>Guests</u>: Gordon and Sheila MacRae
Ed was included in the MacRae routine.

T 36. PERSON TO PERSON (CBS, June 24, 1960)
<u>Host</u>: Charles Collingwood. <u>Guest</u>: Gordon MacRae

T 37. ED SULLIVAN SHOW (CBS, July 31, 1960)
<u>Host</u>: Ed Sullivan. <u>Guests</u>: Gordon and Sheila MacRae.
Gordon and Sheila performed songs from OUR LOVE STORY album
including "When the Children are Asleep."

T 38. BELL TELEPHONE HOUR "Salute to Autumn" (NBC, October
13, 1961)
<u>Host</u>: Gordon MacRae. <u>Orchestra</u>: Bell Telephone.
<u>Guests</u>: Sheila MacRae, Anita Bryant, Red Nichols, Jan
Peerce.

T 39. HOME FOR THE HOLIDAYS (NBC, November 23, 1961)
      <u>Sponsor</u>: Mohawk Carpet. <u>Guests</u>: Gordon MacRae, Patrice
Munsel, Carol Haney, Al Hirt.

T 40. CITIES SERVICE HIGHWAY OF MELODY (NBC, December 31,
      1961)
      <u>Hosts</u>: Gordon and Sheila MacRae. <u>Orchestra</u>: Harry
Zimmerman. <u>Guests</u>: George Chakiris, Buddy Ebsen, Kathryn
Grayson, Jack Jones, Rita Moreno, Jan Morgan. <u>Songs by</u>
<u>MacRae</u>: "Louisiana"-MacRae; "Moon River"-MacRae, Ebsen;
"Make Believe"-MacRae, Grayson; "Chicago"-Gordon and
Sheila; "Auld Lange Syne"-Gordon and Sheila.

T 41. CARNIVAL AT SUN VALLEY (ABC, February 23, 1962)
      <u>Guests</u>: Gordon and Sheila MacRae, Louis Armstrong,
Jack Carter, Roberta Peters. <u>Songs by MacRae</u>: "Climb Every
Mountain," Winter Medley-Gordon and Sheila.

T 42. HIGHWAY OF MELODY (NBC, April 22, 1962)
      <u>Hosts</u>: Gordon and Sheila MacRae. <u>Guests</u>: Hugh O'Brien,
Janet Blair, Michael Landon, Juliet Prowse, Mary Costa,
Meredith and Heather MacRae. <u>Songs</u>: "Nothing Like a Dame"-
Gordon, Landon, O'Brien; "Heather on a Hill"-Gordon,
Meredith, Heather; "Sunday in Savannah"-Gordon; "Deep in My
Heart"-Gordon, Costa.

T 43. TALENT SCOUTS (CBS, August 21, 1962)
      <u>Host</u>: Jim Backus. <u>Orchestra</u>: Harry Sosnik. <u>Guest</u>
<u>Talent Scouts</u>: Gordon and Sheila MacRae, Alan King, Tom
Poston, Juliet Prowse, Hildegarde.

T 44. JACK PAAR SHOW (NBC, October 19, 1962)
      <u>Host</u>: Jack Paar. <u>Guests</u>: Gordon and Sheila MacRae,
Woody Allen.

T 45. ED SULLIVAN SHOW (CBS, November 4, 1962)
      The show was a salute to Richard Rodgers.
      <u>Host</u>: Ed Sullivan. <u>Guests</u>: Peter Nero, Diahann
Carroll, Steve Lawrence, Peggy Lee, Gordon MacRae, Roberta
Peters. <u>Songs by MacRae</u>: "Oklahoma," "Surrey With the
Fringe on Top," "Oh What a Beautiful Morning," "If I Loved
You"-MacRae; "Shall We Dance"-MacRae, Peters.

T 46. RED SKELETON SHOW (CBS, December 10, 1962)
      <u>Star</u>: Red Skeleton. <u>Guests</u>: Gordon and Sheila MacRae.

T 47. STUMP THE STARS (CBS, 1963)
      <u>Host</u>: Mike Stokey. <u>Guest Stars</u>: Gordon and Sheila
MacRae. <u>Regulars</u>: Richard Long, Ruta Lee, Tommy Noonan,
Robert Clarey, Beverly Garland, Stubby Kaye. <u>Comment</u>: This
show is available from Video-Sig.

T 48. TONIGHT SHOW (NBC, March 1963)
      <u>Host</u>: Johnny Carson. <u>Co-Host</u>: Ed McMahon. <u>Guests</u>:
Gordon and Sheila MacRae, Jerry Shane.

T 49. JACK PAAR SHOW (NBC, May 17, 1963)
      <u>Host</u>: Jack Paar. <u>Guests</u>: Gordon and Sheila MacRae,

Sam Levenson. Orchestra: Jose Melis. Songs: "Call Me
Irresponsible," "That Wonderful Year"-Gordon and Sheila;
"Where's My Bess"-Gordon.

T 50. JACK PAAR SHOW (NBC, July 5, 1963)
    Host: Jack Paar. Guests: Gordon and Sheila MacRae, Zsa
Zsa Gabor, Jane Mansfield. Songs by MacRae: "If Ever I
Would Leave You," "What Kind of Fool Am I?"-Gordon;
"Sweetest Sounds," "Let Me Entertain You, "Give My Regards
to Broadway"-Gordon and Sheila.

T 51. HOLLYWOOD DEB STARS OF 1964 (ABC, December 28, 1963)
    Hosts: Gordon and Sheila MacRae. Guests: 10 future
stars. Sponsor: Clairol.

T 52. WINTERLAND ON ICE (ABC, December 27, 1964)
    Hosts: Gordon and Sheila MacRae. Guests: Shipstads and
Johnson Ice Follies, Good Time Singers. Songs by MacRae:
"Call Me Irresponsible," "Sleigh Ride"-with Sheila; "If
Ever I Would Leave You," "More," "Oh What a Beautiful
Morning."

T 53. YOUNG MAN FROM BOSTON (1965)
    Music: Allan Friedman. Lyrics: Paul Francis Webster.
Vocals: Gordon MacRae, Kingston Trio.

T 54. AQUA VARIETIES (ABC, February 7, 1965)
    The program came from Miami Beach's Fountainebleau
Hotel.
    Hosts: Gordon and Sheila MacRae. Guests: Mitchell
    Trio, O'Connor Sisters, Aqua Maids and Maniacs.
    Music Director: Richard Haymond. Writer: Selma
Diamond.

T 55. WORLD'S FAIR SPECTACULAR (ABC, April 29, 1965)
    Gordon and Sheila offered a tour of the fair in song
and fact, visiting the entertainment at some of the
National Pavilions.
    Hosts: Gordon and Sheila MacRae. Producer/Director:
    Gil Cates. Guests: New Christy Minstrels, Al Hirt and
    his Sextet. Song by MacRae: "This is My Once a Year
    Day."

T 56. TONIGHT SHOW (NBC, 1966)
    Host: Johnny Carson. Co-Host: Ed McMahon. Guest:
Gordon MacRae. Song by MacRae: "Michelle" from his new
album IF SHE WALKED INTO MY LIFE.

T 57. PASSWORD (CBS, January 23, 1967 to January 26, 1967)
    Host: Allen Ludden. Guests: Gordon MacRae, Arlene
Dahl.

T 58. ED SULLIVAN SHOW (CBS, July 23, 1967)
    Host: Ed Sullivan. Orchestra: Ray Block. Guests:
Gordon MacRae, Ethel Merman, Myron Cohen, Jose Greco.
Songs: "Soliloquy"-MacRae; "You're Just in Love"-MacRae,
Merman.

T 59. PAY CARDS (Syndicated, 1968)
<u>Host</u>: Art James. <u>Guest</u>: Gordon MacRae.

T 60. LINKLETTER SHOW (CBS, 1968?)
<u>Host</u>: Art Linkletter. <u>Guests</u>: Bess Myerson, Gordon MacRae.

T 61. PERSONALITY (NBC, Week of July 15, 1968)
<u>Host</u>: Larry Blyden. <u>Guests</u>: Joan Rivers, Joan Fontaine, Gordon MacRae.

T 62. ED SULLIVAN (CBS, August 4, 1968)
<u>Host</u>: Ed Sullivan. <u>Guests</u>: Gordon MacRae, Carol Lawrence, Ray Charles, Bill Dana. <u>Songs</u>: "I Do! I Do!" "I Love My Wife," "My Cup Runneth Over"-MacRae, Lawrence.

T 63. LET US ENTERTAIN YOU (August 6, 1968)
<u>Host</u>: Robert Morse. <u>Guests</u>: Gordon MacRae, Dave Brubeck, Jim Backus, Hermione Gingold, talented youth from the Professional Children's School in New York.

T 64. SNAP JUDGEMENT (NBC, August 26, 1968 to August 30, 1968)
<u>Guests</u>: Gordon and Meredith MacRae.

T 65. MIKE DOUGLAS SHOW (Syndicated, Week of September 3, 1968)
<u>Host</u>: Mike Douglas. <u>Co-Host</u>: Gordon MacRae. <u>Guests included</u>: Nancy Wilson, Vincent Price, Elizabeth MacRae, Captain Kangeroo, Bobby Goldsboro, Four Seasons, Helen Gurley Brown, Peter Lawford, Martha Raye. <u>Orchestra</u>: Joe Harnell's Sextet.

T 66. MIKE DOUGLAS SHOW (Syndicated, October 1968)
<u>Host</u>: Mike Douglas. <u>Co-Hosts</u>: Peter Lind Hayes, Mary Healy. <u>Guests</u>: Gordon MacRae, Selma Diamond, Julie Budd.

T 67. MATCH GAME (NBC, Week of December 23, 1968)
<u>Host</u>: Gene Rayburn. <u>Guests</u>: Gordon MacRae, Bess Myerson.

T 68. PERSONALITY (NBC, Week of January 6, 1969)
<u>Host</u>: Larry Blyden. <u>Guests</u>: Jack Cassidy, Totie Fields, Gordon MacRae.

T 69. MATCH GAME (NBC, Week of February 3, 1969)
<u>Host</u>: Gene Rayburn. <u>Guests</u>: Gordon and Meredith MacRae.

T 70. JOEY BISHOP SHOW (ABC, March 17, 1969)
<u>Host</u>: Joey Bishop. <u>Guests</u>: Gordon MacRae, Mickey Shaughnessy, Pat O' Brien. <u>Song by MacRae</u>: "Danny Boy."

T 71. JOEY BISHOP SHOW (ABC, April 21, 1969)
<u>Host</u>: Joey Bishop. <u>Co-Host</u>: Regis Philbin. <u>Orchestra</u>: Johnny Mann. <u>Guests</u>: Steve Allen, Jayne Meadows, Gordon MacRae.

T 72. MERV GRIFFIN (Syndicated, April 24, 1969)
Host: Merv Griffin. Guests: Gordon MacRae, Garry
Moore, Richard Deacon, Karen Morrow.

T 73. MATCH GAME (Week of May 12, 1969)
Host: Gene Rayburn. Guests: Gordon MacRae, Edie Adams.

T 74. DEAN MARTIN SHOW (NBC, May 15, 1969)
Host: Dean Martin. Guests: Gordon MacRae, Abbe Lane,
Bob Newhart, Paul Lynde. Songs by MacRae: "Surrey With the
Fringe on Top," "People Will Say We're in Love," "June is
Busting Out All Over," "If I Loved You," "The Game"-MacRae,
Martin, Lynde.

T 75. GORDON MacRAE SHOW (Syndicated, June 21, 1969)
The 60 minute special was produced by Screen Gems.
Host: Gordon MacRae. Guests: Barbara McNair, Rich
Little. Songs by MacRae: "Fireworks," "Oklahoma," "Oh What
a Beautiful Morning," "If I Loved You," "Surrey With the
Fringe on Top," "Soliloquy," "Somewhere," "Here's to Love,"
"If Ever I Would Leave You," "Hello Young Lovers."

T 76. DEAN MARTIN SHOW (NBC, November 20, 1969)
Host: Dean Martin. Guests: Gordon MacRae, Gail Martin,
Dom Deluise, Stanley Myron Handelman, Tommy Tune. Song by
MacRae: "Soliloquy."

T 77. GUY LOMBARDO (ABC, December 31, 1969)
This New Years Eve show was broadcast from the Waldorf
Astoria.
Host: Guy Lombardo. Guest: Gordon MacRae. Songs by
MacRae: "Dear World," "Why Can't I Walk Away?" "Hello Young
Lovers," "Kiss Her Now," "Come Back to Me," "Try to
Remember."

T 78. MATCH GAME (NBC, Late 1960s)
Host: Gene Rayburn. Guests: Gordon MacRae, Jessica
Walters.

T 79. JOEY BISHOP SHOW (ABC, Late 1960s)
Host: Joey Bishop. Guests: Gordon MacRae, Jim McKay.

T 80. DAVID FROST SHOW (Syndicated, Late 1960s/Early 1970s)
Host: David Frost. Guests: James Franciscus, Richard
Crenna, Gene Hackman, Michael Crawford, Gordon MacRae.

T 81. MERV GRIFFIN (Late 1960s/Early 1970s)
Host: Merv Griffin. Guests: Gordon MacRae, Soupy
Sales, Charles Manna, Dr. Joyce Brothers.

T 82. PETER LUPUS' BODY SHOP (Syndicated, 1970s)
Host: Peter Lupus. Guests: Gordon MacRae, Sybil
Henderson (Home Economist).

T 83. YOUR ALL AMERICAN COLLEGE TALENT SHOW (Syndicated,
1970)
Host: Gordon MacRae.

T 84. BEAT THE CLOCK (Syndicated, May 30, 1972)
Host: Jack Narz. Guest: Gordon MacRae.

T 85. MERV GRIFFIN (Syndicated, January 29, 1973)
The program was a salute to Richard Rodgers.
Host: Merv Griffin. Guests: Gordon MacRae, Florence
Henderson, Myoshi Umeki. Songs by MacRae: from OKLAHOMA and
CAROUSEL.

T 86. GRAMMY SALUTES OSCAR (CBS, May 30, 1974)
Host: Gene Kelly. Guests: Gordon MacRae, Frankie
Avalon, Janet Blair, Rosemary Clooney, Dick Haymes, Henry
Mancini, Dennis Morgan, Donald O'Connor, Buddy Rogers,
Dionne Warwick, Jane Withers, John Green, Jack Jones, Tony
Martin, Ann Miller, Gene Nelson, Johnny Mann Singers. Songs
by MacRae: "Gigi," "High Hopes"-MacRae, Clooney, Avalon,
Johnny Mann Singers. Producer: Pierre Cosette.

T 87. McCLOUD (NBC, September 22, 1974)
The episode was entitled "The Barefoot Girls of
Bleeker Street."
Star: Dennis Weaver (Sam McCloud). Regulars: J.D.
Cannon (Peter Clifford), Terry Carter (Broadhurst). Guests:
Gordon MacRae (Sheriff Rodney), Shelly Winters (Thelma),
Kay Lenz (Eve), Whit Bissell, Bill Fletcher, Robyn Milian.
Synopsis: Gordon played murderer, Sheriff Rodney and Shelly
Winters played a discotheque owner, who hires young girls
to promote the sale of liquor and a credit card scam. Kay
Lenz and the father of her baby witness MacRae and his
deputy with stolen money. They are seen and the young man
is killed. Lenz and her sick baby run away to New York,
where she is hired by Winters. MacRae traces Lenz there in
order to silence her, but is stopped by Weaver.

T 88. MERV GRIFFIN (Syndicated, October 18, 1974)
Host: Merv Griffin. Guests: Gordon and Meredith
MacRae, Robert and Alan Alda, Luise Rainer and Daughter,
Franchesia Norsa.

T 89. CBS BICENTENNIAL MINUTES (CBS, January 6, 1975)
MacRae narrated this segment which was shot on
December 12, 1974 at CBS in Los Angeles. The segments told
of an event in our nations birth 200 years prior to the air
date.

T 90. DINAH (Syndicated, February 18, 1975)
The show's theme was Gold Record Week.
Hostess: Dinah Shore. Guests: Gordon MacRae, Shirley
Jones, Rosemary Clooney, Righteous Brothers, Ronnie Schell,
David Essex. Songs: Gordon and Shirley sang an OKLAHOMA
medley.

T 91. MERV GRIFFIN (Syndicated, March 14, 1975)
The show was broadcast from Ceasars Palace in Las
Vegas.
Host: Merv Griffin. Guests: Sandler and Young,
Checkmates (Soul Group), Dick Capri (Comic), Karen Wyman
(Singer), Carazini (Magician), Gordon MacRae. Songs by

MacRae: "Late Late Show," "Surrey With the Fringe on Top,"
"People Will Say We're in Love," "Oklahoma," "Desert Song."
Imitations by MacRae: Crazy Guggenheim, Arthur Godfrey, Joe
E. Lewis. Walk-On: Peter Lind Hayes.

T 92. VAUDEVILLE (Syndicated, July 16, 1975)
    Each show in this series had a different host.
    Host: Gordon MacRae. Guests: Shani Wallis, Jackie
Kahane (Comedian), Jim Rinehart (Juggler), Mr. Electric
(Magician), Russ Sanders Trio (Gymnastics). Songs by
MacRae: "It Had to Be You," "That Old Feeling," "You Are My
Music." Executive Producer: Burt Rosen. Producer: Mort
Green. Director: Jack Scott. Music: George Wyle. Writer:
Mort Green.

T 93. MUSICAL CHAIRS (CBS, October 14, 1975 to October 20,
    1975)
    Host: Adam Wade. Guests: Lou Rawls, Ernestine Jackson,
Gordon and Heather MacRae. Songs by MacRae: "Blue Skies,"
"If I Loved You," "Old Man River," "Stranger in Paradise,"
"Soliloquy," "If She Walked Into My Life," "Sweet Gypsy
Rose," "I Feel Love," "Love Me Or Leave Me," "By the Light
of the Silvery Moon"-Gordon, Heather, "Too Marvelous For
Words"-Gordon, Heather.

T 94. BOB HOPE SPECIAL (NBC, February 13, 1976)
    Host: Bob Hope. Sponsor: Texaco. Guests: Phyllis
Diller, Telly Savalas, Raquel Welch, Andy Williams, Flip
Wilson. Audience Guests: Gordon MacRae, Fred MacMurray,
President Gerald Ford.

T 95. OVER EASY (PBS, February 2, 1978)
    Host: Hugh Downs. Guest: Gordon MacRae. Songs by
MacRae: "I Write the Songs," "What I Did For Love."

T 96. GOOD MORNING AMERICA (ABC, October 16, 1978)
    Host: David Hartman. Guests: Gordon and Meredith
MacRae. Gordon appeared to discuss his forthcoming film
THE PILOT. Song: "Memories"-Gordon and Meredith.

T 97. OVER EASY (PBS, February 19, 1979)
    Host: Hugh Downs. Guest: Gordon MacRae.

T 98. DOWN MEMORY LANE IN MUSIC AND COMEDY (NBC, May 11,
    1979)
    The show highlighted Dean Martin's Variety Series from
1965 to 1974.

T 99. OVER EASY (PBS, October 23, 1979)
    Host: Hugh Downs. Guests: Gordon and Bruce MacRae.
Bruce played the piano and sang "Forever Young" a song he
wrote for his father, Gordon.

T100. HOLLYWOOD AUTISTIC CHILDREN'S TELETHON (January 15,
    1980)
    Gordon appeared with daughter, Meredith.

T101. 100 YEARS OF GOLDEN HITS (NBC, July 19, 1981)
This show was taped in 1978, but didn't air until 1981. It was a special about the recording industry and its changes over the years.
Co-Hosts: John Davidson, William Windom (Thomas Edison). Guests: Ethel Merman, Gordon MacRae, Johnny and June Carter Cash, Gladys Knight, Mills Brothers, Sha Na Na, Don McLean, Glen Campbell, Johnny Ray, Kiss, Foghat, Andy Williams, Marilyn Horne. Songs by MacRae: Medley of Broadway Songs with Ethel Merman. Executive Producer: Pierre Cossette. Producer: Buz Kohan, Walter Miller. Director: Walter Miller. Announcer: Dick Tufeld. Music: Ray Charles. Writer: Buz Kohan, Rod Warren, Philip Pumpian, Ed Hider. Art Director: Romain Johnston.

T102. AN AMERICAN ORIGINAL: THE OREGON SYMPHONY ORCHESTRA (PBS, September 22, 1981.)
The program was recorded at the Portland Civic Auditorium.
Guest Soloist: Gordon MacRae. Conductor: Norman Leyden. Songs by MacRae: "Almost Like Being in Love," "If Ever I Would Leave You," "Gigi," "Get Me to the Church on Time," "Some Enchanted Evening," "This Nearly Was Mine," "If I Loved You."

T103. BOB HOPE PRESENTS A CELEBRATION WITH STARS OF COMEDY AND MUSIC (NBC, October 22, 1981)
The show was a dedication of the Gerald Ford Presidential Museum in Grand Rapids, Michigan.
Host: Bob Hope. Guests: Pearl Bailey, Debbie Boone, Foster Brooks, Glen Campbell, Sammy Davis, Jr., Tony Orlando, Mark Russell, Danny Thomas, Gordon MacRae. Song by MacRae: "New York, New York." Executive Producer: Bob Hope. Producer: William O. Harbach. Director: Tony Charmoli. Music: Les Brown. Special Musical Material: Ray Charles. Writers: Gig Henry, Robert Mills, Fred Fox, Seaman Jacobs.

T104. NEW YEARS EVE BIG BAND CELEBRATION (December 31, 1982)
This 90 minute special was broadcast from Catalina Island, California.
Host: Art James. Guests: King Sisters, Helen Forrest, Gordon MacRae. Orchestra: Alvino Rey.

T105. SINGING FAMILY FEUD (ABC, October 23, 1983 to October 28, 1983)
Host: Richard Dawson. Guests: King Family, Lennon Sisters, MacRae Family, Sister Sledge.

T106. RODGERS AND HAMMERSTEIN-THE SOUND OF AMERICAN MUSIC (PBS, March 9, 1985)
This program tells the Rodgers and Hammerstein story in film clips, stills and interviews.
Hostess: Mary Martin. Guests included: Alfred Drake, John Raitt, Shirley Jones, Gordon MacRae, Yul Brynner, Robert Wise.

Gordon making a recording for Capitol Records,
circa 1959.

6

Discography

<u>78s</u>

D 1. <u>July 24, 1941</u>
Columbia 36295
Recorded in Chicago
Larry Cotton and Donna and her Don Juans (Gordon, Charlie, George) with Horace Heidt and his Musical Knights
   I DON'T WANT TO SET THE WORLD ON FIRE

D 2. <u>July 24, 1941</u>
Columbia 36306
Recorded in Chicago
Larry Cotton and Donna and her Don Juans (Gordon, Charlie, George) with Horace Heidt and his Musical Knights
   MY HEART RUNS AFTER YOU

D 3. <u>August 11, 1941</u>
Columbia 36370
Recorded in Chicago
with Larry Cotton, Fred Lowrey and Horace Heidt and his Musical Knights
   SHEPHERD SERENADE
<u>NOTE</u>: This song hit the charts on November 22, 1941, and was charted for eight weeks, reaching position seven.

D 4. <u>August 11, 1941</u>
Columbia 36380
Recorded in Chicago
with the Don Juans and Horace Heidt and his Musical Knights
   BE HONEST WITH ME

D 5. <u>April 8, 1942</u>
Columbia 36610
Recorded in Hollywood
with Horace Heidt and his Musical Knights
   HEAVENLY HIDEAWAY

D   6. **April 8, 1942**
Columbia 36665
Recorded in Hollywood
with Horace Heidt and his Musical Knights
   WHEN YOUR LIPS MET MINE

D   7. **July 23, 1942**
Columbia 36667
Recorded in Chicago
with Horace Heidt and his Musical Knights
   WHERE THE MOUNTAINS MEET THE SKY

D   8. **1945**
Musicraft 15052
with the Walter Gross Orchestra
   SLOWLY
   IT'S ANYBODY'S SPRING

D   9. **1945**
Musicraft 15065
with the Walter Gross Orchestra
   PRISONER OF LOVE
   THEY SAY IT'S WONDERFUL

D 10. **1945**
Musicraft 15069
with the Walter Gross Orchestra
   YOU GO TO MY HEAD
   I HAVE BUT ONE HEART

D 11. **1946**
Musicraft 15084
with the Walter Gross Orchestra
   THE WAY THE WIND BLOWS
   I'M SO LONESOME I COULD CRY

D 12. **1946**
Musicraft 15089
with the Walter Gross Orchestra
   YOU KEEP COMING BACK LIKE A SONG
   STARS FELL ON ALABAMA

D 13. **1947**
Appollo 1045
with the Jerry Jerome Orchestra
   IF I HAD MY LIFE TO LIVE OVER
   HEARTACHES

D 14. **1947**
Capitol B 463
with the Paul Weston Orchestra
   A FELLOW NEEDS A GIRL
   BODY AND SOUL

D 15. **1947**
Capitol 15002
with the Paul Weston Orchestra
   I STILL GET JEALOUS

I UNDERSTAND
NOTE: I STILL GET JEALOUS hit the charts on November
15, 1947, and was charted for two weeks. It peaked
at position twenty-five.

D 16. 1947
Capitol 15014
with the Paul Weston Orchestra
   AT THE CANDLELIGHT CAFE
   I SURRENDER DEAR
NOTE: AT THE CANDLELIGHT CAFE appeared on the charts
on December 20, 1947, and reached position twenty and
was charted for four weeks.

D 17. 1948
Capitol?
with Jo Stafford
   BE MINE

D 18. 1948
Capitol 15027
with the Carlyle Hall Orchestra
   YOU WERE MEANT FOR ME
   THOUGHTLESS
NOTE: THOUGHTLESS appeared on the charts on February
21, 1948, and was charted for two weeks, climbing to
spot twenty-eight. YOU WERE MEANT FOR ME reached the
charts on March 6, 1948, and climbed to spot
twenty-two and remained charted for two weeks.

D 19. 1948
Capitol 15041
with the Carlyle Hall Orchestra
   THAT FEATHERY FEELIN'
   MATINEE
NOTE: THAT FEATHERY FEELIN' appeared on the charts
on April 30, 1948. It climbed to spot twenty-seven
for a one week charting.

D 20. 1948
Capitol 15072
with the Carlyle Hall Orchestra
   SPRING IN DECEMBER
   IT'S MAGIC
NOTE: IT'S MAGIC appeared on the charts on July 3,
1948, and climbed to spot nine and remained on the
charts for seventeen weeks.

D 21. 1948
Capitol 15091
with the Carlyle Hall Orchestra
   STEPPIN' OUT WITH MY BABY
   EVELYN

D 22. 1948
Capitol 15128
with the Carlyle Hall Orchestra
   I WENT DOWN TO VIRGINIA

          HANKERIN'
NOTE: HANKERIN' appeared on the charts on July 24,
1948, and climbed to position twenty-three for a one
week charting.

D 23. **1948**
          Capitol 15154
          with the Carlyle Hall Orchestra
               AT YOUR COMMAND
               WIN OR LOSE

D 24. **1948**
          Capitol 15178
          with the Starlighters
               HAIR OF GOLD, EYES OF BLUE
               RAMBLING ROSE
          NOTE: HAIR OF GOLD, EYES OF BLUE appeared on the
          charts on August 28, 1948, and climbed to position
          seven and remained charted for fourteen weeks.
          RAMBLING ROSE hit the charts on October 23, 1948, and
          peaked at position twenty-seven, being charted for
          one week.

D 25. **1948**
          Capitol 15207
          with Jo Stafford
               BLUE BIRD OF HAPPINESS
               SAY SOMETHING SWEET TO YOUR SWEETHEART
          NOTE: Both songs hit the charts on October 16, 1948.
          BLUE BIRD OF HAPPINESS was on the charts for four
          weeks and went to position sixteen. SAY SOMETHING
          SWEET TO YOUR SWEETHEART was a top ten song and was
          on the charts for six weeks.

D 26. **1948**
          Capitol 15270
          with Jo Stafford
               MY DARLING, MY DARLING
               GIRLS WERE MADE TO TAKE CARE OF BOYS
          NOTE: MY DARLING, MY DARLING appeared on the charts
          on November 13, 1948, and rose to number one and was
          charted for seventeen weeks.

D 27. **1949**
          Capitol 15304
          with the Carlyle Hall Orchestra
               RAMONA
               DO YOU EVER THINK OF ME

D 28. **1949**
          Capitol 15342
          with Jo Stafford and the Paul Weston Orchestra
               PUSSY CAT SONG
               I'LL STRING ALONG WITH YOU
          NOTE: The PUSSY CAT SONG hit the charts on February
          12, 1949, and peaked at position twenty-six, staying
          charted for two weeks.

D 29. <u>1949</u>
Capitol 15357
   A ROSEWOOD SPINET
   SO IN LOVE
<u>NOTE</u>: SO IN LOVE reached the charts on March 5,
1949, and peaked at spot twenty and was charted for
nine weeks.

D 30. <u>1949</u>
Capitol 15366
   MELANCHOLY MINSTREL
   YOU'RE STILL THE BELLE OF THE BALL

D 31. <u>1949</u>
Capitol 15393
with Jo Stafford and the Paul Weston Orchestra
   A YOU'RE ADORABLE
   NEED YOU
<u>NOTE</u>: A YOU'RE ADORABLE hit the charts on March 19,
1949, and climbed to the fourth spot, staying on the
charts for fifteen weeks. NEED YOU appeared on the
charts on April 2, 1949, and hit position seven and
remained charted for twelve weeks.

D 32. <u>1949</u>
Capitol 15396
with the Paul Weston Orchestra
   I GET UP EVERY MORNING
   THE RIGHT GIRL FOR ME

D 33. <u>1949</u>
Capitol 15425
with the Paul Weston Orchestra
   LITTLE OLD CHURCH NEAR LEICESTER SQUARE
   CHAPTER IN MY LIFE

D 34. <u>1949</u>
Capitol 57-566
with Jo Stafford and the Paul Weston Orchestra
   MY ONE AND ONLY HIGHLAND FLING
   THANK YOU

D 35. <u>1949</u>
Capitol 57-596
with the Frank DeVol Orchestra
   SOME ENCHANTED EVENING

D 36. <u>1949</u>
Capitol 57-598
with the Paul Weston Orchestra
   YOUNGER THAN SPRINGTIME
<u>NOTE</u>: The song appeared on the charts on July 16,
1949, and reached position thirty and was charted for
one week.

D 37. <u>1949</u>
Capitol 57-628
with the Paul Weston Orchestra

TING-A-LING
LOVER'S GOLD

D 38. <u>1949</u>
Capitol 57-679
with the Paul Weston Orchestra
TWO LITTLE, NEW LITTLE, BLUE LITTLE EYES
NOW, NOW, NOW

D 39. <u>1949</u>
Capitol 57-690
with Jo Stafford and the Paul Weston Orchestra
WHISPERING HOPE
NOTE: WHISPERING HOPE hit the charts on August 20,
1949, and rose to the fourth position and was charted
for twenty-three weeks. It became a gold disc.

D 40. <u>1949</u>
Capitol 57-704
with the Paul Weston Orchestra
BODY AND SOUL
A KISS IN THE DARK

D 41. <u>1949</u>
Capitol 57-711
with the Starlighters and the Paul Weston Orchestra
TWENTY-FOUR HOURS OF SUNSHINE
WEDDING OF LILLI MARLENE

D 42. <u>1949</u>
Capitol 57-723
with the Paul Weston Orchestra
WONDERFUL ONE
I WANT YOU TO WANT ME

D 43. <u>1949</u>
Capitol 57-755
with the Paul Weston Orchestra
PRAIRIE IS STILL
SUNSHINE OF YOUR SMILE

D 44. <u>1949</u>
Capitol 57-777
with the Andy Parker Orchestra and the Plainsmen
MULE TRAIN
DEAR HEARTS AND GENTLE PEOPLE
NOTE: MULE TRAIN reached the charts on November 26,
1949, and peaked at the fourteenth position,
remaining on the charts for four weeks. DEAR HEARTS
AND GENTLE PEOPLE appeared on the charts on December
24, 1949 for two weeks and climbed to position
nineteen.

D 45. <u>1949</u>
Capitol 57-782
with Jo Stafford and the Paul Weston Orchestra
BIBBIDI BOBBIDI BOO
ECHOES

NOTE: Both records hit the charts on December 24,
1949, BIBBIDI BOBBIDI BOO peaked at number thirteen
and stayed on the charts for seven weeks and ECHOES
rose to position eighteen for five weeks on the
charts.

D 46. 1949
       Capitol 768
       with Jo Stafford and the Paul Weston Orchestra
          WUNDERBAR
          I'LL STRING ALONG WITH YOU

D 47. 1950
       Capitol 812
       with the Paul Weston Orchestra
          JUST ONE MORE CHANCE
          I'M YOURS

D 48. 1950
       Capitol 842
       with the Starlighters and the Paul Weston Orchestra
          POISON IVY
          HALF A HEART IS ALL YOU LEFT ME

D 49. 1950
       Capitol 858
       with Jo Stafford and the Paul Weston Orchestra
          DEARIE
          MONDAY, TUESDAY, WEDNESDAY
       NOTE: DEARIE made the charts on March 11, 1950, and
       climbed to the number ten spot and was charted for
       eleven weeks.

D 50. 1950
       Capitol 924
       with Paul Weston's Dixie Eight
          OH OH OPHELIA
          TWO FACED HEART

D 51. 1950
       Capitol 935
       with the Paul Weston Orchestra
          AS WE ARE TODAY
          KISSES AND TEARS

D 52. 1950
       Capitol 959
       with the Paul Weston Orchestra
          THIS IS HEAVEN TO ME
          RIVER OF SMOKE

D 53. 1950
       Capitol 1021
       with the Les Baxter Chorus and the Paul Weston
       Orchestra
          HONGI TONGI HONKI POKI
          STARS AND STRIPES FOREVER

D 54. <u>1950</u>
      Capitol 1061
      with Jo Stafford
          ROSARY

D 55. <u>1950</u>
      Capitol 1214
      with the Frank DeVol Orchestra
          YOUR GONNA LOSE YOUR GAL (with the Ewing Sisters)
          YOU LOVE ME

D 56. <u>1950</u>
      Capitol 1289
      with the Frank DeVol Orchestra
          USE YOUR IMAGINATION
          I AM LOVED

D 57. <u>1951</u>
      Capitol 1307
      with Jo Stafford and the Bill Loose Orchesra
          TO THINK YOU'VE CHOSEN ME
          HOLD ME HOLD ME

D 58. <u>1951</u>
      Capitol 1545
      with the Carmen Dragon Orchestra
          LAST NIGHT WHEN WE WERE YOUNG
          CUBAN LOVE SONG

D 59. <u>1951</u>
      Capitol 1642
      with Jo Stafford
          I'LL STRING ALONG WITH YOU
          WHISPERING HOPE
      (See D82)

D 60. <u>1951</u>
      Capitol 1659
      with Jo Stafford
          BEYOND THE SUNSET
          WUNDERBAR
      (See D83)

D 61. <u>1951</u>
      Capitol 1705
      with the Carmen Dragon Orchestra
          OLD MAN RIVER
          ON A SUNDAY AT CONEY ISLAND (w. the Cheerleaders)

D 62. <u>1951</u>
      Capitol 1750
          DOWN THE OLD OX ROAD (Carlyle Hall Orchestra)
          CUDDLE UP A LITTLE CLOSER (Paul Weston Orchestra)
      (See D84)

D 63. <u>1951</u>
      Capitol 1807
      with Gisele MacKenzie and the Bill Loose Orchestra

        LOVER'S GOLD
        ROSARY HILL

D 64. <u>1951</u>
      Capitol 1836
        LAUGHING AT LOVE (Paul Weston Orchestra)
        BE MY GUEST (Van Alexander Chorus and Orchestra)

D 65. <u>1951</u>
      Capitol 1846
      with the Van Alexander Orchestra and Chorus
        MY LOVE
        HOW CLOSE

D 66. <u>1951</u>
      Capitol 1941
      with the Paul Weston Orchestra
        BABY DOLL
        GREEN ACRES AND PURPLE MOUNTAINS

D 67. <u>1951</u>
      Capitol 1990
        NINE HUNDRED MILES
        CALL HER YOUR SWEETHEART

D 68. <u>1951</u>
      Capitol 2010
      with the Van Alexander Orchestra
        THESE THINGS SHALL PASS
        GENTLE HANDS

D 69. <u>1951/1952</u>
      Capitol SM 100
      with Gisele MacKenzie and the Billy May Orchestra
        MY BUICK, MY LOVE AND I

D 70. <u>1952</u>
      Capitol 2047
      with the Van Alexander Orchestra
        NO OTHER GIRL FOR ME
        IF SOMEONE HAD TOLD ME

D 71. <u>1952</u>
      Capitol 2196
      with the Van Alexander Orchestra
        THERE'S A LULL IN MY LIFE
        BLAME IT ON MY YOUTH

D 72. <u>1953</u>
      Capitol 2311
      with the Van Alexander Orchestra and Chorus
        BROTHERLY LOVE
        STRAIGHT AND NARROW

D 73. <u>1953</u>
      Capitol 2465
      with the Axel Stordahl Orchestra
        HOMIN' TIME

    C'EST MAGNIFIQUE
NOTE: C'EST MAGNIFIQUE appeared on the charts on
June 6, 1953, and went to position twenty-nine and
was charted for one week. (see D87)

D 74. **1953**
    Capitol 2652
    with the Van Alexander Orchestra
        STRANGER IN PARADISE
        NEVER IN A MILLION YEARS
    NOTE: STRANGER IN PARADISE hit the charts on
    December 5, 1953, and climbed to the twenty-nineth
    position for a one week charting.

D 75. **1954**
    Capitol 2760
        FACE TO FACE (George Greeley Orchestra)
        BACKWARD TURN BACKWARD (Van Alexander Orchestra)
    NOTE: FACE TO FACE hit the charts on June 12, 1954,
    and climbed to position thirty and was charted for
    one week.

D 76. **1954**
    Capitol 2784
    with the Van Alexander Orchestra
        OPEN YOUR ARMS
        CONEY ISLAND BOAT (with June Hutton)

45s

D 77. **1950**
    Capitol F1168
    with the Frank DeVol Orchestra
        PIGSKIN POLKA
        LOVE'EM ALL

D 78. **1950**
    Capitol F1193
    with the Frank DeVol Orchestra
        JUST THE WAY YOU ARE
        HONESTLY I LOVE YOU

D 79. **1951**
    Capitol F1317
    with the Frank DeVol Orchestra
        YOU DYED YOUR HAIR CHARTREUSE
        HONKY TONKY TEN CENT DANCE

D 80. **1951**
    Capitol F1374
    with the Frank DeVol Orchestra
        LOVE MEANS LOVE
        WAIT FOR ME

D 81. **1951**
    Capitol F1471
    with the Carmen Dragon Orchestra
        I'M YOURS TO COMMAND

I'LL BUY YOU A STAR

D 82. <u>1951</u>
Capitol F1642
with Jo Stafford
    WHISPERING HOPE
(See D59)

D 83. <u>1951</u>
Capitol F1659
with Jo Stafford
    BEYOND THE SUNSET
    WUNDERBAR
(See D60)

D 84. <u>1951</u>
Capitol F1750
    DOWN THE OLD OX ROAD (Carlyle Hall Orchestra)
    CUDDLE UP A LITTLE CLOSER (Carmen Dragon)
(See D62)

D 85. <u>1952</u>
Capitol F2114
with the Van Alexander Orchestra and Chorus
    PEACE IN THE VALLEY
    MANSION OVER THE HILLTOP

D 86. <u>1953</u>
Capitol F2352
with the Frank DeVol Orchestra
    CONGRATULATIONS TO SOMEONE
    HOW DO YOU SPEAK TO AN ANGEL?
<u>NOTE</u>: CONGRATULATIONS TO SOMEONE made the charts on
March 28, 1953, and peaked at twenty-eight and was
charted for two weeks.

D 87. <u>1953</u>
Capitol F2465
with the Axel Stordahl Orchestra
    HOMIN' TIME
    C'EST MAGNIFIQUE
(See D73)

D 88. <u>1953</u>
Capitol F2652
with the Van Alexander Orchestra
    STRANGER IN PARADISE
    NEVER IN A MILLION YEARS
(See D74)

D 89. <u>1954</u>
Capitol F2672
    HIGH ON A WINDY HILL

D 90. <u>1954</u>
Capitol F2927
    CARA MIA
    COUNT YOUR BLESSINGS

D 91. <u>1954</u>
Capitol F2988
with the Van Alexander Orchestra
    LOVE CAN CHANGE THE STARS
    HERE'S WHAT I'M HERE FOR

D 92. <u>1955</u>
Capitol F3085
with the Van Alexander Orchestra and Chorus
    YOU FORGOT
    TIK-A-TEE

D 93. <u>1955</u>
Capitol F3122
with the Van Alexander Orchestra and Chorus
    BELLA NOTTE
    FOLLOW YOUR HEART

D 94. <u>1955</u>
Capitol F3191
with the Van Alexander Orchestra and Chorus
    JIM BOWIE
    WHY BREAK THE HEART THAT LOVES YOU?
<u>NOTE</u>: Song credits for JIM BOWIE (Clare-MacRae-Steiner)

D 95. <u>1955</u>
Capitol F3284
with the Van Alexander Orchestra
    A WONDERFUL CHRISTMAS
    WOMAN IN LOVE

D 96. <u>1956</u>
Capitol F3315
with the Van Alexander Orchestra and Chorus
    NEVER BEFORE AND NEVER AGAIN
    FATE

D 97. <u>1956</u>
Capitol F3384
with the Van Alexander Orchestra and Chorus
    WHO ARE WE
    I'VE GROWN ACCUSTOMED TO HER FACE
<u>NOTE</u>: I'VE GROWN ACCUSTOMED TO HER FACE hit the
charts on May 12, 1956, and went to position ninety-
six for three weeks on the charts.

D 98. <u>1956</u>
Capitol F3438
with the Van Alexander Orchestra
    I ASKED THE LORD
    ONE MISTY MORNING

D 99. <u>1956</u>
Capitol F3519
with the Van Alexander Orchestra
    WITHOUT LOVE
    OBEY

D100. <u>1957</u>
Capitol F3641
with the Van Alexander Orchestra
    LONELY
    TILL WE MEET AGAIN

D101. <u>1958</u>
Capitol F4033
with the Van Alexander Orchestra
    A MAN ONCE SAID
    THE SECRET
<u>NOTE</u>: THE SECRET hit the charts on September 15,
1958, and reached position eighteen and was charted
for thirteen weeks.

D102. <u>1959</u>
Capitol F4116
with the Van Alexander Orchestra
    FLY LITTLE BLUEBIRD
    LITTLE DO YOU KNOW

D103. <u>1959</u>
Capitol F4179
Produced by Voyle Gilmore
with the Van Alexander Orchestra
    PALACE OF LOVE
    STRANGER

D104. <u>1959</u>
Capitol 4323
Produced by Voyle Gilmore
with the Van Alexander Orchestra
    SOUND OF MUSIC
    WHEN DID I FALL IN LOVE?

D105. <u>1960</u>
Capitol 4483
Produced by Manny Kellem
with the Richard Weiss Orchestra
    IF EVER I WOULD LEAVE YOU
    DOLCE FAR NIENTE

D106. <u>1961</u>
Capitol 4626
Produced by Voyle Gilmore
with the Van Alexander Orchestra
    ORDINARY PEOPLE
    IMPOSSIBLE

D107. <u>1966</u>
Capitol 5779
Produced by Tom Morgan
with arranger Norman Leyden
    I DON'T THINK I'M IN LOVE
    ALL

D108. <u>1969</u>
Capitol 2329

Produced by Tom Morgan
with arranger Claus Ogerman and his Orchestra
    ONLY LOVE
    KNOWING WHEN TO LEAVE

LPs

D109. APPLE BLOSSOM
Mac/Eddy JN 122
12" (1988)
A complete RAILROAD HOUR broadcast with Jeanette Mac-
Donald (April 18, 1949) (See D195)

D110. BEST THINGS IN LIFE ARE FREE
Capitol T-765
12" (1956)
with the Van Alexander Orchestra and Chorus
MacRae sings songs from the film.
Side One
    BEST THINGS IN LIFE ARE FREE
    BUTTON UP YOUR OVERCOAT
    IT ALL DEPENDS ON YOU
    SONNY BOY
    JUST A MEMORY
    ONE MORE TIME
Side Two
    BIRTH OF THE BLUES
    TOGETHER
    YOU TRY SOMEBODY ELSE
    WITHOUT LOVE
    YOU'RE THE CREAM IN MY COFFEE
    BEST THINGS IN LIFE ARE FREE

D111. BITTERSWEET
Mac/Eddy JN 117
12" (1987)
A complete RAILROAD HOUR broadcast with Jeanette Mac-
Donald (January 31, 1949) (See D198)

D112. BY THE LIGHT OF THE SILVERY MOON
Capitol H-422 (10"-1953)
Capitol FBF-422 (Extended playing 45s, 2 record set)
Caliban 6019 (12"-Recorded from film, See F14)
NOTE: The Capitol version contains songs from the
film with June Hutton and the Axel Stordahl Orchestra
and Chorus.
Side One
    MY HOME TOWN-MacRae
    YOUR EYES HAVE TOLD ME SO-MacRae/Hutton
    BE MY LITTLE BABY BUMBLE BEE-MacRae/Hutton
    I'LL FORGET YOU-Hutton
Side Two
    JUST ONE GIRL-MacRae
    BY THE LIGHT OF THE SILVERY MOON-MacRae/Hutton
    AIN'T WE GOT FUN-MacRae/Hutton
    IF YOU WERE THE ONLY GIRL-MacRae/Hutton

D113. CAROUSEL

Capitol W/SW-694 (ST) (12"-1956)
Capitol EDM (extended playing 45s, 4 record set)
with Shirley Jones, Barbara Ruick, Cameron Mitchell,
Claramae Turner, Robert Rounseville, and the Alfred
Newman Orchestra and Chorus.
Side One
    CAROUSEL WALTZ-Orchestra
    YOU'RE A QUEER ONE, JULIE JORDAN-Jones/Ruick
    IF I LOVED YOU-Jones/MacRae
    MISTER SNOW-Ruick
    JUNE IS BUSTING OUT ALL OVER-Turner/Ruick
Side Two
    SOLILOQUY-MacRae
    BLOW HIGH, BLOW LOW-Mitchell
    WHEN THE CHILDREN ARE ASLEEP-Ruick/Rounseville
    REAL NICE CLAMBAKE-Ruick/Turner/Rounseville/
    Mitchell
    STONE CUTTERS CUT IT ON STONE-Mitchell
    WHAT'S THE USE OF WONDERING-Jones
    IF I LOVED YOU-MacRae
    YOU'LL NEVER WALK ALONE-Turner/Jones
NOTE: CAROUSEL hit the music charts on February 25,
1956, and climbed to the number two position for one
week, but remained charted for fifty-nine weeks. It
became a gold disc on July 15, 1964. (See D199)

D114. **CHRISTMAS AT BOYS TOWN**
Sandcastle Records-SCR-1043
12" (1978)
Tom Morgan produced this album with soloist MacRae
and the Boys Town Choir under the direction of Frank
D. Szynskie
Side One (Songs with MacRae)
    HE IS BORN
    THE FIRST NOWELL
    AWAY IN THE MANGER
    SILENT NIGHT
    O HOLY NIGHT
Side Two (Songs with MacRae)
    GREENSLEEVES (WHAT CHILD IS THIS?)
    ADESTE FIDELES
    WHITE CHRISTMAS

D115. **COWBOY'S LAMENT**
Capitol T-834
Stetson Hat-3054
12" (1957)
with the Van Alexander Orchestra
Side One
    COWBOY'S LAMENT
    SAN ANTONIO ROSE
    SOOTHE MY LONELY HEART
    LAST ROUNDUP
    HOW GREEN WAS MY VALLEY
    OKLAHOMA HILLS
Side Two
    RED RIVER VALLEY
    TUMBLING TUMBLEWEEDS

        WAGON WHEELS
        GREEN GROW THE LILACS
        COWBOY'S SERENADE
        I WENT TO THE CITY

D116. DESERT SONG
        Capitol W/SW-1842 (12"-January 1963)
        Angel S-37319 (12"-1978)
        with Dorothy Kirsten, the Rodger Wagner Chorale, and
        the Van Alexander Orchestra (See D200, D206)
        Side One
            RIFF SONG-MacRae
            WHY DID WE MARRY SOLDIERS-Kirsten
            FRENCH MILITARY MARCHING SONG-Kirsten
            ROMANCE-Kirsten
            THEN YOU WILL KNOW-MacRae/Kirsten
        Side Two
            DESERT SONG-MacRae/Kirsten
            LET LOVE GO-MacRae
            ONE FLOWER-MacRae
            ONE ALONE-MacRae
            SABRE SONG-Kirsten/MacRae
            FINALE-All

D117. DESERT SONG
        Capitol L-351 (10"-1953)
        Capitol FBF-351 (Extended playing 45s, 2 record set)
        with Lucille Norman, Thurl Ravenscroft, Bob Sands,
        and the George Greeley Orchestra
        Side One
            OVERTURE
            PROLOGUE-Sands/Male Chorus
            RIFF SONG-MacRae/Male Chorus
            WHY DID WE MARRY SOLDIERS-Girls Chorus
            FRENCH MARCHING SONG-Norman/Girls Chorus
            THEN YOU WILL KNOW-MacRae/Norman
        Side Two
            DESERT SONG-MacRae
            LET LOVE COME-Ravenscroft
            ONE FLOWER-Sands
            ONE ALONE-MacRae
            DUET-MacRae/Norman
            SABRE SONG-Norman
            FINALE-Norman/MacRae

D118. DESERT SONG
        Titanian 505 (12"-Recorded from film, See F15)

D119. DESERT SONG/ROBERTA
        Capitol T-384
        12" (1953)
        with Lucille Norman and the George Greeley Orchestra
        and Chorus
        (For songs see D117 and D154)

D120. GORDON MacRAE
        Galaxy 4805
        Rondo-lette A5

```
12" (1958)
with the Walter Gross Orchestra
```
Side One
    THEY SAY IT'S WONDERFUL
    PRISONER OF LOVE
    YOU GO TO MY HEAD
    STARS FELL ON ALABAMA
    YOU KEEP COMING BACK LIKE A SONG
    FULL MOON AND EMPTY ARMS
Side Two
    LOVE IS THE SWEETEST THING
    OH BUT I DO
    TALKING IS A WOMAN
    FLATTERY
    IT'S ANYBODY'S SPRING
    I'M SO LONESOME I COULD CRY

D121. GORDON MacRAE AND ORCHESTRA
Royale 18155
10" (1955)
Songs by MacRae
    YOU GO TO MY HEAD
    FULL MOON AND EMPTY ARMS
    IT'S ANYBODY'S SPRING
    YOU KEEP COMING BACK LIKE A SONG

D122. GORDON MacRAE AND THE WALTER GROSS ORCHESTRA
Royale 18106
10" (1955)
Songs by MacRae
    STARS FELL ON ALABAMA
    THEY SAY IT'S WONDERFUL
    LOVE IS THE SWEETEST THING
    PRISONER OF LOVE

D123. GORDON MacRAE IN CONCERT
Capitol T/ST-980
12" (April 1958)
with the Van Alexander Orchestra
Side One
    BEGIN THE BEGUINE
    SO IN LOVE
    LOST IN THE STARS
    OL' MAN RIVER
    SUMMERTIME
    I BELIEVE
Side Two
    WATER BOY
    I LOVE THEE
    STRANGER IN PARADISE
    DANNY BOY
    WHERE OR WHEN
    WITHOUT A SONG

D124. GORDON MacRAE SINGS
Capitol H-231
10" (1952)
with the Paul Weston Orchestra

Side One
    I SURRENDER DEAR
    YOU WERE MEANT FOR ME
    SUNSHINE OF YOUR SMILE
    BODY AND SOUL
Side Two
    A KISS IN THE DARK
    JUST ONE MORE CHANCE
    I UNDERSTAND
    I'M YOURS

D125. GORDON MacRAE SINGS
Evon 320 (12"-1958)
Royale EP319 (Long playing 45) * songs on 45 version.
Side One
    THEY SAY IT'S WONDERFUL*
    PRISONER OF LOVE*
    YOU GO TO MY HEAD
    STARS FELL ON ALABAMA*
    YOU KEEP COMING BACK LIKE A SONG
Side Two
    LOVE IS THE SWEETEST THING
    OH BUT I DO
    TALKING IS A WOMAN
    FLATTERY
    IT'S ANYBODY'S SPRING*

D126. GORDON MacRAE SINGS BROADWAY'S BEST
Sutton SU/SSU-292
12" (1958)
with the Paul Lavalle Orchestra
Songs by MacRae
    STARS FELL ON ALABAMA
    THEY SAY IT'S WONDERFUL
    EVERYBODY KNEW BUT ME
    TALKING IS A WOMAN

D127. GORDON MacRAE SINGS SONGS FOR LOVERS
Ember FA-2007
12" (1965)
Side One
    THEY SAY IT'S WONDERFUL
    YOU GO TO MY HEAD
    STARS FELL ON ALABAMA
    YOU KEEP COMING BACK LIKE A SONG
    FULL MOON AND EMPTY ARMS
Side Two
    LOVE IS THE SWEETEST THING
    OH BUT I DO
    TALKING IS A WOMAN
    FLATTERY
    I'M SO LONESOME I COULD CRY

D128. GORDON MacRAE SINGS WITH THE WALTER GROSS ORCHESTRA
Allegro/Royale 1606
12" (1952)
Side One
    THEY SAY IT'S WONDERFUL

     PRISONER OF LOVE
     YOU GO TO MY HEAD
     STARS FELL ON ALABAMA
     YOU KEEP COMING BACK LIKE A SONG
     FULL MOON AND EMPTY ARMS
Side Two
     LOVE IS THE SWEETEST THING
     OH BUT I DO
     TALKING IS A WOMAN
     FLATTERY
     IT'S ANYBODY'S SPRING
     I'M SO LONESOME I COULD CRY

D129. HALLOWED BE THY NAME
Capitol T/ST-1466
12" (1960)
Produced by Voyle Gilmore
with the Van Alexander Orchestra
Side One
     BEAUTIFUL ISLE OF SOMEWHERE
     JESUS LOVES ME
     NEARER MY GOD TO THEE
     ONWARD CHRISTIAN SOLDIERS
     BIRTHDAY OF A KING
     23rd PSALM
Side Two
     ABIDE WITH ME
     LITTLE BROWN CHURCH
     ROCK OF AGES
     HOLY, HOLY, HOLY
     HALLELUJAH
     LORDS PRAYER

D130. HIGHLIGHTS FROM THE WORLD'S GREATEST OPERETTAS
Capitol T-1510
12" (January 1961)
Produced by John Pallidino
with Lucille Norman, Marguerite Piazza, Dorothy
Warenskjold
Orchestras and Choruses conducted by Carmen Dragon,
George Greeley and Paul Weston
Side One
     STOUT-HEARTED MEN-MacRae/Chorus
     LOVER COME BACK TO ME-Norman
     WANTING YOU-MacRae/Norman
     SOFTLY AS IN A MORNING SUNRISE-MacRae
     MOONBEAMS-MacRae/Norman
     YESTERDAYS-Norman
     TOUCH OF YOUR HAND-MacRae/Norman
     DESERT SONG-MacRae
Side Two
     SONG OF THE VAGABONDS-MacRae/Chorus
     SOMEDAY-Norman
     ONLY A ROSE-MacRae
     VILIA-Norman
     DEEP IN MY HEART-Warenskjold/MacRae
     JUST WE TWO-Warenskjold/MacRae
     I'M FALLING IN LOVE WITH SOMEONE-MacRae

AH SWEET MYSTERY OF LIFE-Piazza/MacRae

D131. IF SHE WALKED INTO MY LIFE
Capitol T/ST-2578
12" (September 1966)
Produced by Tom Morgan
with arranger/conductors: Marian Evans, Norman
Leyden, and Van Alexander
Side One
    IF SHE WALKED INTO MY LIFE
    YESTERDAY
    SOMEWHERE
    YOUNG & WARM & WONDERFUL
    IMPOSSIBLE DREAM
    STRANGERS IN THE NIGHT
Side Two
    I WANT TO BE WITH YOU
    MICHELLE
    SHADOW OF YOUR SMILE
    DEAR HEART
    WHO CAN I TURN TO

D132. KISMET
Capitol W/SW-2022 (12"-October 1964)
Angel S-37321 (12"-1978)
Produced by Dick Jones
with Dorothy Kirsten, Richard Levitt, Bunny Bishop,
Sally Terri, the Rodger Wagner Chorale, and
the Van Alexander Orchestra (See D202)
Side One
    OVERTURE
    SANDS OF TIME-Levitt
    RHYMES HAVE I-MacRae/Kirsten
    FATE-MacRae
    NOT SINCE NINEVEH-Bishop
    BAUBLES, BANGLES AND BEADS-Kirsten/Chorus
    STRANGER IN PARADISE-MacRae/Kirsten
Side Two
    NIGHT OF MY NIGHTS-MacRae
    AND THIS IS MY BELOVED-MacRae/Kirsten
    OLIVE TREE-MacRae
    ZABBEDIYA, SAMARIS DANCE-Terri
    FINALE-MacRae/Kirsten/Chorus

D133. KISS ME KATE
Capitol H-157 (10"-1949)
Capitol CDF-157 (Long playing 45s, 4 record set)
with Jo Stafford and the Paul Weston Orchestra
Side One
    WUNDERBAR-MacRae/Stafford
    WERE THINE THAT SPECIAL FACE-MacRae
    ALWAYS TRUE TO YOU IN MY FASHION-Stafford
    SO IN LOVE-MacRae
Side Two
    WHY CAN'T YOU BEHAVE-Stafford
    BIANCA-MacRae/Chorus
    I HATE MEN-Stafford
    TOO DARN HOT-Orchestra/Chorus

NOTE: KISS ME KATE was charted on April 22, 1949, for
two weeks, reaching spot nine.

D134. LAST COMMAND
Citadel CT-7019
12" (1955)
Max Steiner composed and conducted the music for this
soundtrack in which MacRae sings the main title.
JIM BOWIE

D135. LOOK FOR THE SILVER LINING
Titania 504 (12"-Recorded from the film, See F2)

D136. MEMORY SONGS
Capitol T-428
12" (1955)
with Jo Stafford and the Paul Weston Orchestra
(All are Duets.)
Side One
WUNDERBAR
NEED YOU
LONG, LONG AGO
JUANITA
IN THE GLOAMING
LAST NIGHT
Side Two
BEYOND THE SUNSET
WHISPERING HOPE
STARS OF THE SUMMER NIGHT
SWEET AND LOW
LOVE'S OLD SWEET SONG
NOW THE DAY IS OVER

D137. MERRY WIDOW
Capitol L-335 (10"-1952)
Capitol FBF-335 (Extended playing 45s, 2 record set)
with Lucille Norman and the George Greeley Orchestra
and chorus
Side One
OVERTURE
IN MARSOVIA-Norman/Chorus
GIRLS AT MAXIMS-Girls
MAXIMS-MacRae
POLKA-Norman/Chorus
OH COME AWAY-Norman/MacRae
FOLK SONG-Mixed Chorus
VILIA-Norman
Side Two
GIRLS, GIRLS, GIRLS-MacRae
BUTTERFLIES-Girls Chorus
LOVE IN MY HEART-MacRae
I AM FREE-Norman/Chorus
OH COME AWAY-Norman/MacRae
TWO ROYAL CHILDREN-MacRae
MAXIM'S-MacRae
I AM FREE-Norman/Chorus
FINALE-I LOVE YOU SO-Norman/MacRae

D138. MERRY WIDOW
Mac/Eddy JN 120
12" (1988)
A complete RAILROAD HOUR broadcast with Jeanette Mac-
Donald (March 7, 1949) (See D203)

D139. MOTION PICTURE SOUNDSTAGE
Capitol T-875
EMI/Capitol 1183
12" (September 1957)
with the Van Alexander Orchestra (See D205)
Side One
    SINGING IN THE RAIN
    DANCING IN THE DARK
    YOU'RE A SWEETHEART
    CABIN IN THE SKY
    HOORAY FOR LOVE
    LOVE IS A MANY SPLENDORED THING
Side Two
    JALOUSIE
    PENNIES FROM HEAVEN
    LAURA
    EASY TO LOVE
    FLIRTATION WALK
    GOODNIGHT SWEETHEART

D140. NAUGHTY MARIETTA
Capitol L-468 (10"-1954)
Capitol FBF-468 (Extended playing 45s, 2 record set)
with Marguerite Piazza and the George Greeley
Orchestra and Chorus
Side One
    OVERTURE
    TRAMP, TRAMP, TRAMP-MacRae/Chorus
    NAUGHTY MARIETTA-Piazza
    IT NEVER, NEVER CAN BE LOVE-MacRae/Piazza
    ITALIAN STREET SONG-Piazza
Side Two
    ENTR'ACTE
    LOVES OF NEW ORLEANS-Girls Chorus
    LIVE FOR TODAY-MacRae/Piazza
    I'M FALLING IN LOVE WITH SOMEONE-MacRae
    AH, SWEET MYSTERY OF LIFE-MacRae/Piazza

D141. NAUGHTY MARIETTA
Mac/Eddy JN115
12" (1987)
A complete RAILROAD HOUR broadcast with Jeanette Mac-
Donald (January 7, 1949) (See D207)

D142. NAUGHTY MARIETTA/RED MILL
Capitol T-551
12" (1954)
NAUGHTY MARIETTA is with Marguerite Piazza and the
George Greeley Orchestra and Chorus. RED MILL is
with Lucille Norman and the Carmen Dragon Orchestra
and Chorus
(For songs see D140 and D153)

D143. NEW MOON
    Capitol H-217 (10"-1950)
    Capitol FBF-217 (Extended playing 45s, 2 record set)
    with Lucille Norman and the Paul Weston Orchestra
        OVERTURE
        STOUT-HEARTED MEN-MacRae/Chorus
        MARIANNE-MacRae
        ONE KISS-Norman
        WANTING YOU-MacRae/Norman
        SOFTLY AS IN A MORNING SUNRISE-MacRae/Chorus
        LOVER COME BACK TO ME-Norman
        FINALE-MacRae/Norman/Chorus

D144. NEW MOON
    Capitol W/SW-1966 (12"-October 1963)
    Angel S-37320 (12"-1978)
    Produced by Dick Jones
    with Dorothy Kirsten, Earle Wilkie, James Tippey,
    Jeannine Wagner, Richard Robinson, Rodger Wagner
    Chorale, and Van Alexander Orchestra (See D206, D208)
    Side One
        PRELUDE
        MARIANNE-MacRae
        GIRL ON THE PROW-Kirsten/Wilkie
        SOFTLY AS IN A MORNING SUNRISE-MacRae
        ONE KISS-Kirsten/Girls
    Side Two
        STOUT-HEARTED MEN-MacRae/Tippey
        WANTING YOU-MacRae/Kirsten
        LOVER COME BACK TO ME-Kirsten
        TRY HER OUT AT DANCES-Wagner/Robinson
        FINALE-Kirsten/MacRae

D145. OKLAHOMA
    Capitol WAO/SWAO-595 (12"-1955)
    Capitol FDM-595 (long playing 45s, 4 record set)
    with Shirley Jones, Gloria Grahame, Gene Nelson,
    Charlotte Greenwood, James Whitmore, Rod Steiger,
    Jay C. Flippen, and the Jay Blackton Orchestra and
    Chorus
    Side One
        OVERTURE
        OH WHAT A BEAUTIFUL MORNING-MacRae
        SURREY WITH THE FRINGE ON TOP-MacRae/Greenwood/
        Jones
        KANSAS CITY-Nelson/Greenwood/Chorus
        I CAN'T SAY NO-Grahame
        MANY A NEW DAY-Jones/Chorus
    Side Two
        PEOPLE WILL SAY WE'RE IN LOVE-MacRae/Jones
        POOR JUD IS DEAD-MacRae/Steiger
        OUT OF MY DREAMS-Jones/Chorus
        FARMER AND THE COWMAN-MacRae/Nelson/Greenwood/
        Flippin/Whitemore/Grahame
        ALL OR NOTHING-Grahame/Nelson
        OKLAHOMA-MacRae/Greenwood/Jones/Whitemore/Flippin
    NOTE: OKLAHOMA hit the charts on September 17, 1955,
    and peaked at number one for four weeks but remained

charted for three hundred and five weeks. The album
became a gold disc on July 8, 1958. (See D210)

D146. OKLAHOMA/CAROUSEL/KING AND I
Capitol STOL-1790
12" (May 10, 1958)
Contained the three soundtracks

D147. OLD RUGGED CROSS
MFP/EMI 5798
12" (Originally released by Capitol as WHISPERING
HOPE-1962. Released in late 1970s under this title
and again after 1986)
Duets with Jo Stafford and the Paul Weston Orchestra
(See D173, D211)

D148. ONLY LOVE
Capitol ST-125
12" (January 1969)
Tom Morgan produced this album, which was arranged
and conducted by Claus Ogerman.
Side One
        ONLY LOVE
        DEAR WORLD
        KISS HER NOW
        DID I EVER REALLY LIVE
        AND SHE WAS BEAUTIFUL
        IN VINO VERITAS
Side Two
        KNOWING WHEN TO LEAVE
        WHY CAN'T SHE SPEAK
        WHAT DOES SHE THINK
        WHOEVER YOU ARE I LOVE YOU
        WHY CAN'T I WALK AWAY

D149. ON MOONLIGHT BAY
Caliban 6006
12" (Recorded from film, see F9 for songs)

D150. OPERETTA FAVORITES
Capitol T-681
12" (February 1956)
with the George Greeley and Carmen Dragon Orchestras
and Choruses
Side One
        STUDENT MARCHING SONG
        DRINKING SONG
        SERENADE
        EVERY DAY IS LADIES DAY
        IN OLD NEW YORK
        YOU'RE DEVASTATING
        DON'T ASK ME NOT TO SING
        LOVELY TO LOOK AT
        FASHION SHOW
Side Two
        RIFF SONG
        ONE ALONE
        DESERT SONG

        TRAMP, TRAMP, TRAMP
        FALLING IN LOVE WITH SOMEONE
        MAXIM'S
        LOVE IN MY HEART
        GIRLS, GIRLS, GIRLS
        TWO ROYAL CHILDREN

D151. **OUR LOVE STORY**
        Capitol T/ST-1353
        12" (April 1960)
        with Sheila MacRae and the Van Alexander Orchestra
        Side One
            OUR LOVE STORY-Gordon/Sheila
            I MET A GIRL-Gordon
            WONDERFUL GUY-Sheila
            LOVE IS A SIMPLE THING-Gordon/Sheila
            GLAD THERE IS YOU-Sheila
            THAT'S FOR ME-Gordon
        Side Two
            LOVE AND MARRIAGE-Gordon/Sheila
            ALL THE THINGS YOU ARE-Gordon
            MY BABY JUST CARES FOR ME-Sheila
            WHEN THE CHILDREN ARE ASLEEP-Gordon/Sheila
            AND THIS IS MY BELOVED-Gordon
            HAPPY ANNIVERSARY-Gordon/Sheila

D152. **PRISONER OF LOVE**
        MGM E-104
        10" (1953)
        with the Walter Gross Orchestra
        Side One
            PRISONER OF LOVE
            I'M SO LONESOME I COULD CRY
            I HAVE BUT ONE HEART
            FULL MOON AND EMPTY ARMS
        Side Two
            YOU GO TO MY HEAD
            STARS FELL ON ALABAMA
            YOU KEEP COMING BACK LIKE A SONG
            THEY SAY IT'S WONDERFUL

D153. **RED MILL**
        Capitol L-530 (10"-1954)
        Capitol FBF-530 (Extended playing 45s, 2 record set)
        with Lucille Norman and the Carmen Dragon Orchestra
        and Chorus
        Side One
            OPENING CHORUS
            IF YOU LOVE BUT ME-Norman
            ISLE OF YOUR DREAMS-MacRae/Norman
            WHISTLE IT-Chorus
            WHEN YOU'RE PRETTY AND THE WORLD IS FAIR-Chorus
            MOONBEAMS-MacRae/Norman
        Side Two
            GOSSIPS SONG-Chorus
            I WANT YOU TO MARRY ME-Norman
            EVERY DAY IS LADIES DAY WITH ME-MacRae/Chorus
            BECAUSE YOU'RE YOU-MacRae/Norman

STREETS OF NEW YORK-MacRae/Chorus
FINALE-MacRae/Norman/Chorus

D154. ROBERTA
Capitol L-334 (10"-1952)
Capitol FBF-334 (Extended playing 45s, 2 record set)
with Lucille Norman, Anne Triola,and the George
Greeley Orchestra and Chorus
Side One
    OVERTURE
    LET'S BEGIN-Male Chorus
    YOU'RE DEVASTATING-MacRae
    MADRIGAL-Male Chorus
    YESTERDAYS-Norman
    SOMETHING HAD TO HAPPEN-Triola
    DON'T ASK ME NOT TO SING-MacRae/Chorus
    I WON'T DANCE-MacRae/Triola/Chorus
Side Two
    SMOKE GETS IN YOUR EYES-Norman/Chorus
    LET'S BEGIN-MacRae/Triola
    LOVELY TO LOOK AT-MacRae
    FASHION SHOW-MacRae/Triola
    I'LL BE HARD TO HANDLE-Triola
    THE TOUCH OF YOUR HAND-MacRae/Norman
    FINALE-MacRae/Norman/Chorus

D155. ROMANTIC BALLADS
Capitol T-537 (12"-April 1955)
Capitol EAP 1-537 (Extended playing 45)
with the Frank DeVol Orchestra
Side One
    THERE'S A LULL IN MY LIFE*
    STRANGER IN PARADISE*
    CUDDLE UP A LITTLE CLOSER
    YOUNGER THAN SPRINGTIME
    RAMONA
    I DON'T WANT TO WALK WITHOUT YOU
Side Two
    SOME ENCHANTED EVENING
    FACE TO FACE
    C'EST MAGNIFIQUE
    SO IN LOVE
    NEVER IN A MILLION YEARS*
    HIGH ON A WINDY HILL*
NOTE: * indicates songs appearing on EAP version

D156. SEASONS OF LOVE
Capitol T/ST-1146
12" (March 1959)
Produced by Voyle Gilmore
with the Van Alexander Orchestra
Side One
    INDIAN SUMMER
    SPRING IS HERE
    LONG HOT SUMMER
    I'LL REMEMBER APRIL
    IT MIGHT AS WELL BE SPRING
    JUNE IN JANUARY

Side Two
 AUTUMN LEAVES
 MY FUNNY VALENTINE
 SEPTEMBER SONG
 SUMMER IN YOUR EYES
 WHEN IT'S SPRINGTIME IN THE ROCKIES

D157. SONGS FOR AN EVENING AT HOME
Capitol T/ST-1251
12" (October 1959)
with Meredith and Sheila MacRae and the Van Alexander
Orchestra
All songs are by Gordon except where noted
Side One
 A HOUSE WITH LOVE IN IT
 SMILE
 ALWAYS
 BELLS OF ST. MARY'S
 WHISPERING HOPE-Gordon/Meredith
 MEDLEY: IN THE GOOD OLD SUMMERTIME/LET ME CALL
 YOU SWEETHEART/TAKE ME OUT TO THE BALL GAME
Side Two
 HOME
 LOVE'S OLD SWEET SONG
 THREE BLIND MICE-Alexander Orchestra
 SWEETHEART OF SIGMA CHI
 TREES
 A PERFECT DAY

D158. SONGS FOR CHRISTMAS
Capitol EAP 1-9021 (Extended playing 45-1955)
with Jo Stafford and the Paul Weston Orchestra and
Chorus
 HARK THE HERALD ANGELS SING
 THE FIRST NOEL
 O COME ALL YE FAITHFUL
 GESU BAMBINO
 DECK THE HALLS
 O COME O COME EMMANUAL
 JOY TO THE WORLD
 IT CAME UPON THE MIDNIGHT CLEAR
 O LITTLE TOWN OF BETHLEHEM
 GOD REST YE MERRY GENTLEMAN
 SILENT NIGHT

D159. SOUTH PACIFIC
Capitol H-163 (10"-1949)
Capitol CDF-163 (Extended playing 45s, 4 record set)
with Peggy Lee, Margaret Whiting, and the Dave
Barbour, Frank DeVol Orchestras, and the Jeff
Alexander Singers
Songs by MacRae
 SOME ENCHANTED EVENING
 YOUNGER THAN SPRINGTIME
NOTE: The album hit the music charts on June 17,
1949, and rose to fourth place, remaining charted
for six weeks.

D160. **SPOTLIGHT ON GORDON MacRAE AND JOHNNY KING**
Tiara TST-520/TMT-7520
12"
Songs by MacRae
    PRISONER OF LOVE
    YOU KEEP COMING BACK LIKE A SONG
    FULL MOON AND EMPTY ARMS
    TALKING IS A WOMAN

D161. **STARLIFT**
Titania 510
12" (Recorded from the film, See F10 for songs)

D162. **STUDENT PRINCE**
Capitol L-407 (10"-1953)
Capitol FBF-407 (Extended playing 45s, 2 record set)
with Dorothy Warenskjold, Harry Stanton, and the
George Greeley Orchestra and Chorus
Side One
    OVERTURE
    PROLOGUE-Chorus
    GOLDEN DAYS-Stanton/MacRae
    STUDENT'S MARCHING SONG-MacRae/Chorus
    DRINKING SONG-MacRae/Chorus
    COME BOYS-Warenskjold/Chorus
    IN HEIDELBERG FAIR-Warenskjold
    GAUDEAMUS-Chorus
    DUET-MacRae/Warenskjold
Side Two
    MAGIC OF SPRINGTIME-MacRae/Warenskjold
    DEEP IN MY HEART, DEAR-MacRae/Warenskjold
    SERENADE-MacRae/Chorus
    JUST WE TWO-Warenskjold/MacRae
    FINALE-MacRae/Warenskjold/Chorus

D163. **STUDENT PRINCE**
Capitol W/SW-1841 (12"-January 1963)
Angel S-37318 (12"-1978)
with Dorothy Kirsten, Earle Wilkie, Richard Robinson,
William Felber, the Roger Wagner Chorale, and the Van
Alexander Orchestra (See D206, D216)
Side One
    OVERTURE
    GOLDEN DAYS-Wilkie/MacRae
    STUDENT'S MARCHING SONG, DRINKING SONG, COME BOYS-
    Kirsten/students
    ARRIVAL AT HEIDELBERG, IN HEIDELBERG FAIR,
    GAUDEAMUS IGITUR-MacRae/Kirsten/Wilkie/Felber/
    Robinson/Chorus
Side Two
    DEEP IN MY HEART, DEAR-MacRae/Kirsten
    DRINKING SONG (Reprise)-MacRae/Students
    SERENADE-MacRae/Students
    JUST WE TWO-MacRae/Kirsten

D164. **STUDENT PRINCE/MERRY WIDOW**
Capitol T-437
12" (1954)

with Lucille Norman, Dorothy Warenskjold, and the
George Greeley Orchestra and Chorus
(See D137 and D162 for songs)

D165. SUNDAY EVENING SONGS
Capitol H-247
10" (1952)
with Jo Stafford and the Paul Weston Orchestra
(All are Duets)
Side One
    LONG LONG AGO
    JUANITA
    IN THE GLOAMING
    LAST NIGHT
Side Two
    STARS OF THE SUMMER NIGHT
    SWEET AND LOW
    LOVE'S OLD SWEET SONG
    NOW THE DAY IS OVER

D166. TEA FOR TWO
Caliban 6031
12" (Recorded from the film, see F6 for songs)

D167. THERE'S PEACE IN THE VALLEY
Capitol T/ST-1916
12" (1963)
with Jo Stafford and the Paul Weston Orchestra
(All are Duets)
Side One
    HE BOUGHT MY SOUL AT CALVARY
    SOMEBODY BIGGER THAN YOU AND I
    I BELIEVE
    SHEPHERD, SHOW ME HOW TO GO
    ALL THROUGH THE NIGHT
    I MAY NEVER PASS THIS WAY AGAIN
Side Two
    YOU'LL NEVER WALK ALONE
    OH, HOLY MORNING
    HE
    NEARER MY GOD TO THEE
    THE LORD IS MY SHEPHERD
    PEACE IN THE VALLEY

D168. THIS IS GORDON MacRAE
Capitol T-1050
12" (September 1958)
Side One
    IF I FORGET YOU
    ENDLESS LOVE
    WHEN YOU KISS ME
    SAYONARA
    NEVER TILL NOW
    TILL WE MEET AGAIN
Side Two
    I'VE GROWN ACCUSTOMED TO HER FACE
    CARA MIA
    NOW

```
        WHO ARE WE
        COUNT YOUR BLESSINGS
        C'EST MAGNIFIQUE
```

D169. THREE SAILORS AND A GIRL
Capitol L-485 (10"-1953)
Capitol FBF-485 (Extended playing 45s, 2 record set)
with Jane Powell, George Greeley Orchestra and Chorus
Side One
    YOU'RE BUT OH SO RIGHT-MacRae/Chorus
    KISS ME OR I'LL SCREAM-Powell
    FACE TO FACE-MacRae
    LATELY SONG-Powell/MacRae/Chorus
Side Two
    THERE MUST BE A REASON-MacRae/Powell
    WHEN IT'S LOVE-Powell/MacRae
    SHOW ME A HAPPY WOMAN-Powell
    MY HEART IS A SINGING HEART-Powell/MacRae
    HOME IS WHERE THE HEART IS-MacRae/Powell

D170. VAGABOND KING
Capitol H-218 (10"-1950)
Capitol FBF-218 (Extended playing 45s, 2 record set)
with Lucille Norman, Paul Weston Orchestra and Chorus
    OVERTURE
    SONG OF THE VAGABONDS-MacRae/Chorus
    SOMEDAY-Norman
    LOVE ME TONIGHT-MacRae/Norman
    TOMORROW-MacRae/Norman
    NOCTURN-Chorus
    HUGUETTE WALTZ-Chorus
    FINALE-MacRae/Norman/Chorus

D171. VAGABOND KING/NEW MOON
Capitol T-219
12" (1950)
with Lucille Norman and the Paul Weston Orchestra
(See 143 and 170 for songs)
NOTE: The NEW MOON hit the charts on July 14, 1950
and rose to number ten for a charting of one week.

D172. WEST POINT STORY
Titania 501
12" (Recorded from the film, see F7 for songs)

D173. WHISPERING HOPE
Capitol T/ST-1696
12" (1962)
with Jo Stafford and the Paul Weston Orchestra
(All are Duets)
Side One
    WHISPERING HOPE
    ABIDE WITH ME
    IN THE GARDEN
    BEYOND THE SUNSET
    BEAUTIFUL ISLE OF SOMEWHERE
    IT'S NO SECRET
Side Two

    I FOUND A FRIEND
    OLD RUGGED CROSS
    ROCK OF AGES
    STAR OF HOPE
    NOW THE DAY IS OVER
    A PERFECT DAY
(See D145)

D174. YOUNG MAN FROM BOSTON
Unnamed label-MXWR-4546
(1965-TV)
Music by Allan Friedman and lyrics by Paul Francis
Webster and vocals by Gordon MacRae and the Kingston
Trio

COMPILATION RECORDS

D175. AMERICA IS 200 YEARS OLD...AND THERE'S STILL HOPE
Capitol ST-11538 (12"-1976)
Bob Hope Comedy Album (Various celebrities, see D194)
Gordon played Thomas Jefferson in "Declaration of
Independence" and sang "Freedom Policy" with Hope.
NOTE: Charted on July 4, 1976, for four weeks, peak-
ing at one hundred seventy-five.

D176. BROADWAY AND HOLLYWOOD SHOWSTOPPERS
Capitol SL-6645
12" (1970s?)
(various artists)
Song by MacRae
    IF SHE WALKED INTO MY LIFE

D177. CELEBRATION OF RICHARD RODGERS
Private live recording of the Friends of the Theatre
and Music Collection of the Museum of the City of New
York
(1972)
(Various Artists)
Songs by MacRae
    OKLAHOMA MEDLEY

D178. COMMAND PERFORMANCE
Ronco MSD-2005
12" (1973)
Excerpts from the ED SULLIVAN SHOW by various
artists.
Song by MacRae
    SOLILOQUY

D179. DINO, GORDON, BOB
Brigade P-1310-S
12"
Songs by Dean Martin, Gordon MacRae, Bob Eberly
Songs by MacRae
    THAT OLD DEVIL MOON
    HEARTACHES
    I WANT TO BE LOVED

D180. ENCHANTED EVENINGS WITH RICHARD RODGERS AND OSCAR HAMMERSTEIN
ZIV International Z-101
The album was produced by William Hammerstein and Mandum Fox for MT Productions
<u>Song by MacRae and Shirley Jones</u>
    PEOPLE WILL SAY WE'RE IN LOVE

D181. FIRESTONE PRESENTS YOUR CHRISTMAS FAVORITES-VOL 3
Firestone SLP/MLP-7008
12" (1964)
with Martha Wright, Franco Corelli, Roberta Peters, Columbus Boys Choir. Joe Harnell conducted the Orchestra and Choir, Donald Bryant directed the Boys Choir
<u>Songs by MacRae</u>
    GO TELL IT ON THE MOUNTAIN
    SLEIGH RIDE
    WHITE CHRISTMAS (with Martha Wright)

D182. I FEEL A SONG COMING ON
Capitol PRO-139

D183. JANE POWELL
Cutain Calls CC-100-4
12" (1975)
MacRae and Powell's songs came from the soundtrack of the RAILROAD HOUR's-MUSIC IN THE AIR (1949)
    I'VE TOLD EVERY LITTLE STAR
    THE SONG IS YOU
(See D201)

D184. JUST FOR VARIETY-VOL 1

D185. JUST FOR VARIETY-VOL 15
Capitol T-1007
12"
<u>Song by MacRae</u>
    WHO ARE WE (with the Van Alexander Orchestra)

D186. KATHRYN GRAYSON-LET THERE BE MUSIC
Azel Records AZ-102
12"
Gordon and Kathryn's song came from the soundtrack of the DESERT SONG
    DESERT SONG

D187. LET'S GO TO CHURCH
Capitol T-1042
<u>Songs by MacRae</u>
    GENTLE HANDS
    I ASKED THE LORD
    PEACE IN THE VALLEY

D188. MAGIC MOMENTS FROM MUSICALS OF RODGERS AND HAMMERSTEIN
GRT 9DM-8
12" (1978) 4 record set

GRT Music Productions in Association with Ziv
International
<u>Song by MacRae and Shirley Jones</u>
    PEOPLE WILL SAY WE'RE IN LOVE

D189. NEW ALBUM PREVIEW
Capitol PRO 568/569
12" (April 1958)
<u>Song by MacRae</u>
    SO IN LOVE (with the Van Alexander Orchestra)

D190. SHOWSTOPPERS
Capitol SL-6524
12"
(Various Artists)
<u>Songs by MacRae</u>
    C'EST MAGNIFIQUE
    STRANGER IN PARADISE

D191. STEREO POP SPECTACULAR
Capitol CD-2007
12"
(Various Artists)
<u>Song by MacRae</u>
    STRANGER IN PARADISE

D192. THREE OF A KIND
Design DLP-911
12" (1959)
with Johnny Desmond and John Gary
<u>Songs by MacRae</u>
    STARS FELL ON ALABAMA
    TALKING IS A WOMAN
    IT'S ANYBODY'S SPRING

D193. TODAY'S TOP HITS BY TODAY'S TOP ARTISTS
Capitol H-9116
10"
(Various Artists)

CASSETTES/8-TRACKS/CDs

D194. AMERICA IS 200 YEARS OLD...AND THERE'S STILL HOPE
available on cassette and 8-track (1976) (See D175)

D195. APPLE BLOSSOMS
available on cassette from Mac/Eddy (1988) (see D109)

D196. BEST OF BROADWAY
available on cassette-Capitol 4XL-9393 (1986)
<u>Side One</u>
    STRANGER IN PARADISE
    YOUNGER THAN SPRINGTIME
    I'VE GROWN ACCUSTOMED TO HER FACE
    SUMMERTIME
    ALWAYS
<u>Side Two</u>
    MY FUNNY VALENTINE

SOME ENCHANTED EVENING
SEPTEMBER SONG
IT MIGHT AS WELL BE SPRING

D197. BITTERSWEET
available on cassette, Demand Performance-DPC-128
(1987) a complete radio broadcast with Dorothy Kirsten

D198. BITTERSWEET
available on cassette, Mac/Eddy (1987) (See D111)

D199. CAROUSEL
available from Capitol on 8-track, cassette(4XT-694),
CD-CDP-7466352 (CD-1987) (See D113)

D200. DESERT SONG
available on cassette, Angel-4XS-37319 (1978) and on
CD with Dorothy Kirsten (See D116, D206)

D201. JANE POWELL
available on cassette, Curtain Calls-CCC-100/4 (1975)
(See D183)

D202. KISMET
available on cassette, Angel 4xs-3721 (1978)
with Dorothy Kirsten (See D132)

D203. MERRY WIDOW
available on cassette, Mac/Eddy (1988) (See D138)

D204. MLLE MODISTE
available on cassette, Demand performance-DPC-104
(1986) a complete radio broadcast with Dorothy Kirsten

D205. MOTION PICTURE SOUNDSTAGE
available on cassette, Capitol TC-EMS-1183 (See D139)

D206. MUSIC OF SIGMUND ROMBERG
on CD, Angel CDM7-69052-2 (1987)
Most songs from the albums STUDENT PRINCE, DESERT
SONG, NEW MOON. (See D163, D116, D144)

D207. NAUGHTY MARIETTA
available on cassette, Mac/Eddy (1987) (See D142)

D208. NEW MOON
available on cassette, Angel 4XS-37320 (1978) and on
CD with Dorothy Kirsten (See D144, D206)

D209. NEW MOON
available on cassette, Demand Performance-DPC-127
(1987) a complete radio broadcast with Dorothy Kirsten

D210. OKLAHOMA
available from Capitol on 8-track, cassette (4XT-595),
CD-CDP-7466312 (CD-1987) (See D145)

D211. OLD RUGGED CROSS

available on cassette, Music for Pleasure-TC-MFP-
5798 (See D147)

D212. PRINCESS PAT
available on cassette, Demand Performance-DPC-102
(1986) a complete radio broadcast with Dorothy Kirsten

D213. ROBIN HOOD
available on cassette, Demand Performance-DPC-109
(1986) a complete radio broadcast with Dorothy Kirsten

D214. ROSE MARIE
available on cassette, Demand Performance-DPC-130
(1987) a complete radio broadcast with Dorothy Kirsten

D215. SARI
available on cassette, Demand Performance-DPC-101
(1986) a complete radio broadcast with Margaret
Truman, Francis X. Bushman

D216. STUDENT PRINCE
available on cassette, Angel 4XS-37318 (1978) and on
CD with Dorothy Kirsten (See D163, D206)

D217. STUDENT PRINCE
available on cassette, Demand Performance-DPC-126
(1987) a complete radio broadcast with Dorothy Kirsten

D218. VAGABOND KING
available on cassette, Demand Performance-DPC-129
(1987) a complete radio broadcast with Dorothy Kirsten

D219. YOU'LL NEVER WALK ALONE
available on cassette, Capitol-4XL-9536
(1987)
with Jo Stafford
(All Duets)
Side One
    I BELIEVE
    NEARER MY GOD TO THEE
    ABIDE WITH ME
    ROCK OF AGES
    YOU'LL NEVER WALK ALONE
Side Two
    WHISPERING HOPE
    OLD RUGGED CROSS
    IN THE GARDEN
    PEACE IN THE VALLEY

NOTE: The source for all charted singles up to 1954 is
Joel Whitburn's Pop Memories 1890-1954.
    The source for all charted singles after 1954 is
Joel Whitburn's Top Pop Singles 1955-1986.
    The source for all charted LP's (except OKLAHOMA and
CAROUSEL) is Joel Whitburn's Top LP's 1945-1972.
    The source for the charted LP's OKLAHOMA, CAROUSEL
and AMERICA IS 200 YEARS OLD...AND THERE'S STILL HOPE is
Joel Whitburn's Top Pop Albums 1955-1985.

Gordon and Sheila at opening night party for Broadway's DRAT THE CAT, October 10, 1965. Photograph courtesy of Irv Steinberg.

Pictured with Elizabeth and Gordon at their El Moracco wedding reception on September 25, 1967, are Gordon's children Gar, Heather, Meredith, and Bruce. Photograph courtesy of Irv Steinberg.

With Carol Lawrence in I DO! I DO!, 1967-1968. Photograph courtesy of Joseph Abeles Studio.

As host of radio's RAILROAD HOUR, NBC, 1948-1954. Photograph courtesy of Warner Bros. Inc.

With Shirley Jones singing "People Will Say We're in Love" in Rodgers & Hammerstein's OKLAHOMA! Copyright © 1955 Estate of Richard Rodgers and Estate of Oscar Hammerstein II. Copyright renewed. All rights reserved. Courtesy of The Rodgers and Hammerstein Organization.

As host of TV's GORDON MacRAE SHOW, NBC, 1956.

Fairmont Hotel concert, Dallas, 1978. Photograph by Andy Hanson, Dallas.

7

Sheet Music

Most of the partial list of Sheet Music that follows was
released in connection with MacRae's films. He is pictured
on all songs except where noted with NP (not pictured) in
which case his name appears on the cover. The dates
of film music correspond to those of the film and not
necessarily to the songs original publication date.

SM 1. ALL ER NOTHIN' (1955)
SM 2. BEST THINGS IN LIFE ARE FREE (1956)
SM 3. BUTTON UP YOUR OVERCOAT (1956)
SM 4. BY THE LIGHT OF THE SILVERY MOON (1953)
SM 5. DEAR HEARTS AND GENTLE PEOPLE (1949)
SM 6. DESERT SONG (1953)
SM 7. FACE TO FACE (1953)
SM 8. FARMER AND THE COWMAN (1955)
SM 9. GENTLE HANDS (1951)
SM10. HOME IS WHERE THE HEART IS (1953)
SM11. I CAN'T SAY KNOW (1955)
SM12. IF I HAD A TALKING PICTURE OF YOU (1956)
SM13. IF I LOVED YOU (1956)
SM14. I KNOW THAT YOU KNOW (1950)
SM15. IT ALL DEPENDS ON YOU (1956)
SM16. I WANT TO BE HAPPY (1950)
SM17. JUNE IS BUSTING OUT ALL OVER (1956)
SM18. KANSAS CITY (1955)
SM19. KISS ME OR I'LL SCREAM (1953)
SM20. LATELY SONG (1953)
SM21. LITTLE OLD CHURCH NEAR LEICESTER SQUARE (1949)
SM22. LONELY (1957)
SM23. LONG BEFORE I KNEW YOU (1950)
SM24. LOOK FOR THE SILVER LINING (1949) NP
SM25. MANY A NEW DAY (1955)
SM26. MATINEE (1948)
SM27. MISTER SNOW (1956)
SM28. MY HEART IS A SINGING HEART (1953)
SM29. NEED YOU (1949)
SM30. OH WHAT A BEAUTIFUL MORNING (1955)
SM31. OKLAHOMA (1955)
SM32. ONE MORE CHANCE (1950)
SM33. ON MOONLIGHT BAY (1951)

SM34. OUT OF MY DREAMS (1955)
SM35. PEOPLE WILL SAY WE'RE IN LOVE (1955)
SM36. POOR JUD IS DEAD (1955)
SM37. RAMBLING ROSE (1948)
SM38. A REAL NICE CLAMBAKE (1956)
SM39. RIVER OF SMOKE (1950)
SM40. ROSE OF TRALEE (1950)
SM41. SAY SOMETHING SWEET TO YOUR SWEETHEART (1948)
SM42. THE SECRET (1958)
SM43. SHOW ME A HAPPY WOMAN (1953)
SM44. SONNY BOY (1956)
SM45. SUNNY SIDE UP (1956)
SM46. SURREY WITH THE FRINGE ON TOP (1955)
SM47. TEA FOR TWO (1950)
SM48. THERE MUST BE A REASON (1953)
SM49. TOGETHER (1956)
SM50. UNDERNEATH A WESTERN SKY (1950)
SM51. WHAT'S THE USE OF WONDERING (1956)
SM52. WHEN IT'S LOVE (1953)
SM53. WHEN THE CHILDREN ARE ASLEEP (1956)
SM54. WHY BREAK THE HEART THAT LOVES YOU (1955)
SM55. WITHOUT LOVE (1956)
SM56. YOU'LL NEVER WALK ALONE (1956)

ADDENDA

SM57. AIN'T WE GOT FUN (1953)
SM58. AS WE ARE TODAY (1950)
SM59. BE MY LITTLE BABY BUMBLE BEE (1953)
SM60. CAROUSEL WALTZ (1956)
SM61. CHRISTMAS STORY (1951)
SM62. CRAZY RHYTHM (1950)
SM63. DAUGHTER OF ROSIE O'GRADY (1950)
SM64. DO-DO-DO (1950)
SM65. I'LL FORGET YOU (1953)
SM66. I'M FOREVER BLOWING BUBBLES (1951)
SM67. JUST ONE GIRL (1953)
SM68. KING CHANTICLEER (1953)
SM69. LOVE YA (1951)
SM70. THE ONLY GIRL IN THE WORLD (1953)
SM71. SOLILOQUY (1956)
SM72. TELL ME (1951)
SM73. TILL WE MEET AGAIN (1951)
SM74. TIME ON MY HANDS (1949)
SM75. YOUR EYES HAVE TOLD ME SO (1953)

Night Clubs and Concerts

NC 1. HOLLYWOOD BOWL-Hollywood, California (1948)
This was a benefit. MacRae met Horace Heidt for the first time since leaving the band.

NC 2. WILSHIRE EBELL-Hollywood, California (May 6, 1949)
with Jane Powell and Howard S. Swan directing the Occidental College Glee Club
The proceeds benefited the Hollywood Kiwanis Club's Youth Fund.

NC 3. STRAND THEATRE-New York (January 1950)
with Patrice Wymore

NC 4. CAPITOL THEATRE-New York (February 1950)

NC 5. EL RANCHO VEGAS-Las Vegas (1950)
with Anthony, Allyn and Hodges, Cover Girls and the Sterling Young Orchestra

NC 6. HOLLYWOOD COLISEUM-Hollywood, California (1951)
<u>Songs</u>: "God Bless America," "The Loveliest Night of the Year."

NC 7. DESERT CIRCUS-Palm Springs (1952)
To raise money for charity many celebrities participated in a Kangaroo Court including: Marjorie Main (Judge), Bing Crosby, Greer Garson, Gordon and Sheila MacRae, Dean Martin, Jerry Lewis, Bob Hope, Lucille Ball, and Randolph Scott.

NC 8. AMBASSADOR HOTEL (Cocoanut Grove)-Los Angeles (January 31, 1952)
with the Van Alexander Orchestra
<u>Songs</u>: "Luck Be a Lady," "We Kiss in a Shadow," "The Little White Cloud," "I Have Dreamed," "Body and Soul," International Girl Medley: "Charmaine," "Laura," "Annie Laurie," "Laura," "Peggy O'Neill," Gershwin Medley: "Lisa," "But Not For Me," "Summertime."
<u>Impressions</u>: Maurice Chevalier, Bing Crosby
<u>Comment</u>: Meredith appeared at the early show and

sang "Carry Me Back to Old Virginny" and "How Much is That Doggy in the Window?"

NC 9. DENVER RED ROCKS-Denver, Colorado (1953)
   with Sheila MacRae

NC10. CAPITOL THEATRE-New York (1953)

NC11. CASINO TORONTO-Toronto, Canada (May 1953)
   with Sheila MacRae and the Van Alexander Orchestra
   Songs: "Nobody But You," "How Do You Speak to an Angel," "I Believe," "Begin the Beguine," with Sheila: "Baby Bumble Bee," "By the Light of the Silvery Moon," "Jealous."
   Impressions: Bing Crosby, Humphrey Bogart, James Cagney.
   Review: Variety (June 3, 1953) felt that Gordon was more than a singer, that he was a "good comedy actor." He was okay as a dancer and had an easy approach with his audience.

NC12. COTTON BOWL-Dallas (October 18, 1953)
   MacRae performed in the State Fair of Texas East Texas Day Show.

NC13. BAKER HOTEL (Murial Room)-Dallas (October 25, 1953)
   with Sheila MacRae and the Van Alexander Orchestra
   Bob Kirk replaced Alexander when Van had to return to California.

NC14. EL RANCHO VEGAS-Las Vegas (November 18, 1953)
   with Sheila MacRae, Buddy Hackett, Zerby's, Dot Dee Dancers, Iris Menshell and Van Alexander conducting the Bob Ellis Orchestra (during MacRae's spot)
   Songs: "Donkey Serenade," "No Other Love," "Stranger in Paradise." Sheila: "Glad to be Mrs. Gordon MacRae." Gordon did a Celtic Sword Dance in full costume.
   Review: Variety (November 25, 1953) felt that Gordon could and should have done the act alone.
   Comment: At the early show Meredith sang "Carry Me Back to Old Virginny" and Heather and Gar sang "How Much is That Doggie in the Window?"

NC15. BROADMOOR HOTEL-Colorado Springs (1954)
   Sammy Cahn made a special arrangement of Gordon's film songs with Sheila playing his various film partners.

NC16. CASINO THEATRE-Toronto, Canada (1954)

NC17. LATIN CASINO-Philadelphia (January 31, 1955 to
   February 5, 1955)

NC18. EL RANCHO VEGAS-Las Vegas (June 8, 1955)
   with Sheila MacRae, Van Alexander, Morty Gunty, Billy Daniel, El Rancho Girls, and the Ted Fio Rito Orchestra
   Songs: "Granada," "You'll Never Walk Alone," "You Forgot to Tell Me."
   Skits: "This is Your Life'-with Sheila on mike off

stage and an OKLAHOMA reinactment.
    Review: Variety (June 15, 1955) felt the act had
"clever continuity" and that Gordon hadn't ever been in
"better voice."

NC19. HOLLYWOOD BOWL-Hollywood, California (July 1955)
    with the Johnny Green Symphony Orchestra
    Songs: Rodgers and Hammerstein hits.

NC20. AMBASSADOR HOTEL-Los Angeles (July 11, 1956)
    with Prullie and Tallow and Van Alexander conducting
the Freddy Martin Orchestra
    Songs: "This is Your Life"-traces his life, MY FAIR
LADY medley, "Soliloquy."
    Impressions: Marlon Brando, Gary Cooper, Humphrey
Bogart, Bing Crosby, Arthur Godfrey.
    Review: Variety (July 18, 1956) said that MacRae used
his "excellent voice" advantageously when he recreated
some of the roles he had done in films, which he did with
"savvy and humor," also evident in his "sly takeoffs."

NC21. CHICAGOLAND MUSIC FESTIVAL-Chicago's Soldier Field
    (August 1957)
    Co-star: Roberta Peters. Festival Director and Host:
Philip Maxwell. Announcer: Pierre Andre. Sponsor: Chicago
Tribune Charities Inc. Comment: It was the 8th annual
festival broadcast on WGN radio between 8:05 to 10 p.m.
before an expected audience of 80,000.

NC22. COCOANUT GROVE-Los Angeles (September 1, 1957)
    with Sheila MacRae
    Songs: Selections from OKLAHOMA and CAROUSEL.
    Impressions: James Cagney, Arthur Godfrey, Mortimer
Snerd, Nat Cole, Elvis Presley. Sheila did an impression of
Laurie from OKLAHOMA with a Kathryn Hepburn twist.
    Review: Variety (September 4, 1957) felt that the
patrons would find the evening "both rewarding and
exhilerating."

NC23. COTTON BOWL-Dallas (October 15, 1957)

NC24. CHEZ PAREE-Chicago (January 31, 1958)
    with Sheila MacRae, Van Alexander conducting for
MacRae, Miss Loni Adorables, and the Ted Fio Rito
Orchestra.
    Songs: "Singing in the Rain," "Easy to Love," "Cabin
in the Sky," "Soliloquy," "I'll Never Forget You."
    Impressions: Arthur Godfrey and his Lipton Tea
commercial, Zsa Zsa Gabor, Jane Mansfield.
    Review: Variety (February 5, 1958) considered the act
"well-paced" and that MacRae's "rich baritone" made up most
of the act.

NC25. AMBASSADOR HOTEL (Cocoanut Grove)-Los Angeles (June
    20, 1958)
    with Sheila MacRae, Norton and Patricia, Van
Alexander conducting the Freddy Martin Orchestra
    Songs: "Nice People," "Some Enchanted Evening," "Oh

What a Beautiful Morning," "Surrey With the Fringe on Top,"
"Oklahoma."
 Impressions: Dinah Shore, Perry Como.
 Review: Variety (June 25, 1958) felt that the act was
"smart" and "sharply-programmed." MacRae used his "big,
rich voice" advantageously. Sheila was a "handsome,
charming foil."
 Comment: The Gower Champions, Lisa Kirk, and Carol
Channing were in the audience.

NC26. WALDORF-ASTORIA (Empire Room)-New York (October 1958)
 with Sheila MacRae
 Songs: Excerpts from OKLAHOMA, "Some Enchanted
Evening," "You'll Never Walk Alone," "Young Love"-as Tab
Hunter, "Blue Suede Shoes"-as Elvis Presley. With Sheila:
"I Remember It Well," "I've Grown Accustomed to Your Face."
 Impressions: Kathryn Hepburn, Lena Horne, Dinah
Shore, Zsa Zsa Gabor.
 Review: Billboard (November 3, 1958) felt the act was
"great" and that the conversation and dances were "bright."
The impressions were "sharp" and that Gordon's voice was
"mellower and better trained" than in his movie days.

NC27. WALDORF-ASTORIA-New York (1959)
 with the Van Alexander Orchestra, the Sea Chanters
(choral unit with the Navy Band)
 MacRae was guest soloist in a tribute to Douglas
MacArthur. Joining MacArthur was President Dwight David
Eisenhower.

NC28. HARRAH'S- Lake Tahoe (1959)
 with Sheila MacRae and magician Mr. Ballentine
 Songs: "You Are Beautiful," "I Enjoy Being a
Girl"-Sheila, "I Remember It Well"-Gordon and Sheila.

NC29. KENTUCKY STATE FAIR HORSE SHOW (September 19, 1959)
 Songs: "Without a Song," "Blue Suede Shoes"-as Elvis
Presley, "Young Love"-as Tab Hunter, Selections from
OKLAHOMA and CAROUSEL, Medley from his films with Doris
Day, "Desert Song," "Stranger in Paradise," "Begin the
Beguine," "You'll Never Walk Alone."

NC30. BEVERLY HILLS-Cincinatti, Ohio (September 29, 1959)
 with Sheila MacRae, Isabela and Miguel, Moro Landers
Dancers, Dan Kellarney, Martin Skiles conducting the
Gardner Benedict Orchestra for the MacRaes, Jimmy Wilber
Trio, Larry Vincent.
 Songs: "You Out There," "One Alone," "Oh What a
Beautiful Morning"-with Sheila, Medley from OKLAHOMA and
CAROUSEL.
 Impressions: Arthur Godfrey, James Cagney, Perry
Como, Zsa Zsa Gabor, Lena Horne, Kathryn Hepburn, Dinah
Shore.
 Review: Variety (October 7, 1959) said that the
MacRaes got a "tremendous ovation" after finishing their
"sterling musical tab." The applause that followed their
singing, impressions and dancing was "solid."

NC31. WALDORF-ASTORIA-New York (October 1959)
        with Sheila MacRae, Emil Coleman, Norman Leyden
conducting the Bela Babai Orchestra
        <u>Songs</u>: "Everything is Coming Up Roses"-Sheila, With
Gordon: "Together," "I Remember It Well," "We're in Love
With New York," Gordon: "One Alone," "Lost in the Stars,"
"So in Love," "Small World," OKLAHOMA medley.
        <u>Impressions</u>: Kathryn Hepburn, Lena Horne, Judy
Holliday, Dinah Shore, James Cagney, Edward R. Morrow,
Arthur Godfrey, Cary Grant, Perry Como.
        <u>Review</u>: <u>Variety</u> (October 21, 1959) felt that Gordon
was good at mimicry but he "really shines" when singing.

NC32. MOTORAMA SHOW-Toronto, Canada (December 4, 1959)
        with Sheila MacRae
        <u>Songs</u>: "Surrey With the Fringe on Top," "Oh What a
Beautiful Morning," "Oklahoma," "So in Love," "I Remember
It Well"-with Sheila, "If I Loved You," "Tea for Two," "One
Alone," "I Got the Jewels"-Sheila, "And This is My
Beloved."
        <u>Impressions</u>: Kathryn Hepburn, Arthur Godfrey, James
Cagney, Zsa Zsa Gabor, Perry Como, Dinah Shore.

NC33. LATIN CASINO-New Jersey (Late 1950s/Early 1960s)
        with Sheila MacRae, Comic Bob Melven, Moro Landers
Dancers
        <u>Songs</u>: Medley of show tunes, OKLAHOMA medley.
        <u>Impressions</u>: Louis Prima, Arthur Godfrey, Dean
Martin, Perry Como, Keely Smith, Zsa Zsa Gabor, Lena Horne,
Dinah Shore.

NC34. SHARE INC. (Late 1950s/Early 1960s)
        with Tony Curtis, Dean Martin, Frank Sinatra

NC35. COCOANUT GROVE-Los Angeles (September 23, 1960)
        with Sheila MacRae, Bob Devaye Trio, Van Alexander
conducting the Freddy Martin Orchestra. <u>Material Written by</u>
Shirley Henry, Harry Crane. <u>Choreographer</u>: Miriam Nelson
        <u>Songs</u>: "If I Loved You," "So in Love," "Stranger in
Paradise."
        <u>Impressions</u>: Arthur Godfrey, Dean Martin, Perry Como.
        <u>Review</u>: <u>Variety</u> (September 28, 1960) said that
MacRae's "great voice" was in "top form." His impressions
were "first rate."

NC36. HARRAH'S-Lake Tahoe (November 30, 1960)
        with Sheila MacRae, Francis Brunn, Dorben Singers and
Dancers, Van Alexander conducting the Leighton Noble
Orchestra. A Russ Hall Production.
        <u>Songs</u>: "If I Loved You," "On Moonlight Bay," "By the
Light of the Silvery Moon," "Tea For Two," OKLAHOMA medley,
"I Remember It Well"-with Sheila.
        <u>Review</u>: <u>Variety</u> (December 7, 1960) felt that the act
consisting of songs and conversation was "pleasant," and
that they did some "slick impressions."

NC37. FAIRMONT-San Francisco (January 10, 1961)
        with Sheila MacRae, Van Alexander and the Ernie

Heckscher Orchestra
     Songs: "It's Showtime"-with Sheila, "If I Loved You," "So in Love," "This Could Be the Start of Something Big"-Sheila, Songs from OKLAHOMA and CAMELOT, "I've Grown Accustomed to Her Face," "I Remember It Well"-with Sheila.
     Impressions: Louis Prima, Keely Smith, Arthur Godfrey, Zsa Zsa Gabor, Dean Martin, Carol Channing, Edward R. Morrow, Lena Horne, Perry Como, Dinah Shore.
     Review: Variety (January 18, 1961) thought that Gordon had a "good, powerful voice" and that although a little hoarse in the lower range, sang his songs "well." Sheila doesn't sing as well but has "great vivacity."

NC38. WALDORF-ASTORIA (Empire Room)-New York (April 1961)
     with Sheila MacRae
     Songs: "Do Re Mi," Songs from MY FAIR LADY, CAMELOT, CAROUSEL, OKLAHOMA, "Make Someone Happy," "Oh What a Beautiful Morning," "Surrey With the Fringe on Top," "If I Loved You."
     Impressions: "An Evening With Everybody"-Louis Prima, Keely Smith, Arthur Godfrey, Zsa Zsa Gabor, Edward R. Morrow, Dean Martin, Lena Horne, Dinah Shore, Marilyn Monroe, Perry Como, Carol Channing, Ed Sullivan.
     Review: New York Times (April 5, 1961) Milton Esterou felt that a "delightful hour" was the result of Gordon's "rich baritone" and Sheila's songs and impressions.

NC39. COCOANUT GROVE-Los Angeles (July 4, 1961) 18 days
     with Sheila MacRae, the Swinging Four, Van Alexander and the Dick Stabile Orchestra. Staged by Miriam Nelson
     Songs: "Make Someone Happy," "If Ever I Would Leave You," "Long Hot Summer," "Porgy's Lament," OKLAHOMA medley.
     Impressions: Louis Prima, Kelly Smith, Arthur Godfrey, Zsa Zsa Gabor, Dean Martin, Carol Channing, Edward R. Morrow, Perry Como, Dinah Shore, Lena Horne.
     Review: Variety (July 12, 1961) felt that the show was "shrewdly framed" and that the songs and comedy "can play any situation." It was nice to see performers that had enough "facets of genuine talent" not to have to use gimmicks.

NC40. SHOREHAM HOTEL (Blue Room)-Washington D.C. (April 3, 1962)
     with Sheila MacRae and the Bob Cross Orchestra
     Impressions: Lena Horne, Carol Channing, Dinah Shore, Edward R. Morrow, Arthur Godfrey.
     Review: Variety (April 11, 1962) felt that the MacRaes were a "smash" and that the act was "well-written" and had a "lively pace."

NC41. AMBASSADOR HOTEL (Cocoanut Grove)-Los Angeles (June 1962)
     with Sheila MacRae, Van Alexander and the Freddy Martin orchestra. Material Written by Martin Ragaway, Shirley Henry, Lynn Duddy, Jerry Bresler. Choreographer: Miriam Nelson.
     Songs: OKLAHOMA medley, "Gigi," "Tonight," "If Ever I Would Leave You."

Impressions: "So Nice to Have a Camera in the White House"-John Fitzgerald Kennedy and Jackie, Elizabeth Taylor as Cleopatra, Louis Prima, Zsa Zsa Gabor, Carol Channing, Dinah Shore, Dean Martin, Perry Como, David Brinkley.
Review: Variety (June 20, 1962) thought that the MacRaes were "one of the best man-wife acts in show business" and that Gordon hadn't ever been in "better voice."

NC42. WALDORF-ASTORIA (Empire Room)-New York (September 1962)
with Sheila MacRae. Musical Director: Harry Frohman with Milt Shaw and the Bill Snyder Orchestra. Special Songs: Lynn Duddy, Jerry Bresler, Shirley Henry, Martin Ragaway, Martin Roth. Choreographer: Miriam Nelson. Lighting: Leslie Wheel and Claire Carter.
Songs: from CAROUSEL and OKLAHOMA, "The Sweetest Sounds," "You Deserve a Great Show," "Gigi," CAMELOT and LOST IN THE STARS medley, "I Believe in You," "Here's to Everyone in Love," "I've Grown Accustomed to Your Face."
Impressions: Dinah Shore, Zsa Zsa Gabor, Dean Martin, Louis Prima, Elizabeth Taylor, Edward R. Morrow, George Burns, Carol Channing, John Fitzgerald Kennedy and Jackie.
Review: Variety (September 26, 1962) felt that the MacRaes offered a "double-featured barrage of talent" and that Gordon performs an "engaging solo singalong."

NC43. COCOANUT GROVE-Los Angeles (December 28, 1963)
with Sheila and Meredith MacRae, Craig Smith, Mike Storm and the Freddy Martin Orchestra. Material Written by Shirley Henry, Harry Crane, Jack Lloyd. Staged by Miriam Nelson.
Impressions: Dean Martin, Bo Belinsky, Frank Fontaine, Red Skeleton, Lucille Ball, Elizabeth Taylor, Carol Channing, Judy Garland, Peggy Lee, Barbara Streisnd.
Review: Variety (January 1, 1964) thought that the best and biggest part of the show was Gordon's songs and his "growing adeptness" in satire. Sheila's impressions were "brisk and biting."

NC44. DIPLOMAT-Hollywood, Florida (March 1965)
with Sheila MacRae
Arthur Godfrey, Lucille Ball and Gary Morton were present.

NC45. NUGGETS SPARKS-Sparks, Nevada (July 22, 1965)
with Sheila MacRae, Eddie Peabody, Don Bagley and the Foster Edwards orchestra
Songs: OKLAHOMA medley, "If I Loved You," "Who Can I Turn To," "Here's To Love," "Hello Young Lovers," "Try a Little Tenderness," "People"-with Sheila, "Will You Still Be Mine,"-with Sheila.
Impressions: "That Was the Week That Was"-Frank Fontaine's Crazy Guggenheim, Elizabeth Taylor, Carol Channing, Barbara Streisand, Zsa Zsa Gabor.
Review: Variety (July 28, 1965) felt that Gordon had never been in "better voice" and that Sheila has her impressions "down to perfection" both in look and voice.

NC46. COMMONWEALTH CLUB-North Park, Texas (August 1965)
with Ernie Johnson's Band
Songs: OKLAHOMA medley, "It Only Takes a Moment,"
"More."
Impressions: Dean Martin, Frank Fontaine's Crazy
Guggenheim.
Review: Dallas Morning News (August 20, 1965) Francis
Raffetto said MacRae was in "fine voice."

NC47. QUEEN ELIZABETH-Montreal, Canada (May 1966)
with Froio Troio Girls, Frank Pavan Trio, and the
Nick Martin Orchestra
Songs: Hits from OKLAHOMA, "If Ever I Would Leave
You."
Review: Variety (May 25, 1966) thought that MacRae
performed with "socko showmanship" and his singing was
"smooth" and "effortless" that was a reminder of the days
of singers with big voices.

NC48. DIPLOMAT-Hollywood, Florida (August 30, 1966)
with Joey Villa, Host: George Foster, Jimmy Leyden
conducting the Van Smith Orchestra
Review: Variety (September 7, 1966) thought MacRae
was best when he stayed in his range and that most of his
performance was "well-performed and well-received."

NC49. CENTURY PLAZA HOTEL (Westside Room)-Los Angeles (March
1967) 3 weeks
with Van Alexander conducting the Frankie Ortega
Orchestra. "Walking Happy Routine" devised by Miriam
Nelson. Jack Carter introduced MacRae.
Songs: "Rhymes Have I," "Strangers in the Night,"
"Come Back to Me," "Here's to Everyone in Love," OKLAHOMA
medley, "If Ever I Would Leave You," "Shadow of Your
Smile," "Impossible Dream."
Impressions: "Walking Happy" included the walking
habits of Dean Martin, Cary Grant, Jimmy Durante.
Review: Citizen News (March 9, 1967) Nadine Edwards
felt that MacRae "induced poignancy and heartwarmth" into
the songs he sang and displayed "emotional depth" that many
singers aren't able to do.

NC50. HOTEL ROOSEVELT-New Orleans (March 30, 1967 to April
19, 1967)
with the Leon Kelner Orchestra
Songs: "Strangers in the Night," "If Ever I Would
Leave You," "Try a Little Tenderness," Medleys from
OKLAHOMA and CAROUSEL.
Review: Variety (April 5, 1967) thought that MacRae
had "rich pipes" and had "accrued poise" and the use of his
range was "top drawer."

NC51. WALDORF-ASTORIA-New York (April 1967)
with Norman Leyden conducting the orchestra. Act by
Lynn Duddy, Jerry Bresler, Sammy Cahn. Staged by Miriam
Nelson
Songs: "Draw Me a Circle," "Rhymes Have I," "If She
Walked Into My Life," "Come Back to Me," "Impossible

Dream."
    Impressions: "Walking Happy" (written by Sammy Cahn
and Jimmy Heussan) was the lead-in for impressions of Dean
Martin and Jimmy Durante.
    Review: Variety (April 26, 1967) felt that because of
the blend between conversation, impressions and songs,
MacRae was a "song stylist for all seasons."

NC52. MADISON SQUARE GARDEN-New York (April 1967)
    This was a benefit with Sheila for Israel.

NC53. A GEORGETOWN CLUB (December 8, 1967)
    Carol Lawrence and MacRae did a short version of I DO
I DO at the wedding eve dinner of Lynda Bird Johnson and
Marine Captain Charles S. Robb.

NC54. WHITE HOUSE-Washington D.C. (January 25, 1968)
    Carol Lawrence and MacRae in a 30-minute version of
I DO I DO at a dinner honoring Vice-President Hubert
Humphrey and Supreme Court Justice Earl Warren.

NC55. SHOREHAM (Blue Room)-Washington D.C. (November 19,
        1968 to November 23, 1968)
        with his musical director, James Leyden

NC56. DRAKE HOTEL-Chicago (January 22, 1969)
        with the Bill Snyder Orchestra
        Songs: "Impossible Dream," OKLAHOMA medley, Dramatic
reading of "America."
        Review: Variety (January 29, 1969) felt that his
songs were "crowd-pleasing" and that he chose songs that
suited his voice "perfectly." He also did well in
conversation with the audience.

NC57. HARRAH'S (South Shore Room)-Lake Tahoe (February
        1969)
        with Brian Farnon Orchestra, Maggie Banks Dancers,
and Jimmy Guppo (slight of hand and ESP expert)
        Review: Los Angeles Times (March 1, 1969) John Scott
said that the act was "well-assembled" and that MacRae's
voice was "sonorous and well-paced." It appeared that
MacRae sang effortlessly.

NC58. STATE FAIR MUSIC HALL-Dallas (May 25, 1969)
        Songs: OKLAHOMA and CAROUSEL medleys, "Dear World,"
"Impossible Dream."
        Impressions: Dean Martin, Arthur Godfrey, Jack
Benny, Frank Fontaine's Crazy Guggenheim.

NC59. HOTEL PLAZA (Persian Room)-New York (January 1970)
        with James Leyden and the Bert Farber Orchestra
        Songs: "Is That All There Is," "Gentle on My Mind,"
"I've Gotta Be Me," "I, Yes Me, That's Who," "America the
Beautiful," songs from OKLAHOMA and CAROUSEL.
        Impressions: "Walking Happy"-Jack Benny, Arthur
Godfrey, Jackie Gleason, Dean Martin, Frank Fontaine's
Crazy Guggenheim, Joe E. Lewis.
        Review: Variety (February 4, 1970) felt that MacRae

knew his way around a song and that he was a "slick songster."

NC60. LATIN CASINO-New Jersey (March 2, 1970 to March 8, 1970)
    with Billy Baxter, Jack Curtis and the Lew Krouse Orchestra
    Songs: OKLAHOMA and CAROUSEL medleys, "Gentle on My Mind," "I've Gotta Be Me," "My Way," "Is That All There Is."
    Impressions: "Walking Happy"-Jack Benny, Arthur Godfrey, Dean Martin, Jackie Gleason, Frank Fontaine's Crazy Gugenheim.
    Review: Evening Bulletin-Philadelphia (March 4, 1970) Frank Brookhouser said MacRae's style was varied and that his impressions were "well-done." His stories were "well-told" and his humor and casualness were "delightful."

NC61. HAROLD'S-Reno (September 8, 1970)
    with the Four Step Brothers and the Don Conn Orchestra
    Songs: "Oklahoma," "Gentle on My Mind," "I've Gotta Be Me," "Impossible Dream," "I, Yes Me, That's Who," "My Way," "America," "Oh What a Beautiful Morning," "It's Magic," "Let it Snow," "I Heard That Song Before."
    Impressions: "Walking Happy"-Jack Benny, Dean Martin, Jackie Gleason.
    Review: Variety (September 16, 1970) felt that when he did what he did best the "results sparkle" demonstrating the "uniqueness" of his talent as well as his potential.

NC62. DRAKE HOTEL-Chicago (October 1, 1970)
    with the Dick Judson Orchestra
    Songs: "I've Gotta Be Me," "My Kind of Town," OKLAHOMA medley, "America."
    Impressions: Jackie Gleason, Arthur Godfrey, Dean Martin.
    Review: Variety (October 7, 1970) felt that MacRae's singing was the best part of the show.

NC63. FAIRMONT (Venetian Room)-San Francisco (January 17, 1972)
    with Gordon Munford conducting the Ernie Heckscher Orchestra
    Songs: "Late Late Show"-Medley of his movie songs.
    Impressions: Jack Benny, Arthur Godfrey, Dean Martin.
    Review: Variety (January 26, 1972) felt that the "Late Late Show" was "fun" because you saw MacRae, when he was younger, singing his old movie songs. He was also a "good mimic."

NC64. HOTEL ST. REGIS-New York (March 1972)
    with Gordon Munford conducting the George Cort Orchestra
    Review: Variety (March 22, 1972) felt that MacRae's old songs were sung in a "robust and melodic style,"

reminiscent of the times when a singer had to have a voice.

NC65. IMPERIAL THEATRE-New York (March 26, 1972)
in "A Celebration of Richard Rodgers" presented by the
Friends of the Theatre and Music Collection of the Museum
of the City of New York. Many stars performed the music of
Rodgers. MacRae sang an OKLAHOMA medley. (see D177)

NC66. DESERT INN-Las Vegas (November 25, 1972)
with Phyllis Diller and Gordon Munford conducting the
Carleton Hayes Orchestra
    Songs: from OKLAHOMA
    Review: Variety (December 6, 1972) felt that MacRae
had a "fine rapport" with the audience and that his act was
done "very well."

NC67. THUNDERBIRD-Las Vegas (December 15, 1973)
with Marilyn Michaels, the Golddiggers, and Gordon
Munford leading the Joe Berlingerri Orchestra. Produced by
Sidney Gothrid. Presented by Barton Cohen.
    Songs: "If," "MacArthur Park," "Bad Bad Leroy
Brown," "Is That All There Is," "Late Late Show"-medley
with songs from OKLAHOMA and LOOK FOR THE SILVER LINING.
    Review: Variety (December 19, 1973) said that
MacRae's "big rich tones" filled his collection of songs.

NC68. FAIRMONT (Venetian Room)-Dallas (April 10, 1974 to
        April 13, 1974)
    Songs: "The Most Beautiful Girl in the World," "If,"
"Is That All There Is," medleys from ON MOONLIGHT BAY,
DESERT SONG, BY THE LIGHT OF THE SILVERY MOON, OKLAHOMA,
CAROUSEL (complete with stills)
    Review: Dallas Morning News (April 11, 1974) Phillip
Wuntch said MacRae's voice was "strong and hearty" and that
he told some "good-natured" stories.

NC69. FAIRMONT-Atlanta (July 2, 1975)
with Gordon Munford conducting the Earl Heckscher
Orchestra
    Songs: "I Didn't Promise You a Rose Garden,"
"MacArthur Park," "People Will Say We're in Love," medley
of hits.
    Review: Variety (July 9, 1975) said that MacRae was
"dapper and spry."

NC70. NEW ORLEANS SUMMER POPS-New Orleans (July 1976)
in duets with Amy Weston, daughter of Jo Stafford.

NC71. CONDO CIRCUIT-Florida (1977)
Producer Jerry Grant organized this road show aimed
at retirement condos between Miami and Palm Beach. Each
act usually had a name star, a master of ceremonies and a
3-5 piece orchestra.

NC72. VETERANS MEMORIAL AUDITORIUM-Providence, Rhode Island
        (April 16, 1977)
in "An Evening of Rodgers and Hammerstein" with Gordon
Munford conducting the orchestra.

Songs: "People Will Say We're in Love," "If I Loved
You," "This Nearly Was Mine," "Some Enchanted Evening,"
"Soliloquy."
Review: Providence Sun Journal (April 17, 1977)
Martha Smith said the audience appeared "blissfully happy"
laughing and applauding the old songs. The early part of
the show was "less than enchanted" but MacRae sang the
"Soliloquy" with "tremendous sensitivity and style."

NC73. FAIRMONT HOTEL (Venetian Room)-San Francisco (August
5, 1977) 2 weeks
Songs: "You'll Never Walk Alone," "People Will Say
We're in Love," "Desert Song," "Oh What a Beautiful
Morning," "I Write the Songs," "I Won't Last a Day Without
You," "Sweet Gypsy Rose," "MacArthur Park," "What the World
Needs Now," "So in Love," "Lover," "All the Way," "And I
Love You So," "You Are Love," "What I Did For Love," "Late
Late Show"-"On Moonlight Bay," "Tea For Two," "By the
Light of the Silvery Moon," "Soliloquy.
Review: San Francisco Examiner (August 5, 1977)
Cynthia Rebins felt that MacRae's emphasis was on style
more so than interpretation. His special material-"Nob
Hill" and "The Late Late Show" were "crowd pleasers." His
family show would appeal to those who wanted a "good
evening's entertainment."
Comment: Bruce MacRae handled the lights and slide
show the first week and became his father's conductor the
second. Meredith paid a surprise visit on opening night.

NC74. SS ROTTERDAM (October 1, 1977)
in "Come to the Cabaret" with Helen O'Connell, Jerry
Van Dyke, the Amazing Randi, and Lee Castle and the Jimmy
Dorsey Orchestra.

NC75. FAIRMONT (Venetian Room)-Dallas (1978)

NC76. SS ROTTERDAM AND SS STATENDAM (October 7, 1978 to
October 14, 1978)
in a "Tribute to Rodgers and Hammerstein" with Lois
Hunt, Earl Wrightson, Elaine Malbin and the Lester Lanin
Orchestra.

NC77. COUNTRY DINNER PLAYHOUSE-Dallas (Late 70s)
with Gordon Munford
Songs: "MacArthur Park," "My Sweet Gypsy Rose,"
"Send in the Clowns," "Oklahoma," "Tea For Two," "On
Moonlight Bay," "I'm in the Mood For Love," "What I Did For
Love," "My Way."
Review: John Neville said MacRae was a "complete
entertainer" with "charm" and "charisma" and it was nice to
see a performer who didn't need gimmicks.

NC78. PLAYBOY RESORT AND COUNTRY CLUB (1978)

NC79. FAIRMONT (Venetian Room)-Dallas (1979)
with Jane Powell

NC80. BRIDGES AUDITORIUM-Claremont, California (January

1979)
     with George Gobel and Gordon Munford conducting.
     Songs: "Oklahoma," "Desert Song," "Soliloquy," "I
Write the Songs," "What I Did For Love," "My Way."
     Review: Los Angeles Times (January 30, 1979) Richard
Houdek felt MacRae's best moments were when he sang the
movie hits he did with Doris Day and June Haver as well as
the hits from OKLAHOMA, CAROUSEL, and the DESERT SONG.

NC81. FOX THEATRE-San Diego (December 1979)
     in "4 Guys 4" with Jack Carter, Donald O'Connor, Billy
Daniels. Loeb and Weems assembled and produced the tour.

NC82. SAHARA-Reno (January 13, 1980)
     in "4 Guys 4" with Billy Daniels, Jack Carter, Donald
O' Connor.
     Songs: "Four of a Kind"-all, "Late Late Show"-medley
of MacRae's movie songs.
     Review: Variety (January 23, 1980) felt that "The
Late Late Show" was "excellently written" and "fared
well," as did most of his jokes. Some of his other songs
weren't as strong.

NC83. MUSIC HALL AT FAIR PARK-Dallas (March 15, 1980)
     in "An Evening with Gordon MacRae and Anna Maria
Alberghetti."
     with Gordon Munford conducting the orchestra
     Songs: "I Write the Songs," "Some Enchanted
Evening," "I'm Getting Married in the Morning," "Gigi,"
"This Nearly Was Mine," "Edelweiss," "MacArthur Park,"
"Salute to Beautiful Girls," "The Late Late Show."

NC84. FAIRMONT (Venetian Room)-Dallas (1981)
     with Billy Daniels

NC85. FLINT CENTER-San Jose Mecury (October 1981)
     This was a big band benefit for Foothill-DeAnza
Colleges Foundation with Connie Haines and the Alvino Rey
Orchestra.

NC86. HOLIDAY HOUSE-Pittsburgh, Pennsylvania (November 3,
     1982)
     in "Great Stars of the Silver Screen" produced and
directed by Paul Blane.
     with Patti Andrews, Morey Amsterdam, Roberta
Sherwood, Gloria DeHaven, Forrest Tucker and the Randy
Purcell Orchestra
     Songs: He sang his movie hits including songs from
OKLAHOMA.
     Review: Variety (November 17, 1982) thought MacRae
was in "fine voice" but should drop some of his "dumb
jokes."
     Comment: This was MacRae's first appearance since
his stroke in January 1982.

NC87. MISHLER THEATRE-Altoona, Pennsylvania (November 1982)
     with Anna Maria Alberghetti
     Songs: from OKLAHOMA and CAROUSEL.

Review: Classic Images (February 1983) Ted Reinhart
felt no other singer achieved the "richness and vitality"
MacRae had in each song. Miss Alberghetti's duets with
MacRae were "magnificent" and their harmony "unexcelled."
Comment: Mr. Reinhart, a western singer, and his
wife, Ruth got to meet Gordon (Ted's idol) at the concert
and they became friends.

NC88. CLARIDGE HOTEL (Palace Room)-Atlantic City, New
    Jersey (May 6, 1983 to May 8, 1983)
    with Martha Raye
    With his arm in a sling, he told the audience about
his stroke. He joked and sang new songs and those
associated with him. He did a tribute to woman and his
"Late Late Show" routine consisted of his film songs. He
sang a song he'd written and was to record for Capitol
Records, but nothing materialized. He looked and sang well.

NC89. GREENVILLE CONCERT-Greenville, South Carolina (June
    14, 1983)
    Sponsored by the North Greenville Alcoholism Treatment
Program. It was to make up for the October 25, 1978 concert
when he was too drunk to remember lyrics.

ADDENDA

NC90. SACRAMENTO MUSIC CIRCUS-Sacramento, California
    (Summer 1955)

NC91. CALIFORNIA STATE FAIR-Sacramento, California
    (September 1-3, 1955)
    in a tribute to Rodgers & Hammerstein with Marion
Bell. Host: Will Rogers, Jr. Producers: Russell Lewis and
Howard Young. Conductor: James Gutherie. Script: Robert
Young, Jr. Songs: from Rodgers & Hammerstein musicals
including OKLAHOMA and CAROUSEL.

Annotated Bibliography

B 1. Ardmore, Jane. "What Next, Gordon?" Unknown magazine.
1953.
Gordon is free-lancing in pictures. He wants to
tackle television, night clubs, and Broadway. Several
pictures of MacRae.

B 2. Asher, Jerry. "Don't Wait to Marry." <u>Screenland</u>. Date
unknown.
Although Gordon and Sheila had many hardships in
their early marriage, they felt the experience strengthened
their marriage. Miscellaneous pictures of the couple.

B 3. Askew, Rual. "Mr. MacRae Facing Two 'Large Moments'."
<u>Dallas Morning News</u>. July 13, 1955.
Tells of MacRae's appearance in CAROUSEL in Dallas,
of the New York premiere of OKLAHOMA on September 14, 1955.
There is a picture of MacRae in the theatre reading
CAROUSEL.

B 4. Balling, F.D. "The Boys From Syracuse." <u>Silver</u>.
December 1949.

B 5. "Barbecued Beefcake." <u>Movie World</u>. September 1952.
Pictures of MacRae and Dean Martin with their wives
at a barbecue.

B 6. Barnes, Clive. "I Do! I Do! Does Well With New
Couple-Slight Play Begins Second Year." <u>New York
Times</u>. November 28, 1967.
Review of Carol Lawrence and MacRae in I DO! I DO!
Lawrence and MacRae are pictured.

B 7. Bartlett, Maxine. "Casualness For the Gordon
MacRaes." <u>Los Angeles Times Home Magazine</u>. May 26,
1957.
The MacRae's home is featured in pictures.

B 8. Baskette, Kirtly. "No Time For Modesty." <u>Modern
Screen</u>. July 1952.
Discusses Gordon being a go-getter. Several photos

with Gordon, Sheila and the children.

B 9. Bernstein, Bob. "Gordon MacRae a Comic Revelation."
       Billboard. November 3, 1958.
       Review of Gordon and Sheila's appearance at the
Waldorf-Astoria.

B 10. "Between Shows." Movies. February 1951.
       Nine pictures of MacRae's activities between
performances of his night club act.

B 11. "Big Family Outing." Movie Life. July 1956.
       Nine pictures of the MacRaes having fun at a rustic
camp at Lake Tahoe.

B 12. Billboard. August 2, 1952.
       Brief summary of MacRae's career in films, radio,
records, including a picture of Gordon.

B 13. _____. February 8, 1986.
       MacRae's obituary.

B 14. Bowman, Harry. "Music Hall Show Headed by MacRae."
       Dallas Morning News. May 26, 1969.
       Discuses MacRae's appearance at the State Fair Music
Hall.

B 15. Boxoffice. August 5, 1974.
       Reports on a tax lien made on MacRae for back taxes
for 1966, 1971, 1972, 1973.

B 16. _____. February 3, 1975.
       The article describes MacRae's Public Service Award
for fund raising efforts in 1974 for the Arthritis
Foundation.

B 17. _____. July 21, 1975.
       Discusses MacRae's prestige license plate in Nebraska
with "Gordo" on it.

B 18. Brookhouser, Frank. "At the Latin: Oklahoma Only
       Opener." The Philadelphia Evening Bulletin. March 4,
       1970.
       Review of MacRae's act at the Latin Casino, including
a portrait of MacRae.

B 19. Brooks, Caroline. "How Dopey Can He Get?" Modern
       Screen. November 1951.
       Discusses his forgetting things when Sheila isn't with
him.   MacRae and family pictured.

B 20. Bruce, Jon. "Gordon MacRae: One Musical Too Many?"
       Unknown magazine. 1952.
       Although MacRae is thankful for his musical films, he
doesn't want to become type-cast. Many pictures of Gordon
and his family at home in the pool.

B 21. "Cancer Kills Actor Gordon MacRae, 64." Associated

Press. <u>Delaware County Sunday Times</u>. January 26, 1986.
MacRae's obituary.

B 22. "Career Man Gordon MacRae." <u>Movie Spotlight</u>. November 1951.
MacRae's life and career in pictures. Gordon is also pictured on the cover.

B 23. "Carousel is Movie Clambake Too." <u>Life</u>. February 6, 1956.
An article on CAROUSEL with nine pictures. Shirley Jones is on the cover.

B 24. "Carter Added." <u>Hollywood Reporter</u>. December 21, 1979.
Jack Carter replaced ailing Dick Haymes in the "4 Guys 4" act with members MacRae, Donald O'Connor, and Billy Daniels.

B 25. "Catching Up With Gordon MacRae." <u>Modern Screen</u>. July 1974.
Tells about what Gordon has been doing since leaving the movies, about his divorce from Sheila and his new life since marrying Elizabeth Schrafft. Portrait of MacRae and a picture of Gordon and Shirley Jones in OKLAHOMA

B 26. Churchill, Reba and Bonnie. "He'll Never Learn." <u>Motion Picture and Television Magazine</u>. October 1953.
Tells about Gordon's outspokenness often (unintentionally) ruffling feathers. Pictured with Sheila and Jane Powell at party for THREE SAILORS AND A GIRL cast.

B 27. <u>Citizen News</u>. September 26, 1967.
Announcement of the wedding of Gordon to Elizabeth Schrafft in New York at St. Peter's Lutheran Church. The couple are pictured.

B 28. "Clan MacRae." <u>TV Yearbook</u>. 1956.
Short profile on MacRae with a picture of Gordon and the family.

B 29. <u>Classic Images</u>. February 1986.
MacRae's obituary.

B 30. "Comedy Hour Signs MacRae as Permanent Singing Host." <u>Down Beat</u>. October 6, 1954.
Gordon signed for his first TV series the COLGATE COMEDY HOUR.

B 31. "Croon Guy Gordon MacRae." Unknown magazine. 1950.
The article discusses his love for travel, golf, clothes, cars, and his versatility as an entertainer. Several pictures of Gordon.

B 32. <u>Daily Variety</u>. May 19, 1948.
Review of BIG PUNCH

B 33. _____. June 4, 1949.
      Review of LOOK FOR THE SILVER LINING.

B 34. _____. January 10. 1950.
      Review of BACKFIRE

B 35. _____. July 9, 1951.
      Review of ON MOONLIGHT BAY.

B 36. _____. February 17, 1956.
      Review of CAROUSEL.

B 37. _____. September 24, 1956.
      Review of BEST THINGS IN LIFE ARE FREE.

B 38. Dallas Morning News. October 25, 1953.
      Review of Gordon and Sheila's appearance at the
Baker Hotel's Murial Room. Gordon and Sheila are pictured.

B 39. "A Day With MacRae." Filmland. December 1952.
      Pictures of MacRae getting ready for the studio.

B 40. "A Day With MacRae." Filmland. January 1953.
      Conclusion of MacRae's day filming DESERT SONG

B 41. Denton, Charles. "MacRae Finds Singing Just Isn't
      Enough." Philadelphia Inquirer. September 6, 1959.
      Gordon talks about the need to have more than one
talent in order not to have a narrow scope.

B 42. "Divorce Shatters Sheila and Gordon MacRae Marriage."
      Movie Mirror. 1967.
      Divorce ended more than twenty years of marriage, as
well as a top night club act. Gordon and Sheila are
pictured.

B 43. Down Beat. June 30, 1954.
      Brief summary of MacRae's life and career.

B 44. Dumont, Lou. "Historical Tape Recordings." Hobbies.
      March 1978.
      Gives background information about the RAILROAD HOUR
and its stars.

B 45. _____. "Historical Tape Recordings." Hobbies. April
      1978.
      Gives a complete RAILROAD HOUR log provided by Ray
Stanich. MacRae is pictured.

B 46. Edwards, Nadine. "Gordon Welcomed Back to LA." Citizen
      News. March 9, 1967.
      Review of MacRae's return to the Century Plaza Hotel
for three weeks after an absence of a year and a half.

B 47. Eidge, Frank. "Condo Circuit New Show Biz Wrinkle."
      United Press. June 5, 1977.
      Discusses the condo Circuit set up by agent-producer
Jerry Grant, where famed older stars tour Florida's condos

Pictured are MacRae and Myron Cohen.

B 48. "The End of a Beautiful Dream." Unknown magazine.
      1967.
      How after making it through the lean years, Gordon
and Sheila were unable to resolve their differences and
divorced. They were now pursuing their own careers.
Gordon and Sheila are pictured.

B 49. English, Mary. "MacRae Rated Top Pop Singer, Has
      Everything But Hit Disc." Down Beat. March 24, 1954.
      Tells about having trouble getting a hit disc even
though he is rated by professionals and Capitol Records as
about the best singer in pops both in voice and in
musicianship. Pictured with Carmen Dragon.

B 50. "Escape From Hollywood." Movie Pix. 1953.
      The MacRaes get away to Lake Arrowhead for fishing
and skiing. Several pictures of them fishing, water
skiing, and motor boating.

B 51. Esterow, Milton. "Being a Blueprint of Gordon
      MacRae's Climb Up the Show Business Scale." New York
      Times. December 11, 1955.
      Discusses taking a chance leaving Warners and seeking
and getting the leads in OKLAHOMA and CAROUSEL.

B 52. _____. "Gordon MacRaes in Harmony." New York Times.
      April 5, 1961.
      Review of Gordon and Sheila's Waldorf-Astoria's
Empire Room act with pictures of the couple.

B 53. _____. "On a Baritone's Score." New York Times.
      December 11, 1955.
      Discusses MacRae's climb up the show business scale.

B 54. "Face in the Mirror." Unknown magazine. 1967.
      An article on Sheila MacRae and Jane Kean joining the
"Honeymooners." Sheila talks about her role in the show.
She also talks about her career with Gordon, including her
nervousness before a show. Sheila and Jane are pictured.

B 55. "Family Fling by the MacRaes." Life. June 9, 1961.
      Talks about Sheila joining Gordon's act and
developing one of the classiest acts of impressions and
songs. Gordon and Sheila are pictured in the act and
around their pool with the children.

B 56. "Family Honeymoon." Movie Stars Parade. April 1949.
      Although Gordon and Sheila have been married for
awhile and have three children, they still act like
newlyweds. Several pictures of them and the children.

B 57. "Film Singer Selected as Father of the Year." Los
      Angeles Times. June 8, 1950.
      Gordon was selected as Father of the Year by the
Music Trade Association. He is pictured with Meredith,
Heather, and Gar.

B 58. "First Photo." Los Angeles Times. November 12, 1954.
     Announcement of the birth of Bruce MacRae, who is
pictured with Gordon and Sheila.

B 59. Flint, Peter. "Gordon MacRae Dies, Star of Movie
     Musicals." New York Times. January 25, 1986.
     Obituary. He is pictured with Shirley Jones in
OKLAHOMA, and in a portrait.

B 60. "Friendly Divorce." Unknown paper. 1968.
     Pictures of Gordon and Elizabeth, Sheila and Ron,
along with Meredith attending Heather's opening in WHERE I
BELONG.

B 61. Goldfarb, Susan. "Wives Rally at Singer's Deathbed."
     Globe. December 24, 1985.
     Talks about MacRae's last battle with cancer and
Sheila and Elizabeth gathering at his bedside.

B 62. "The Good Life." Screen Annual. Summer 1954.
     Article on getting away with Sheila for a day of deep
sea fishing. Eight pictures at sea, fishing.

B 63. "Gordon Goes Golfing." Television and Screen Guide.
     September 1951.
     Pictures of MacRae on the golf course.

B 64. "Gordon MacRae Always In Time." Movie Life. February
     1953.
     Pictures of Gordon and Sheila out for the evening
with Marge and Jeff Chandler.

B 65. "Gordon MacRae-Baby-Sitter." Movie Life. February
     1952.
     Pictured at the MacRae home baby sitting his
children.

B 66. "Gordon MacRae Denies Drunk Driving, Trial Set."
     Hollywood Citizen News. December 13, 1955.
     Report of his being involved in an auto accident and
being charged with drunk driving, complete with photos.

B 67. "Gordon MacRae-Family Man." Movie Life. October 1952.
     MacRae liked to spend time at home with his family.
They are often in the pool. Miscellaneous pictures of the
family in the pool and around the yard.

B 68. "Gordon MacRae Gets License to Marry." Los Angeles
     Times. September 15, 1967.
     Announces the forthcoming wedding of MacRae to
Elizabeth Schrafft.

B 69. "Gordon MacRae-His Second Life Is Better." Family
     Weekly. November 10, 1968.
     Tells about MacRae's life with new wife, Elizabeth,
and their daughter, Amanda. Pictured with Elizabeth and
Amanda.

B 70. "Gordon MacRae: Horace Heidt Happened to Be
       Listening." Unknown magazine and date.
       The article discusses his discovery by Heidt and his
rise to star of radio and films, as well as his marriage
and family. There are miscellaneous pictures of MacRae.

B 71. "Gordon MacRae Joins 1944 Cast." Hollywood Reporter.
       February 25, 1980.
       Tells of MacRae getting a role in THE BIG BROADCAST
OF 1944.

B 72. "Gordon MacRae Oklahoma Star." Chicago Tribune.
       January 25, 1986.
       Obituary. Pictured with Shirley Jones in OKLAHOMA.

B 73. "Gordon MacRae Radio's Most Versatile Singer." Look.
       July 5, 1949.
       Tells of his many roles on the RAILROAD HOUR with
pictures of several characters.

B 74. "Gordon MacRae, Singing Film Star Dies in Nebraska."
       Variety. January 29, 1986.
       Obituary.

B 75. "Gordon MacRae, 64, Singer Famed For Oklahoma."
       Chicago Sun Times. January 25, 1986.
       Obituary with portrait of MacRae.

B 76. "Gordon MacRae, 64, Star of Movie Musicals and a
       Popular Singer." Philadelphia Inquirer. January 25,
       1986.
       Obituary with a picture of him in OKLAHOMA.

B 77. "Gordon MacRae Star of Colorful Western." Unknown
       paper. 1950.
       A small article about MacRae in RETURN OF THE
FRONTIERSMAN opening at the Blue Mouse Theatre.

B 78. "Gordon MacRae: We Think Birth is a Miracle."
       Unknown magazine and date.
       Gordon and Sheila felt that the solid road to God was
through his universe, including the mysteries of birth and
death. They only answered the childrens questions when
asked and just enough to satisfy their curiousity.
Pictures of Gordon and the family.

B 79. "Gordon MacRae's Confidence Game." TV World. June
       1957.
       Talks about knowing what you want and going after it.
Pictured in dressing room and at home.

B 80. "Gordon MacRae's Double Life." Unknown magazine.
       1954.
       His double life is that of movie star and as family
man. Miscellaneous pictures of Gordon.

B 81. "Gordon MacRae's Happy Voice Finds Fame a Willing
       Listener." Los Angeles Times. February 11, 1951.

Discusses his not being changed by success.

B 82. "Gordon MacRae's Problem." <u>Movie Life</u>. February 1968.
      Talks about Gordon's drinking problem and its effect
on his career, as well as, his split with Sheila and
marriage to Elizabeth. Portrait on cover of article and he
is pictured kissing both wives.

B 83. "Gordon MacRae's Stepfather Dies." <u>Los Angeles
      Examiner</u>. August 28, 1953.
      Announcement of the death of Philip Osborne at age
71.

B 84. "Gordon MacRae's Wife Has Baby Boy." <u>Time</u>. April 7,
      1954.
      Announces the birth of Bruce MacRae.

B 85. "Gordon Takes a Bow." <u>Movie Stars Parade</u>. May 1952.
      Pictured at his appearance at the Ambassador Hotel
with friends.

B 86. Gould, Bernard. "Sheila MacRae's Premonitions Saved
      Her Ex-Hubby's Life Twice." <u>Midnight</u>. Date unknown.
      Two premonitions Sheila made while Gordon was in the
military. Sheila is pictured putting on makeup and with
Gordon in "One Sunday Afternoon" on LUX VIDEO THEATRE.

B 87. Gould, Helen. "Who's Inhibited?" <u>Filmland</u>. January
      1955.
      Talks about some people taking confidence as conceit.
Pictures of Gordon, Sheila and the family.

B 88. Graham, Sheila. "Gordon MacRae Sings Anywhere,
      Anytime." <u>Philadelphia Evening Bulletin</u>. June 2,
      1952.
      He sings anywhere and that's what was sometimes taken
as conceit, in reality it was self-confidence.

B 89. _____. "MacRaes Likely Will Reconcile." <u>Citizen News</u>.
      May 11, 1967.
      Tells some of the reasons contributing to the divorce
and the hope of a reconciliation.

B 90. "Grand Slam-But Fast." <u>TV Headliner</u>. July 1956.
      Discusses his success. Several photos.

B 91. Hannah, Marilyn. "My Mother's Divorce Gave Me Courage
      to Leave My Husband." <u>TV Picture Life</u>. Date unknown.
      Discusses Meredith's divorce from Richard Berger, as
well as her parent's divorce and their remarriages.
Miscellaneous pictures.

B 92. Harford, Margaret. "MacRaes Charm in Musical."
      Unknown paper. July 23, 1964.
      Review of Gordon and Sheila's appearance in BELLS ARE
RINGING at the Melodyland Theatre.

B 93. _____. "Sheila Gets Into Hubby's Act." <u>Los Angeles</u>

<u>Mirror</u>. July 1, 1961.
Discusses Sheila getting into Gordon's act, and their appearance at the Cocoanut Grove and Waldorf-Astoria.

B 94. Harris, Harry. "TV's Busy Husband." <u>Philadelphia Evening Bulletin</u>. May 20, 1953.
Mentions Sheila joining Gordon for his fourth and final time as substitute for Eddie Fisher on TUNE TIME.

B 95. Hazlett, Tim. "Oklahoma." <u>TV Broadway Movie Magazine</u>. March 1956.
Article on the making of OKLAHOMA. MacRae and Jones pictured on cover.

B 96. "Hefty Gordon Turned Heavy For His McCloud Assignment." Unknown paper. 1974.
Response to a viewers question if it was MacRae she saw in McCLOUD. Gordon is pictured.

B 97. "He Grabbed the Brass Ring." <u>Cue</u>. January 21, 1956.
Gordon was the only one who believed he'd play the leads in both OKLAHOMA and CAROUSEL.

B 98. "Here's Your Choice." <u>Movie Life</u>. February 1955.
Pictured are the top rated stars female and male according to reader's ballots.

B 99. "Hi Court Heaves MacRae Tax Plan." <u>Los Angeles Times</u>. January 9, 1962.
U.S. Supreme Court turned down Gordon's plea for a review of an adverse IRS ruling.

B100. "His Charm Worked." Unknown paper. April 26, 1948.
Picture of MacRae lulling baby Michael asleep. Michael is to be given to parents by the Native Sons and Daughters Adoption Agency.

B101. Hochstein, Rollie. "Over-35 Housewives Who Transformed Their Lives." <u>Family Circle</u>. October 1972.
Discusses becoming a housewife after Meredith's birth and rejoining Gordon in clubs and TV. She married Ron Wayne and is striking out on her own career.

B102. Holland, Jack. "What I Owe My Wife." <u>Movie Stars Parade</u>. Date unknown.
MacRae says even though they quarreled and separated their love was there and strong enough to save their marriage. He owes her his success. Gordon and Sheila are pictured.

B103. "Hollywood In New York." <u>Movie Life</u>. December 1950.
The article is about Patrice Wymore and Gordon appearing at the Strand Theatre in New York. MacRae and Wymore are pictured in his dressing room.

B104. <u>Hollywood Reporter</u>. August 15, 1950.
Review of TEA FOR TWO.

B105. _____. March 25, 1953.
     Review of BY THE LIGHT OF THE SILVERY MOON.

B106. Hopper, Hedda. "Born to Sing." Chicago Tribune.
     February 11, 1951.
     Discusses Gordon's being a master of ceremonies for
MINATURE MINSTRELS, his being discovered by Horace Heidt,
and agent Dick Dorso suggesting MacRae change to his
natural voice so he wouldn't sound like Frank Sinatra.

B107. _____. "Gordon MacRae-He Just Had to Play Curly."
     Chicago Tribune Magazine. Date unknown.
     Discussion of MacRae going from page boy to star of
OKLAHOMA in eight years. Pictured with Shirley Jones in
OKLAHOMA.

B108. _____. "Gordon MacRae Receives Lead in Film
     Carousel." Los Angeles Times. August 26, 1955.
     The announcement of MacRae replacing Sinatra in
CAROUSEL.

B109. _____. "Singer MacRae Eyes Footlights." Chicago
     Tribune. 1955.
     Mentions that eight years ago he was broke, now he
owns a big home, belongs to the Lakeside Golf Club, and
owns 4800 acres in Wyoming near a producing oil well.
Portrait of MacRae.

B110. Houdek, Richard. "MacRae, Gobel Pair Up at Bridge."
     Los Angeles Times. January 30, 1979.
     A review of MacRae and George Gobel's concert at
Bridges Auditorium.

B111. Howe, Velica. "With the Fan Clubs." Movie Play. July
     1954.
     Discussion of stars' fan clubs including MacRae's and
the club publications. MacRae is pictured.

B112. "Investment: Eleven Years of Marriage, Return: Three
     Husky Dividends." Unknown magazine. 1952.
     Mentions Sheila giving up acting to raise a family.
It profiles the children, and mentions the probability of
Sheila returning to work. Miscellaneous pictures of MacRae
and family.

B113. Jackson, George. "Warm Welcome for MacRae." Los
     Angeles Herald Examiner. March 9, 1967.
     Review of MacRae's return to the Century Plaza Hotel.

B114. "Jane Powell, MacRae Soloists for Oxy Glee Clubs
     Tonight." Los Angeles Examiner. May 6, 1949.
     Announcement of concert with the Occidental College
Glee Club at the Wilshire Ebell Theatre, benefiting the
Hollywood Kiwanis Club's Youth Fund.

B115. "Keeping it in the Clan." TV Guide. July 14, 1956.
     Discusses Sheila's writing and assisting in the
production of the GORDON MacRAE SHOW. Miscellaneous

pictures on the set and with the children. Gordon and
Sheila are on the cover.

B116. Keith, Broghan. "Meredith MacRae: Heartbreak and
      Happiness." <u>Screenplay</u>. Date unknown.
      An article on Gordon and Sheila's divorce and
Meredith's divorce from Richard Berger and of meeting and
marrying Greg Mullavey. Miscellaneous pictures.

B117. "Lanquor, Curls, and Tonsils." <u>Time</u>. September 15,
      1947.
      Several crooners discussed. MacRae is described as
Destiny's Boy. He felt that his career as a crooner was
predestined. Gordon is pictured.

B118. "Las Vegas Vagabond." <u>Movie Stars Parade</u>. May 1951.
      Talks about MacRae's appearance at the El Rancho
Vegas and his spare time activities. Several pictures.

B119. Lee, Marilyn. "MacRae Tops in 5 Media." <u>Los Angeles
      Examiner</u>. October 18, 1953.
      A discussion on MacRae's fame in five media and his
versatility in music. Cartoon characterization of MacRae.

B120. Leston, Jim. "At Home With Gordon MacRae." <u>American
      Home</u>. January 1961.
      The article discusses the MacRae home in the San
Fernando Valley and their interest in antique collecting.
Six pictures show their home inside and out.

B121. Levine, Al. Unknown paper and date.
      Gordon (pictured with Mrs. Skitch Henderson) was
hosting a celebrity brunch at New York's Daly's Dandelion
owned by Skitch Henderson.

B122. Levy, Paul. "Singer Gordon MacRae: God Helped Me Win
      12-Year Battle With Booze." <u>National Enquirer</u>. March
      3, 1981.
      Discussion of his battle with booze and how and why
he stopped. MacRae is pictured.

B123. Lewine, Frances. "Stage All Set For White House
      Wedding at 4p.m." <u>Greeneville (Tennessee) Sun</u>.
      December 9, 1967.
      Tells of the wedding preparations for Lynda Bird
Johnson's wedding and of Carol Lawrence and MacRae doing
excerpts from I DO! I DO! at her wedding eve dinner.

B124. <u>Life</u>. May 2, 1955.
      Article and colored pictures on OKLAHOMA

B125. Linet, Beverly, "The MacRae Touch." <u>TV Headliner</u>.
      March 1954.
      Tells how MacRae has succeeded at what ever project
he touched. MacRae talks to Eddie Fisher about getting
into TV.

B126. Lloyd, Jack. "MacRae's Windup Shocks Cynics."

Philadelphia Inquirer. May 4, 1970.
Review of MacRae's appearance at the Latin Casino.

B127. Longacre, Fred. "Patrice Points Out...the Girls and
      Boys of Filmland With Sweet and Lovely Singing
      Voices." Unknown magazine. 1953.
      Patrice Munsel discusses her film debut in MELBA and
compares the opera to Hollywood including her thoughts on
several film singers including MacRae who is pictured.

B128. Los Angeles Times. April 17, 1967.
      Announcement of Sheila's divorce from Gordon in
Juarez, Mexico for incompatibility. Both are pictured.

B129. _____. March 19, 1978.
      Easter time with Gordon and his new daughter and his
grandchildren.

B130. Ludden, Allen. "Let's Talk it Over." Movie Stars
      Parade. June 1952.
      MacRae served as guest consultant, giving advice to
his fans. He is pictured.

B131. McClay, Howard. "MacRae Riding High in Oklahoma
      Film." Los Angeles Daily News. October 1, 1954.
      Discusses how MacRae got the role of Curly in the film
OKLAHOMA.

B132. "MacRae Career Accented by Steady Progress to
      Stardom." Dallas Morning News. May 15, 1955.
      A review of his career, of his meeting Sheila and his
doing CAROUSEL in Dallas. Portrait of MacRae.

B133. "MacRae for Martin." Newsweek. March 1, 1948.
      MacRae replaced Tony Martin on radio's TEXACO STAR
THEATRE. Picture of MacRae.

B134. "The MacRae Gang." Movieland. May 1951.
      Three pictures of Gordon and family.

B135. MacRae, Gordon. "They Call Me Lovelorn Luke." Unknown
      magazine. 1953.
      He kept trying to win Sheila over and he finally
married her. He believed that one shouldn't wait for
conditions to be perfect before marrying, because the
struggle and goal setting helps create a lasting bond.
There are pictures of Gordon and his family.

B136. _____. "Happy-Go-Lucky Family." Unknown magazine and
      date.
      Sheila doesn't worry him with the little problems at
home and she understands his moods. She helps his morale
when he's down. They enjoy the outside and their friends

B137. _____. "I Believe in Marrying." Movie Stars Parade.
      August 1953.
      Discusses Gordon and Sheila's early period of
marriage. Pictures of Gordon with family.

B138. _____. "A Letter to My Son." Movie Stars Parade. April
      1952.
      A letter Gordon wrote to his son, Gar several years
before giving it to him, expressing his feelings. There's
a picture of Gordon and an insert of Gar.

B139. _____. "Listen Kate." Photoplay. April 1953.
      Dispels the rumor that Kathryn Grayson was a terror
on the set. There is a picture of both stars.

B140. _____. "MacRae Tells Plight of an Actor." Hollywood
      Citizen News. June 16, 1958.
      MacRae discusses the need of versatility in order to
stay alive in show business.

B141. _____. "P.S. I Got the Job." American Magazine. March
      1952.
      The article discusses pursuing a show business career
and his father's advice to sing anywhere, which resulted in
his being discovered by the Heidt organization. MacRae is
pictured.

B142. _____. "Ready, Able and Praying." Photoplay. April
      1958.

B143. _____. "The Role I Liked Best." Saturday Evening
      Post. January 30, 1954.
      Gordon talks about his role in WEST POINT STORY.
Pictured with Doris Day in a scene from the film.

B144. _____. "Terror on Route 99." Unknown magazine. 1952.
      On a weekend trip to Palm Springs, the MacRaes take a
cut off to get there faster and loose their brakes on a
hill. The MacRaes are pictured with horses.

B145. _____. "Watch Out for Jealousy." Screen Stars. 1952.
      Gordon shares how he and Sheila deal with the
jealousy between the children. There is a picture of
Gordon and his family.

B146. _____. "Why I Pray." Motion Picture. Date unknown.
      Gordon believes prayer can help you through troubled
times. MacRae is pictured.

B147. _____. "You Can't Win With Women." Motion Picture.
      1952.
      Gordon talks about himself and Gar living in a house
with women. Several pictures with his family.

B148. "MacRae Hits Tax Charges." Mirror News. October 23,
      1958.
      Discusses MacRae's tax problems brought about by a
company handling his investments.

B149. "MacRae in Cast of '44'." Variety. February 27, 1980.
      Announces MacRae's addition to the cast of the BIG
BROADCAST OF 1944.

B150. "MacRae in Pilot." <u>Hollywood Reporter</u>. December 18,
       1978.
       Mentions Gordon's return to film in THE PILOT after
twenty-two years.

B151. "MacRae Marries Social Figure." <u>Los Angeles Times</u>.
       September 27, 1967.
       Announces Gordon's marriage to Elizabeth Schrafft.

B152. "MacRae Pays Fine of $300 in Traffic Crash." Unknown
       paper. December 17, 1955.
       MacRae appeared in Van Nuys Municipal Court to change
his mind about having a jury hear his case on a drunk
driving charge. The judge found him guilty and imposed the
$300 fine.

B153. "The MacRaes and the Nelsons Step Out." <u>Movie Life</u>.
       May 1952.
       Pictures of each family getting ready to go out
together.

B154. "MacRaes Appeal Gov't Tax Dispute to Supreme Court."
       <u>Variety</u>. November 28, 1961.
       Gordon and Sheila go to U.S. Supreme Court to appeal
IRS claim of back taxes.

B155. "MacRae's Beautiful Morning." <u>Look</u>. December 27,
       1955.
       Discusses Gordon's getting OKLAHOMA and CAROUSEL and
his enjoyment of family life. There are pictures of
OKLAHOMA, CAROUSEL, the family on vacation, and rehearsals
for Las Vegas.

B156. "MacRae's Bedtime Round-Up." <u>Filmland</u>. 1952.
       Article in pictures of tiring the kids out (as
cowboys) to get them to bed.

B157. "MacRaes Form Their Own Show-Business Machine."
       Unknown paper. 1960.
       Mentions the MacRaes working together on a record OUR
LOVE STORY, on a TV pilot NO PLACE LIKE HOME, and the
desire to work together in films and on Broadway.

B158. "The MacRaes: From Sun-Up to Star-Up Melody and
       Laughter." Unknown magazine and date.
       Discusses things that go on at the MacRae household
from sun-up to star-up. Picture of Gordon holding Heather
on their big shaggy dog.

B159. MacRae, Sheila. "Champagne for Breakfast." <u>Motion
       Picture</u>. 1950.
       Although it was nice to try things on a special
occasion (like a champagne breakfast) it was her life with
Gordon she'd remember and treasure. The couple are
pictured.

B160. _____. "The Day He Proposed." <u>Motion Picture and
       Television Magazine</u>. June 1953.

Discusses MacRae's marriage proposal to Sheila.
Picture of Gordon and Sheila framed in a heart.

B161. _____. "Gordie's No Square." <u>Movies</u>. June 1955.
       Discusses his becoming more relaxed, understanding,
and patient. He had a good memory for things he wanted to
remember. Miscellaneous pictures.

B162. _____. "The Lowdown on MacRae." <u>Modern Screen</u>.
       August 1951.
       Sheila talks about her ten-year marriage, a lovely
home, and three children. She remembers New York when they
were starting out. Pictures of MacRae and his family.

B163. _____. <u>Movie Stars Parade</u>. 1952.
       Sheila tells how to win a man and how to hold on to
him. Gordon and Sheila are pictured.

B164. _____. "My Guiding Star." <u>Photoplay</u>. April 1951.
       Discusses Gordon's persistance and eventual success
in getting Sheila to date him, as they didn't get along at
first. They eventually fell in love.

B165. _____. "We Were Not Too Young for Love." <u>Radio TV
       Mirror</u>. 1953.
       Sheila discusses the ecstasy and heartache of their
early marriage. Miscellaneous pictures of the MacRae
family.

B166. "MacRae's Loan Set Up Explained." <u>Los Angeles Times</u>.
       October 4, 1958.
       Discusses tax problems caused by a company MacRae let
handle his investments.

B167. "MacRae Stands for Song." <u>Movie Pix</u>. 1953.
       Although he's grateful for the musicals, his desire
is to do a comedy or drama. Several pictures.

B168. "MacRae Star of New Blue Mouse Film." Unknown paper.
       1950.
       Announcement of the opening of RETURN OF THE
FRONTIERSMAN at the Blue Mouse Theatre.

B169. "MacRae's Trio: Always Something Up Their Sleeves."
       <u>Hollywood Family Album</u>. October 1950.
       Discussion of Sheila and his children. MacRae and
family pictured.

B170. "MacRaes Will Star in Bells Are Ringing." <u>Los Angeles
       Times</u>. Date unknown.
       Announces the MacRaes doing BELLS ARE RINGING at the
Valley Music Theatre.

B171. "MacRae Will Aid American Day." <u>Los Angeles Examiner</u>.
       September 17, 1955.
       MacRae and others participated in the telecast of
persons becoming U.S. citizens.

B172. Maddox, Tex. "Men Marriage and Me." <u>TV Star Parade</u>.
    March 1968.
    Discussion of Meredith's life and career, her parents,
and brothers and sister. Some of the men she had dated are
mentioned, as well as her meeting, marrying, and divorcing
Richard Berger. Miscellaneous pictures.

B173. Mallory, Bob. "Gordon MacRae's Secret Battle With the
    Bottle." <u>Star</u>. February 11, 1986.
    Discusses his battle with the bottle, his stroke, and
his death from cancer. Miscellaneous pictures.

B174. Manners, Dorothy. "Cruelty of Fame." <u>Los Angeles
    Herald Examiner</u>. February 18, 1968.
    Discussion of how some offspring of famous parents
find the going difficult. Heather bounded back after her
unhappiness at her parents divorce.

B175. _____. "Gordon MacRae-An Actor As Well As a Singer."
    <u>Los Angeles Herald Examiner</u>. January 28, 1973.
    Discusses MacRae's return to Hollywood to make his
home in Beverly Hills and the difference he found when he
returned. There is a portrait of Gordon.

B176. "Marriage Ends." <u>Citizen News</u>. April 17, 1967.
    Announcement of Sheila's divorce from Gordon in
Juarez, Mexico on the grounds of incompatibility. The
couple is pictured.

B177. Maxwell, Elsa. "That Old MacRae Magic." <u>Photoplay</u>.
    October 1951.
    Tells about what puts you under his spell, his
audition for Jack Warner, and overcoming problems in his
early marriage. There are pictures at home with the
family.

B178. Maynard, John. "You Have to Blow Your Own Horn."
    <u>Motion Picture</u>. Date unknown.
    The article discusses Gordon being a good performer
and knowing it, and that he is confident and doesn't believe
in false modesty. There are pictures of Gordon and his
family.

B179. "Meredith MacRae's Wedding Day-A Touch of India."
    <u>Movie Stars Parade</u>. 1967.
    Article and numerous pictures of Meredith's wedding
to Greg Mullavey at Pacific Palisades on April 19, 1969.

B180. <u>Metronome</u>. April 1950.
    Mentions being unpopular with young jazz fans
because he sang all kinds of songs. MacRae pictured at the
piano.

B181. Mooring, W.H. "Is Gordon MacRae Another Bing?"
    <u>Picturegoer</u>. November 5, 1949.
    He's compared to Bing Crosby by some. His being
discovered and brought to Warners is discussed, their
neighbors opinion of them is mentioned, as well as his

growing up around music. There is a portrait of MacRae and
one of Gordon and June Haver studying the script of LOOK
FOR THE SILVER LINING.

B182. "Mornings Are Beautiful Again." <u>Philadelphia
       Inquirer</u>. November 27, 1981.
       The interview discusses his battle with alcohol and
his recovery. Miscellaneous pictures.

B183. Morris, Jane. "If Only He Were Italian." Unknown
       magazine. 1953.
       Dean Martin tells Jane Morris that Gordon is a
perfectionist and is determined to be tops at whatever he
does. The combination of classical and crooner style makes
him a great singer. He's not a phony and speaks his mind
and would make a great comedian. MacRae and Martin are
pictured golfing.

B184. <u>Movie Fan</u>. 1951.
       A discussion of some strange things that have
happened to Gordon. He also talks about his friendship
with Gene Nelson and his private recordings at home for the
children and Sheila. Several pictures of MacRae.

B185. _____. 1951.
       The article talks about his tackling anything new
that comes along and usually doing well with whatever it
is. Miscellaneous pictures.

B186. _____. 1952.
       The article mentions his drive and ambition, his
desire for perfection. He knows what he wants and goes
after it without being insincere or dishonest. Several
pictures.

B187. "Movie Life of Gordon MacRae." <u>Movie Life</u>. April
       1951.
       Gordon's life story in pictures. It compares Gordon
at work and at play and has pictures of the MacRaes on
vacation in Palm Springs.

B188. _____. <u>Movie Life</u>. February 1955.
       MacRae's life in pictures from a baby to the film
OKLAHOMA.

B189. _____. <u>Movie Life Yearbook</u>. 1951.
       MacRae's life in pictures from child to ON MOONLIGHT
BAY. Pictured on cover.

B190. _____. <u>Movie Life Yearbook</u>. 1954.
       MacRae's life in pictures. Pictured on back cover.

B191. <u>Movie Play</u>. January 1956.
       Article on MacRae.

B192. "Movie Singer MacRae Sued in Auto Crash." Unknown
       paper. February 2, 1956.
       As a result of an accident occurring in December

1955, he was being sued by Mrs. Marion Dunn, a film studio secretary, who said his car struck another car, which pushed into a third car, which struck her car.

B193. Movie Stars Parade. June 1950.
        Article on MacRae.

B194. "Mr. MacRae to Repeat for '57 Fair." Dallas Morning News. August 7, 1957.
        Announces his being featured again in the East Texas Day Show in the Cotton Bowl on October 15, 1957. Portrait of MacRae.

B195. "Mrs. Helen MacRae Osborne." Variety. July 7, 1952.
        Reported the sudden death of Gordon's mother.

B196. Nesbet, Fairfax. "Baritone Also Busy in Dallas."
        Dallas Morning News. October 18, 1953.
        Talks about MacRae's appearance at the Baker Hotel's Murial Room and at the State Fair of Texas East Texas Day Show at the Cotton Bowl.

B197. Neville, John. "MacRae's Show Brings Vaudeville Back to Life." Unknown paper and date.
        Review of MacRae's show at the Country Dinner Playhouse in Dallas.

B198. "New Play in Manhattan." Time. December 1, 1941.
        Review of JUNIOR MISS.

B199. Newsweek. February 3, 1986.
        Obituary.

B200. _____. May 1, 1967.
        Announces Gordon and Sheila's divorce, including a picture of them kissing.

B201. "New York Manner." Unknown magazine. 1950.
        Tells of MacRae's appearance at the New York Strand Theatre and in the films RETURN OF THE FRONTIERSMAN and the DAUGHTER OF ROSIE O'GRADY. Miscellaneous pictures.

B202. New York Times. October 31, 1940.
        Review of the TROJAN HORSE.

B203. _____. March 8, 1946.
        Review of the Broadway show THREE TO MAKE READY. Pictured with Ray Bolger and Garry Davis.

B204. _____. June 24, 1949.
        Review of LOOK FOR THE SILVER LINING.

B205. _____. January 27, 1950.
        Review of BACKFIRE.

B206. _____. March 31, 1950.
        Review of DAUGHTER OF ROSIE O'GRADY.

B207. _____. June 10, 1950.
Review of RETURN OF THE FRONTIERSMAN.

B208. _____. September 2, 1950.
Review of TEA FOR TWO.

B209. _____. December 23, 1950.
Review of WEST POINT STORY.

B210. _____. July 27, 1951.
Review of ON MOONLIGHT BAY.

B211. _____. December 15, 1951.
Review of STARLIFT.

B212. _____. May 24, 1952.
Review of ABOUT FACE.

B213. _____. March 27, 1953.
Review of BY THE LIGHT OF THE SILVERY MOON.

B214. _____. May 21, 1953.
Review of DESERT SONG.

B215. _____. November 23, 1953.
Review of THREE SAILORS AND A GIRL.

B216. _____. October 11, 1955.
Review of OKLAHOMA.

B217. _____. February 17, 1956.
Review of CAROUSEL.

B218. _____. September 29, 1956.
Review of BEST THINGS IN LIFE ARE FREE.

B219. "No New Partners Say the MacRaes." Los Angeles Times.
April 17, 1967.
A report on Sheila's divorce from Gordon in Juarez,
Mexico, complete with picture of the couple.

B220. "No Temper, All Talent." TV-Radio. May 1955.

B221. "Nuptials." Citizen News. September 14, 1967.
Elizabeth Schrafft and MacRae pictured at marriage
license bureau in New York.

B222. "Off We Go." Movie Life. September 1951.
Several pictures of Warner stars at Travis Air Force
Base, which became the idea for STARLIFT.

B223. Okon, May. "Kids and Kidding." Sunday News. January
28, 1962.
Discusses Sheila joining Gordon's act, as well as
writing material for clubs and TV. Pictured with his
family at Christmas.

B224. "One Punch Decks Gordon MacRae." Los Angeles Herald

Examiner. April 27, 1967.
After finishing his second show at the
Waldorf-Astoria's Empire Room, MacRae reportedly danced
with three women, one of whom was the wife of Ralph Houk.
When he returned the women to their tables, he gave each an
affectionate kiss. Houk took exception. Houk reportedly
apologized before leaving.

B225. "On the Level." Movieland. May 1951.
Discusses what MacRae's buddies thought of him.
Miscellaneous pictures.

B226. Oppenheimer, Peer. "Backstage Romance." TV World.
Date unknown.
Discusses how Gordon and Sheila met and married and
the ups and downs of their romance. The couple are
pictured.

B227. _____. "Gordon MacRae: This is My Sheila." TV Stage.
February 1957.
Discusses how Sheila has helped Gordon succeed.
Pictures of Gordon, Sheila and the children.

B228. _____. "Our Marriage is Vulnerable." TV Stage. 1953.
You can't take love or marriage for granted even
after twelve years. After Sheila joined Gordon's act, they
had to juggle time spent with the children, and handle the
problems that come with working on the road. Miscellaneous
pictures.

B229. "Palm Springs Jubilee." Unknown magazine. 1952.
To raise money for charity in Palm Springs, many
stars took part in the annual festivities.

B230. Parsons, Louella. "In Hollywood With Louella
Parsons." Los Angeles Examiner. September 25, 1949.
Discusses MacRae's budding movie career. Picture of
MacRae with pipe.

B231. _____. "Louella O. Parsons in Hollywood." Los Angeles
Examiner. June 1, 1952.
Louella discusses her opinion of MacRae as one of the
"soundest, sanest, and most talented young men in our
town." MacRae is pictured.

B232. _____. "MacRae Given Sinatra Key Role in Carousel."
International News Service. August 26, 1955.
Tells about MacRae getting Frank Sinatra's part in
CAROUSEL after Sinatra left the project.

B233. _____. "MacRae Strives to Lose Rating as
Uncooperative!" Philadelphia Inquirer. August 19,
1951.
Because of his busy schedule the previous year, he
gave fewer interviews and pictures, so the newspaper women
and publicists declared him uncooperative.

B234. _____. "Mr. and Mrs. Gordon MacRae." Los Angeles

Examiner. 1951.
    Discusses his being one of the most popular actors on
screen. He was so busy in films, radio, and with personal
appearances he was declared uncooperative by newspaper
women and publicists.

B235. Peer, Robert. "Happy Though Married." Unknown
      magazine. 1953.
      It's their love for each other that gets them through
anything, and their desire to make life easier and less
worrisome for each other.

B236. Peterson, Marva. "House of MacRae." *Modern Screen*.
      February 1952.
      Pictures of the MacRae home, which had been chosen
the home of the month.

B237. *Photoplay*. 1952.
      A cartoon article showing Gordon taking a rare
vacation from his busy and hectic schedule.

B238. "The Picture Life of Gordon MacRae." *Photoplay*. 1952.
      Article and pictures of MacRae's life to ABOUT FACE.

B239. *Picture Show and Film Pictorial*. May 12, 1951.
      Article on TEA FOR TWO. Gordon and Doris Day on the
cover.

B240. _____. February 2, 1952.
      Full-page photo of Gordon.

B241. _____. April 19, 1952.
      Article on MacRae.

B242. _____. May 17, 1952.
      Review and pictures of ON MOONLIGHT BAY. Gordon and
Doris Day are on the cover.

B243. _____. August 29, 1953.
      Full-page of pictures on DESERT SONG

B244. _____. June 2, 1956.
      Article on CAROUSEL. Shirley Jones and MacRae on
cover.

B245. _____. September 8, 1956.
      Marked the London premiere of OKLAHOMA with critique
and pictures. Gordon and Shirley Jones are on the cover.

B246. _____. January 19, 1957.
      Full-page photo of MacRae.

B247. Pierce, Marjorie. "Colleges Foundation Has Big
      Success With Big Sound." Unknown paper and date.
      Talks about the big band benefit for Foothill-DeAnza
Colleges Foundation.

B248. Pine, Dick. "How the Gordon MacRaes Keep Love

Alive." <u>Movieland</u>. September 1951.
Gordon and Sheila give the do's and don'ts for a
happy marriage. Pictures of Gordon, Sheila, and the
family.

B249. _____. "Temper Temper!" <u>Motion Picture</u>. June 1951.
The article discusses the pet peeves of several
stars. MacRae's is audience rudeness. MacRae is pictured.

B250. _____. "That Certain Feeling." <u>Motion Picture</u>.
February 1950.
Discussion about MacRae having what it takes to out
last the dozens of male singers who came to Hollywood and
didn't last. Pictures of Gordon and Sheila.

B251. <u>Playbill</u>.
From the Broadway productions of THREE TO MAKE READY
and I DO! I DO!.

B252. Policy, Joseph. "Singer Gordon MacRae: God is Guiding
My Recovery From a Crippling Stroke." <u>National
Enquirer</u>. November 1982.
Tells of his stroke and his determination to work
again. Pictured with arm in a sling.

B253. Pollock, Lou. "He Never Said Can't." <u>Modern Screen</u>.
September 1953.
Gordon knew what he wanted and didn't give up until
he got it. Pictured with family in pool and in a full-page
portrait.

B254. <u>Pop Scrapbook</u>. 1953.
A brief profile of MacRae, including a picture.

B255. Pressbooks.
Pressbooks from each of his films, put out by the
studio giving stories, ad campaigns etc. These were used
by theatre owners to publicize the film.

B256. "Private Life of Gordon MacRae." <u>Movie Stars Parade</u>.
July 1952.
On vacation in Palm Springs. Pictured with Moss
Hart, and golfing with Bing Crosby and Dean Martin.

B257. Programs.
Programs and souvenir programs from GOLDEN RAINBOW,
OKLAHOMA at Valley Forge Music Fair, as well as, GUYS AND
DOLLS and his other stage shows. (See Stage appearances)

B258. "Racket at the Racquet Club." <u>Movie Life</u>. July 1951.
Pictures of Gordon and the family vacationing at the
Racquet Club in Palm Springs.

B259. <u>Radio and Television Best</u>. August 1948.
Gordon and Evelyn Knight are pictured in a brief
article concerning radio's TEXACO STAR THEATRE.

B260. Raffetto, Francis. "Commonwealth Has MacRae

Opening." <u>Dallas Morning News</u>. August 20, 1965.
Review of MacRae's show at the Commonwealth Club in
North Park, Texas.

B261. "The Real MacRae." Unknown magazine. April 29, 1947.
After THREE TO MAKE READY, he went to radio's
TEENTIMER CLUB, becoming second to Bing Crosby as the most
heard crooner on radio. MacRae is pictured.

B262. "The Reckless MacRaes: You Can't Take it With You—and
They Don't Care!" Unknown magazine and date.
The article mentions buying things on the spur of the
moment, and about MacRae's confidence. Gordon and Sheila
are pictured at the pool with the children.

B263. Reichle, Bill. "Move Over." <u>Motion Picture</u>. January
1951.
Picture of fans crowded around MacRae at the stage
door of a New York appearance and one of fans crowded
around Frank Sinatra.

B264. Reinhart, Ted. "In Memory of MacRae." <u>Classic Images</u>.
February 1986.
Remembrances by Reinhart of MacRae's career and the
friendship he and wife, Ruth had with Gordon. Picture of
MacRae with Ruth.

B265. _____. "My Day With MacRae." <u>Classic Images</u>. February
1983.
Reinhart tells of himself and his wife, Ruth meeting
MacRae at his concert in Altoona, Pennsylvania. Picture of
MacRae and Reinhart, and one of MacRae in CAROUSEL.

B266. "Return to Youth." <u>TV Guide</u>. June 18, 1955.
Discusses MacRae being hired for the COLGATE COMEDY
HOUR with pictures of Gordon on the set and with his
family.

B267. "Riding the Rails." <u>Movie Stars Parade</u>. February 1952.
Article and pictures of Gordon, Sheila, and the
children at the Valley Model Railroad Shop.

B268. Robins, Cynthia. "Gordon MacRae Acts As If He Wrote
the Songs." <u>San Francisco Examiner</u>. August 15, 1977.
Review of MacRae's appearance at the Fairmont Hotel's
Venetian Room. Large picture of Gordon.

B269. Rounder. "MacRae Grove's Best." <u>Los Angeles News</u>.
August 30, 1957.
Review of Gordon and Sheila's show at the Cocoanut
Grove.

B270. <u>Schwann Catalog</u>.
Various issues listing MacRae's albums and dates of
release.

B271. Scott, John. "Gordon MacRae at Harrah's Tahoe." <u>Los
Angeles Times</u>. March 1, 1969.

Review of MacRae's appearance at Harrahs with
portrait of Gordon.

B272. _____. "Mom, Pop, Four Youngsters-All the MacRaes Get
in Act." Los Angeles Times. September 18, 1960.
Discuses the shows the family did on the summer
circuit.

B273. _____. "Plaza Patrons Hear MacRae." Los Angeles
Times. March 11, 1967.
Tells about MacRae's appearance at the Century Plaza
Hotel complete with portrait of MacRae.

B274. "Screen Annual Presents Musical Stars." Screen
Annual. 1953.
Small profile of MacRae complete with picture.

B275. Screen Stories. April 1950.
Article on MacRae.

B276. Shallert, Edwin. "Singer Gordon MacRae Plays Pugilest
in Picture." Los Angeles Times. June 6, 1948.
Tells about MacRae starting in a dramatic film BIG
PUNCH and his next film LOOK FOR A SILVER LINING. Portrait
of Gordon.

B277. Silden, Isabel. "The Woman Beside Gordon MacRae."
Boston Post TV Eye. Date unknown.
Tells of Sheila's start in show business and her
working with Gordon on his show producing and writing
material. Pictured on show and with family.

B278. "Singer and Bride-To-Be." Los Angeles Times.
September 14, 1967.
Picture of Gordon and Elizabeth leaving license
bureau in New York City.

B279. "Singer Gordon MacRae and Family Moving West So His
Daughter, 3, Can Take a Deep Breath Without Choking."
Unknown paper. 1972.
MacRae and Elizabeth are moving to Las Vegas, from
New York, because they felt it was healthier for their
daughter. Pictured with friends at a golf course.

B280. "Singer Gordon MacRae Dead at 64." Associated Press.
January 25, 1986.
Obituary.

B281. "Singer Gordon MacRae's Son Wed in Church." Los
Angeles Times. January 27, 1970.
Describes son Gar's wedding to Megan Handschumacker.

B282. "Singer in 4-Car Crash, Faces Trial on Jan. 9."
Mirror News. December 14, 1955.
MacRae is involved in a 4-car crash. He wanted a jury
trial. Portrait of Gordon.

B283. "Singer MacRae's Crash Trial Slated January 9." Los

Angeles Times. December 14, 1955.
Discusses MacRae in Van Nuys court after being arrested for drunk driving. Pictured in court.

B284. Skolsky, Sidney. "Hollywood Is My Beat." _Hollywood Citizen News_. Date unknown.
About Gordon going after and usually getting what he wants, such as, the parts in OKLAHOMA and CAROUSEL. Portrait included.

B285. Smith, Cecil. "MacRaes Ponder Show en Famille." _Los Angeles Times_. June 23, 1958.
Discusses Cocoanut Grove show, their desire to do a situation comedy with the whole family, and TV appearances on ED SULLIVAN SHOW and PLAYHOUSE 90. Picture of Gordon and Sheila.

B286. Smith, Martha. "R.I. Festival Pops Gives Concert With MacRae." _Providence Sunday Journal_. April 17, 1977.
Reviews MacRae's concert at Veterans Memorial Auditorium on April 16, 1977.

B287. "Sometimes It Lasts: The Gordon MacRaes." _Movie Stars Parade_. 1953.
Despite financial problems when they married, Gordon and Sheila have been happily married for twelve years and still take a honeymoon, spend their leisure time together. The kids help make a happy family. Several pictures of Gordon, Sheila, and the children.

B288. "Space Getters." _Hollywood Picture Life_. Winter issue 1955-1956.
Discusses doing what you do best.

B289. Speers, W. "MacRae in Hospital and is Very Sick." _Philadelphia Inquirer_. Date unknown.
Tells about MacRae's illness and his stroke in 1982, and of well wishes from Gerald R. Ford, Betty Ford, Norman Cousins, Robert Goulet, and Frank Sinatra. Pictured as he appeared in 1953.

B290. "Spend An Evening With a Beautiful Girl." _Broadcasting_. November 18, 1968.
Announces the first (Carol Lawrence) in the second series of six TV specials highlighting different stars. It also lists the first series of six, which included the GORDON MacRAE SHOW.

B291. Spires, George. "The Big Punch." _Herald_. May 29, 1948.
Review of the film BIG PUNCH.

B292. _Spotlight on Gordon MacRae_. 1959.
The official fan club magazine with articles and pictures by club members about MacRae's activities.

B293. "A Star Can Be Scared." _Movie Stars Parade_. December 1952.

Tells about MacRae's career and of his jitters before
every show. Pictured with Sheila in the living room and in
the DESERT SONG.

B294. Starr, Maxine. "He's Riding High." TV Stage. August
      1956.
      Says MacRae knows what he wants and goes after it.
Miscellaeous pictures with family. He's pictured on cover.

B295. Strait, Raymond. "I Was Raised in Studio City."
      Philadelphia Sunday Bulletin. August 24, 1980.
      Excerpt from interview of Meredith in Strait's book
Star Babies. MacRae pictured at picnic with Heather and
Gar.

B296. Sunday News. January 15, 1950.
      An article on Vaughn Monroe, Tony Martin and Gordon
with a brief biographical and career sketch given. MacRae
pictured.

B297. "Surprise For Sheila, Her Children, a Cake." Unknown
      paper. September 28, 1964.
      Sheila receives a birthday cake from Gordon, who
brought the children to New York from Los Angeles. Picture
of Gordon, Sheila, and the children.

B298. "Taking in the Sun." Movies. August 1952.

B299. "Tax Court Blues Facing 3 Show Biz Couples-Arlens,
      Nelsons, MacRaes." Variety. September 29, 1965.
      Addition of back taxes for 1960-1962 to those of
1954-1959.

B300. Taylor, Kevin. "Platter Pick-Up." Unknown magazine.
      July 1948.
      MacRae is pictured saying he's with Capitol Records,
and with Warners in BIG PUNCH. It also pictures him with
his family and listening to his record collection.

B301. Tepper, Randy. "Silver Spoons." TV Guide. June 11,
      1988.
      Meredith talks about being born famous in connection
with her syndicated series BORN FAMOUS. She mentions
Gordon's alcoholism and news hitting the Los Angeles Times
in 1955, when he was arrested for drunk driving. Meredith
is pictured.

B302. "This Is My Belief." Unknown magazine and date.
      Gordon discusses his beliefs and philosophy of life.
Pictures of Gordon and his family.

B303. "Tops of the Week." Philadelphia Inquirer. August 21,
      1977.
      Announces MacRae's and other artists scheduled
appearances at the Temple University's Music Festival.
MacRae is pictured.

B304. Tusher, Bill. "Hollywood's Happiest Marriage." TV

and <u>Movie Screen</u>. July 1956.
    Gordon and Sheila are devoted and attentive to each
other. She gave him faith, morale support, and confidence.
He's pictured with Gower Champion.

B305. <u>TV Guide</u>.
    Various issues, documenting MacRae's TV appearances.

B306. _____. April 21, 1956.
    Review of the GORDON MacRAE SHOW.

B307. <u>TV Headliner</u>. November 1953.
    Discussion of his happy 12-year marriage and a brief
summary of his career to date. Full-page picture of Gordon
and a smaller one of him and Jane Powell in THREE SAILORS
AND A GIRL.

B308. <u>TV Song Stars</u>. January 1954.
    A short profile of MacRae with picture of Gordon and
Sheila.

B309. <u>TV Views This Week</u>. December 6-12, 1958.
    Article on the musical version of O'Henry's GIFT OF
    THE MAGI. MacRae is pictured in the article and on
the cover.

B310. "Under the Sun in Las Vegas." <u>Movies</u>. June 1951.
    Pictures of MacRae and family in Las Vegas during his
show at the El Rancho Vegas. Gordon is pictured on cover.

B311. <u>US News Today</u>. Date unknown.
    Announces that MacRae is in the hospital fighting
cancer of the mouth.

B312. <u>Variety</u>. March 29, 1950.
    Review of DAUGHTER OF ROSIE O'GRADY.

B313. _____. May 17, 1950.
    Review of RETURN OF THE FRONTIERSMAN.

B314. _____. November 15, 1950.
    Review of WEST POINT STORY.

B315. _____. November 7, 1951.
    Review of STARLIFT.

B316. _____. February 6, 1952.
    Review of his appearance at the Ambassador Hotel.

B317. _____. April 16, 1952.
    Review of ABOUT FACE.

B318. _____. April 29, 1953.
    Review of DESERT SONG.

B319. _____. June 3, 1953.
    Review of his show at the Casino-Toronto.

B320. _____. November 25, 1953.
Review of Gordon and Sheila's appearance at the El
Rancho Vegas on November 18, 1953.

B321. _____. November 25, 1953.
Review of THREE SAILORS AND A GIRL.

B322. _____. April 7, 1954.
Announcement of the birth of Bruce MacRae.

B323. _____. June 15, 1955.
Review of MacRae's show at the El Rancho Vegas on
June 8, 1955.

B324. _____. June 25, 1955.
Review of his appearance at the Cocoanut Grove on
June 20, 1955.

B325. _____. October 12, 1955.
Review of OKLAHOMA.

B326. _____. July 18, 1956.
Review of the July 11, 1956 show at the Ambassador
Hotel.

B327. _____. September 4, 1957.
Review of his appearance at the Cocoanut Grove on
September 1, 1957.

B328. _____. February 5, 1958.
Review of MacRae's act at the Chez Paree Hotel on
January 31, 1958.

B329. _____. October 29, 1958.
Review of his show at the Waldorf-Astoria

B330. _____. October 7, 1959.
Review of MacRae's act at the Beverly Hills Hotel in
Cincinatti on September 29, 1959.

B331. _____. October 21, 1959.
Review of MacRae's show at the Waldorf-Astoria.

B332. _____. September 28, 1960.
Review of the September 23, 1960 Cocoanut Grove show.

B333. _____. December 7, 1960.
Review of Gordon and Sheila's show at Harrah's Lake
Tahoe on November 30, 1960.

B334. _____. January 18, 1961.
Review of the MacRae act at the Fairmont in San
Francisco on January 10, 1961.

B335. _____. April 5, 1961.
Review of MacRae's show at the Waldorf-Astoria.

B336. _____. July 12, 1961.

Review of the July 5, 1961 Cocoanut Grove show.

B337. _____. April 11, 1962.
Review of MacRae's appearance at the Shoreham Hotel's
Blue Room on April 3, 1962.

B338. _____. June 20, 1962.
Review of the Ambassador Hotel show.

B339. _____. September 26, 1962.
Review of MacRae's show at the Waldorf-Astoria.

B340. _____. January 1, 1964.
Review of his Cocoanut Grove show on December 28,
1964.

B341. _____. July 28, 1965.
Review of MacRae's show at the Nugget in Sparks,
Nevada on July 23, 1965.

B342. _____. May 25, 1966.
Review of his show at the Queen Elizabeth Hotel in
Montreal.

B343. _____. September 7, 1966.
Review of his show at the Diplomat in Florida on
August 30, 1966.

B344. _____. April 5, 1967.
Review of MacRae's appearance at the Hotel Roosevelt
in New Orleans on March 30, 1967 to April 19, 1967.

B345. _____. April 26, 1967.
Review of his Waldorf-Astoria show.

B346. _____. January 29, 1969.
Review of his appearance at the Drake Hotel in
Chicago on January 22, 1969.

B347. _____. February 4, 1970.
Review of MacRae's appearance at the Hotel Plaza in
New York on February 1970.

B348. _____. March 11, 1970.
Review of MacRae's act at the Latin Casino in New
Jersey on March 4, 1970.

B349. _____. September 16, 1970.
Review of Gordon's appearance at Harold's in Reno on
September 8, 1970.

B350. _____. October 7, 1970.
Review of his show at the Drake Hotel in Chicago on
October 1, 1970.

B351. _____. January 26, 1972.
Review of his act at the Fairmont in San Francisco.

B352. _____. March 22, 1972.
       Review of his appearance at the Hotel St. Regis in
New York.

B353. _____. December 6, 1972.
       Review of Phyllis Diller and MacRae's appearance at
the Desert Inn in November 1972.

B354. _____. December 19, 1973.
       Review of MacRae's show at the Thunderbird in Vegas.

B355. _____. July 9, 1975.
       Review of Gordon's act at the Fairmont in Atlanta.

B356. _____. January 17, 1979.
       Tells about the filming of THE PILOT and his touring
in SHENANDOAH and of the reunion with his children.

B357. _____. January 23, 1980.
       Review of Gordon's appearance in the act "4 Guys 4"
at the Sahara in Reno on January 13, 1980.

B358. _____. November 17, 1982.
       Review of his appearance at the Holiday House in
Pittsburgh, Pennsylvania in the act "Great Stars of the
Silver Screen."

B359. Walker, H.L. "He Says It With Music." Photoplay.
       January 1950.

B360. Wantch, Phillip. "MacRae Warmth At Venetian Room."
       Dallas Morning News. April 11, 1974.
       Review of MacRae's appearance at the Venetian Room
complete with portrait of MacRae.

B361. Ward, I. E. "The Great Films." Classic Images.
       December 1988.
       Among the films discussed were ON MOONLIGHT BAY and
       BY THE LIGHT OF THE SILVERY MOON. MacRae and Doris
Day are pictured.

B362. _____. "Warner Brothers' Days of Glory-Part II."
       Classic Images. Date unknown.
       Mentions Gordon in reference to Doris Day and ON
MOONLIGHT BAY and BY THE LIGHT OF THE SILVERY MOON.

B363. Webster, Holly R. "Oklahoma Keeps All Its Appeal."
       Unknown paper. August 1967.
       Review of OKLAHOMA at Valley Forge Music Fair.

B364. Weller, Helen Hover. Movieland. March 1950.
       Discusses MacRae getting joy out of life. Pictured
with Sheila.

B365. "West Point Story." Movie Stars Parade. December
       1950.
       An article and 15 pictures on the film.

B366. "Who Dat?" Filmland. 1953.
      MacRae's appearance at the El Rancho Vegas.   Several
      pictures of Gordon, Sheila, and Pinky Lee.

B367. "Who Is King?" Movie Stars Parade. January 1952.
      The article compares the lives and careers of MacRae
and Mario Lanza, as to which is the number one singer.
Many pictures of both.

B368. Who's Who in Television, Radio, and Records. 1958.
      Short summary of MacRae's career with a small
picture.

B369. Williams, Dick. "Upstaged By a Skunk." Unknown paper.
      1959.
      About a skunk being on stage during their performance
of REDHEAD in Warwick, Rhode Island.

B370. Williams, Wylie. "Gordon MacRae Scores Hit in Grove
      Bow." February 1, 1952.
      Review of MacRae's show at the Cocoanut Grove.

B371. Wilson, Earl. "Gordon MacRae's Show Actually a Family
      Affair." Los Angeles Mirror. April 22, 1961.
      Talks about the family working together in ANNIE GET
YOUR GUN.

B372. _____. "Gordon Parades His Paternity." Delaware
      County Daily Times. February 3, 1970.
      Tells about funny stories MacRae told at his Plaza
show about Phil Harris, his new daughter, Amanda, and
golfing with George Gobel and President Nixon.

B373. _____. "Kids of Yesterday Take Over." Delaware County
      Daily Times. 1974.
      About taping of the TV special GRAMMY SALUTES OSCAR.

B374. "Wilson, MacRae and Day Revive a 'Golden Age'." Los
      Angeles Herald Examiner. April 23, 1980.
      A question and answer article on their doing BIG
BROADCAST OF 1944 at the Pantages Theatre.   Pictured with
Don Wilson and Dennis Day.

B375. Wolfers, Larry. "Gordon MacRae-Born to Sing." Chicago
      Sunday Tribune. August 18, 1957.
      Describes MacRae's appearance at the Chicagoland Music
Festival with Roberta Peters, his life and career.   Pictured
with Sheila, Phil Harris, and on the cover of the magazine.

B376. Wood, C. TV Personalities Biographical Sketchbook.
      1956.

B377. Yanqui, Liam. "Famous Offspring Reveal Family
      Secrets." Unknown magazine and date.
      Meredith talks about Heather and her not liking to be
in their parent's limelight, and her not liking to be
introduced by friends as Gordon MacRae's daughter.   She
also relates the time Gordon went to see Heather in HAIR.

There is a picture of Meredith.

B378. "Yodelers' Foursome." Unknown magazine. 1952.
     MacRae, Bing Crosby, Phil Harris, and Dean Martin on
the Thunderbird's golf course between activities at the
Desert Circus at Palm Springs. Many photos of the foursome
both singly and together.

BOOKS

Books were selected that discussed MacRae as a topic or that
included credits or reviews within a media.

B379. Amory, Cleveland and Blackwell, Earl. <u>Celebrity
     Register</u>. N.Y.: Harper & Row, 1963.
     Gives a biographical account of MacRae, with picture.

B380. Amory, Cleveland, editor. <u>International Celebrity
     Register</u>. N.Y.: Celebrity Register LTD, 1959.
     Gives a biographical account of MacRae, with picture.

B381. <u>Annual Obituary 1986</u>. Chicago: St. James Press,
     1989.
     Good summary of MacRae's life and career.

B382. Aylesworth, Thomas and Bowman, John. <u>The World
     Almanac Who's Who of Film</u>. N.Y.: Bison Books, 1987.
     Gives a brief biographical sketch and a listing of
selected films.

B383. Blum, Daniel. <u>Screen World</u>. N.Y.: Biblo and Tannen.
     Reprint of various volumes of <u>Screen World</u> which
gives credits, casts, and pictures of each film.

B384. Brooks, Tim and Marsh, Earle. <u>Complete Directory to
     Prime Time Network TV Shows 1946 to Present</u>. N.Y.:
     Ballantine Books, 1985.
     This paperback encyclopedia lists and describes the
prime time network shows. It includes grids and Emmy
listings.

B385. Brooks, Tim. <u>The Complete Directory to Prime Time TV
     Stars</u>. N.Y.: Ballantine Books, 1987.
     This paperback alphabetically lists stars with a
biographical sketch and a documentation of their TV series.

B386. Buxton, Frank and Owen, Bill. <u>The Big Broadcast 1920-
     1950</u>. N.Y.: Viking Press, 1972.
     An alphabetical listing of radio shows with credits,
cast, type of show and description of each show.
Illustrated. MacRae is pictured on RAILROAD HOUR with
Carmen Dragon and announcer Marvin Miller.

B387. Chamels, Sol and Wolsky, Albert. <u>The Movie Makers</u>.
     N.J.: Derbebooks Inc., 1974.
     Biographical sketch of stars with a sample listing of
films.

B388. Claghorn, Charles Eugene. <u>Biographical Dictionary of</u>
      <u>American Music</u>. N.Y.: Parker Publishing Co., 1973.
      Over 5000 brief biographical sketches of persons
connected with American music from the 17th Century on.

B389. Clark, Al, editor. <u>The Film Yearbook 1987</u>. N.Y.:   St
      Martin's Press, 1987.
      Covers the film year 1986, including the obituary of
MacRae.

B390. Clarke, Donald, editor. <u>The Penguin Encyclopedia of</u>
      <u>Popular Music</u>. N.Y.: Viking Press, 1989.
      Profiles nearly 3000 performers from every field of
music.

B391. Dimmitt, Richard Bertrand. <u>An Actor Guide to the</u>
      <u>Talkies</u>. N.J.: Scarecrow Press, 1967.
      Gives films, the company, release date, character,
and star for some 8000 films between January 1949 and
December 1964.

B392. Dunning, John. <u>Tune In Yesterday-the Ultimate</u>
      <u>Encylopedia of Old-Time Radio 1925-1976</u>. N.J.:
      Prentice-Hall, 1976.
      Lists alphabetically many radio shows with a detailed
description.   Illustrated.

B393. Ephron, Henry. <u>We Thought We Could Do Anything</u>. N.Y.:
      W. W. Norton & Co., 1977.
      Ephron's rememberances of doing films such as
      MacRae's LOOK FOR THE SILVER LINING, CAROUSEL, and
BEST THINGS IN LIFE ARE FREE.   Pictures of Gordon in
CAROUSEL.

B394. Gelb, Alan. <u>The Doris Day Scrapbook</u>. N.Y.:   Grosset &
      Dunlap, 1977.
      This paperback covers Doris Day's life and career in
words and pictures. It covers her films with Gordon. Many
pictures.

B395. Grankos, Larry. <u>Television Drama Series Programming A</u>
      <u>Comprehensive Chronicle, 1947-1959</u>. N.J.:   Scarecrow
      Press, 1980.
      Lists drama series episode by episode.

B396. _____. <u>Television Drama Series Programming A</u>
      <u>Comprehensive Chronicle, 1959-1975</u>. N.J.:   Scarecrow
      Press, 1978.
      Lists drama series episode by episode.

B397. Green, Stanley. <u>Encyclopedia of Musical Film</u>. N.Y.:
      Oxford University Press, 1981.
      Gives a biographical sketch of persons related to the
musical film and a chronological listing of their musical
films, including character played.

B398. Halliwell, Leslie. <u>Halliwell's Film and Video Guide</u>
      6th Edition. N.Y.: Charles Scribner's Sons, 1987.

Gives cast, short credit list, small summary and critique, Academy Awards and availability on video tape.

B399. _____. Halliwell's Filmgoer's Companion-9th Edition. N.Y.: Charles Scribner's Sons, 1988.
Gives a brief biographical sketch and a list of films.

B400. Hirschorn, Clive. The Hollywood Musical. N.Y.: Crown Publishers, 1981.
Covers every film musical, by year, from 1927 with a picture. Each year gives Academy Award winners and nominees and the top money making films of that year.

B401. _____. The Warner Brothers Story. N.Y.: Crown Pubishers, 1979.
Covers every film made by the studio by year. Each film has a picture.

B402. Hodgins, Gordon W. The Broadway Musical-A Complete LP Discography. N.J.: Scarecrow Press, 1980.
Gives various recordings of Broadway shows with record label, year, cast, credits, songs. It has a book and lyric writer index, and performer, song and label indexes.

B403. Hotchner, A.E. Doris Day Her Own Story. N.Y.: William Morrow & Co., 1976.
Doris Day's autobiography includes information on her films with Gordon and an interview with MacRae about his letting her husband, Marty Melcher and lawyer Jerome Rosenthal handle his finances. Pictured in BY THE LIGHT OF THE SILVERY MOON with Day.

B404. Hummel, David. The Collector's Guide to the American Musical Theatre-2 volumes.
Volume one lists shows with credits, songs, and recorded versions. Volume two is an index by performer.

B405. Johnson, Catherine, editor. TV Guide 25 Year Index. PA: Triangle Publications, 1979.
An index to articles on shows and persons printed in TV Guide.

B406. Karney, Robyn, editor. The Movie Star Story. N.Y.: Crescent Books, 1984.
Gives a listing, by decade, of stars with a biographical and career study, including a picture.

B407. Katz, Ephraim. The Film Encyclopedia. N.Y.: Thomas Y. Crowell, 1979.
Gives film terms, biographical sketches, and film credits for persons identified with film.

B408. Kinkle, Rodger D. The Complete Encyclopedia of Popular Music and Jazz 1900-1950. New Rochelle, N.Y.: Arlington House, 1974. Four volume set.
Third volume has biographical sketch of MacRae, film

list, and a sampling of records.

B409. Lloyd, Anne and Fuller, Graham. The Illustrated
      Who's Who of the Cinema. N.Y.: Macmillian Co., 1983.
      Alphabetical listing of persons connected to the
cinema with a biographical account and sampling of films,
with picture.

B410. McNeil, Alex. Total Television. N.Y.: Penguin Books,
      1984.
      This paperback is an encyclopedia listing television
series from 1948 to present. It also lists specials,
season graphs, and Emmys.

B411. Maltin, Leonard. TV Movies and Video Guide-1989
      Edition. N.Y.: Signet, 1988.
      This paperback contains alphabetical listings of over
18,000 films with cast, credits, and a short summary and
review. It has a star rating, and indicates which films
are available on video.

B412. Marx, Kenneth. Star Stats. Los Angeles:
      Price/Stern/Sloan, 1979.
      This paperback gives a computerized printout on star
statistics.

B413. Mawhinney, Paul. Music Master-the 45 rpm Record
      Directory. PA: Record-Rama, 1983. Two Volumes.
      A listing by artist and by title of 45 recordings.

B414. Morino, Marianne. The Hollywood Walk of Fame. CA:
      Ten Speed Press, 1987.
      This paperback gives every performer with a star on
the Walk of Fame and for what category. It gives a brief
statement on each person and the location of the star.

B415. Murrells, Joseph. Million Selling Records From the
      1900s to the 1980s-An Illustrated Directory. N.Y.:
      Arco, 1984.
      It gives the artist and their million-selling records
by year with a biographical summary of each million-selling
artist. Cast and soundtrack million-sellers are listed at
the beginning of the year.

B416. The New York Times Directory of the Film. Arno/Random
      House, 1971.
      Gives sample reviews and a listing, by artist, of
films reviewed by the New York Times. Credits MacRae with
an appearance in EAST SIDE WEST SIDE (1927). Not
confirmed. Includes a picture gallery.

B417. The New York Times Directory of the Theatre.
      Arno/Quadrangle, 1973.
      Gives selected reprints of reviews, a title index,
and a listing, by artist, of plays reviewed by the New York
Times. Credits MacRae with appearances in JOHN (1927), OUR
BETTERS (1928), EXCEEDING SMALL (1928). All unconfirmed.

B418. Nite, Norman. Rock On-the Illustrated Encyclopedia of
      Rock N' Roll. N.Y.: Thomas Y Crowell Co., 1974.
      All Artist's with a top 100 hit during Rock's Golden
      Age has a biographical sketch and a list of 100 hits.

B419. O'Donnell, Monica, editor. Contemporary Theatre, Film
      and TV-Volume 3. Michigan: Gale Research, 1986.
      Gives an up-to-date profile on stars, including
MacRae.

B420. Osborne, Jerry and Hamilton, Bruce. Movie, TV
      Soundtracks and Original Cast Albums Price Guide.
      Arizona: O'Sullivan Woodside & Co., 1981.
      Lists alphabetically various show recordings with
composer, cast, year, record number, and price range.

B421. Osborne, Jerry. Official Price Guide to Records-8th
      Edition. N.Y.: House of Collectibles, 1988.
      MacRae's Capitol 7" singles between 1953-1968 range
from $2-$4. His Capitol 7" EPs range from $54-$57. His
Capitol LPs 10 and 12" range between $54-$69. His 7"
single recordings with Jo Stafford range between $2-$3.
His Capitol (1600 & 1900 series) 10 and 12" LPs with her
between 1962-1963 range between $10-$15. His Capitol 1100
series with Stafford range between $4-$8.

B422. Parish, James Robert and Terrace, Vincent. Actors'
      Television Credits 1948-1988. Volume I-Actors. N.J.:
      Scarecrow Press, 1989.
      Lists, by actor, their television credits by title,
date, and network.

B423. Parish, James Robert and Pitts, Michael. Hollywood
      Songsters. N.Y.: Garland.
      This forthcoming book profiles 100 musical stars in
mini chapters, including their movies, TV series, radio
series, and LP credits.

B424. Pickard, Roy. A Companion to the Movies-1903 to
      Present. N.Y.: Hippocrene Books, 1972.
      Covers each film genre with sample films and a brief
sketch of persons associated with that genre.

B425. Pierce, David. The Film Daily Yearbook Guide to the
      Fifties. MD, 1987.
      Lists all feature films with cast, credits, release
date and date reviewed by Film Daily.

B426. Pitts, Michael and Harrison, Louis. Hollywood on
      Record: The Film Stars' Discography. N.J.: Scarecrow
      Press, 1978.
      It lists each actor's LPs, soundtracks, compilation
LPs, and a sampling of 45s.

B427. Pitts, Michael. Radio Soundtracks: A Reference Guide.
      N.J.: Scarecrow Press, 1986.
      Gives background on radio shows that are available on
tape or records, as well as sources.

B428. Quinlan, David. Quinlan's Illustrated Directory of
      Film Stars. N.Y.: Hippocrene, 1986.
      Gives a brief biographical sketch on some 1700 stars
with 1660 pictures, as well as screen credits, including
film shorts. MacRae is pictured as Curly.

B429. Ragan, David. Who's Who in Hollywood 1900-1976. N.Y.:
      Arlington House, 1976.
      Gives an update on film stars with a sampling of film
credits. A second section does the same for deceased
stars.

B430. Raymond, Jack. Show Music on Record. N.Y.:   Frederick
      Ungar, 1982.
      Lists the various recordings of a show under the
original year of production with performer, and album
number.

B431. Reed, Dena. The Complete Life of Gordon MacRae.
      Pocket, 1955. Illustrated, 64 pages.

B432. Rust, Brian. The American Dance Band Discography
      1917-1942. 2 Volumes. New Rochelle, N.Y.:   Arlington
      House, 1975.
      Gives the recordings by orchestra, date of recording,
and principal musicians and vocalists.

B433. Scheurer, Steven. Movies on TV and Videocassette
      1989-1990 Edition. N.Y.: Bantam Books, 1989.
      This paperback lists films alphabetically with
director, cast, short critique and synopsis. It also
indicates which films are available on video.

B434. Schuster, Mel. Motion Picture Performers: A
      Bibliography of Magazine and Periodical Articles,
      1900-1969. Metuchen, N.J.: Scarecrow Press, 1971.
      Listing of magazine and periodical articles, by star.

B435. _____. Motion Picture Performers: A Bibliography of
      Magazine and Periodical Articles, 1970-1974-
      Supplement I.
      Metuchen, N.J.: Scarecrow Press, 1976.
      Listing, by star, of magazine and periodical articles.

B436. Shipman, David. The Great Movie Stars the
      International Years. Hill and Wang, 1980.
      Profiles over 230 stars from the post-war period.
One of the longer profiles's on MacRae. He is pictured with
Shirley Jones in OKLAHOMA, and under Doris Day's entry.

B437. Slide, Anthony. Great Radio Personalities in Historic
      Photographs. N.Y.: Dover Publications, 1982.
      This paperback lists alphabetically radio
personalities with a picture and a brief sketch of their
lives and radio history.

B438. Strait, Raymond. Star Babies. N.Y.: St Martin's
      Press, 1979.

Strait does chapters based on interviews with children of stars. One of the chapters is on Meredith MacRae who discusses growing up with Gordon and Sheila. Meredith is pictured with Gordon on the set of BY THE LIGHT OF THE SILVERY MOON.

B439. Summers, Harrison, editor. A Thirty-Year History of Radio Programs 1926-1956. N.Y.: Arno/New York Times, 1971.
Lists radio shows by season, giving sponsor, type of show, program, season on the air, length, day, time, and rating.

B440. Terrace, Vincent. Encyclopedia of Television Series, Pilots, and Specials. Three Volumes. New York Zoetrope, 1985-1986.
This three volume encyclopedia lists series, pilots, and specials from 1937-1984, giving casts, credits, running dates, and networks.

B441. _____. Radio's Golden Years. N.Y.: A&S Barnes & Co., 1981.
Alphabetical listing of radio shows from 1930-1960, telling the type of show, host, regulars, announcers, orchestra, sponsor, network, length, and date of first broadcast.

B442. Thomas, Tony and Solomon, Aubrey. The Films of 20th Century Fox. N.J.: Citadel Press, 1979.
Pictorial history of the studio, listing every film by year, with credits, cast, summary and comment. MacRae is pictured in CAROUSEL and BEST THINGS IN LIFE ARE FREE.

B443. Thompson, Howard, editor. The New York Times Guide to Movies on TV. Chicago: Quadrangle Books, 1970.
This paperback gives credits, plots, one-line and capsule reviews of over 2000 films, with a picture of each.

B444. Vallance, Tom. The American Musical. N.Y.: A&S Barnes, 1970.
This paperback encyclopedia lists persons who were in film musicals and their film credits. MacRae is pictured in BEST THINGS IN LIFE ARE FREE.

B445. Variety Film Reviews-1949-1953. Volume 8. N.Y.: Garland, 1983.
Reprints of film reviews appearing in Variety.

B446. _____. 1954-1958. Volume 9. N.Y.: Garland, 1983
Reprints of film reviews appearing in Variety.

B447. Variety Who's Who in Show Business. N.Y.: Garland, 1983.
This paperback gives a brief biographical sketch with selected films, and TV credits for some 6000 persons.

B448. Walker, Leo. The Big Band Almanac. CA: Ward Ritchie Press, 1978.

     This illustrated paperback lists alphabetically
bands, telling when the band was started, where, previous
affiliations, sidemen, vocalists, sponsors, theme song,
recording affiliations, and a biographical account of the
leader and band.

B449. Warren, John. <u>Warren's Movie Poster Price Guide</u>.
      Cleveland, TN: Overstreet Publications, 1986.
      Gives the prices for various size posters for films
between 1930-1969.

B450. Weaver, John. <u>Forty Years of Screen Credits
      1929-1969</u>. 2 Volumes. N.J.: Scarecrow Press, 1970.
      Lists chronologically, by artist, their film credits.

B451. Whitburn, Joel. <u>The Billboard Book of Top 40 Hits</u>.
      N.Y.: Billboard Publications, 1985.
      This paperback lists, by artist, every song to hit
the top 40 with date it reached the charts, its highest
position, weeks charted, and label number. A brief
biographical and career statement is made on each artist.

B452. _____. <u>Pop Memories 1890-1954</u>. Wisconsin: Record
      Research, 1986.
      It lists alphabetically, with a short biographical
sentence, each artist and their records that hit the
charts. It tells when the record hit the charts, highest
position reached, and how long charted. Also there is an
alphabetical listing by song, as well as, achievement
sections.

B453. _____. <u>Top LP's 1945-1972</u>. Wisconsin: Record
      Research, 1973.
      Lists by artist every album to hit the charts,
telling when the album hit the charts, its peak position,
and how long charted.

B454. _____. <u>Top Pop Albums 1955-1985</u>. Wisconsin: Record
      Research, 1985.
      Lists, by artist, every album to hit the charts,
telling when the album hit the charts, its peak position,
and how long charted.

B455. _____. <u>Top Pop Singles 1955-1986</u>. Wisconsin: Record
      Research, 1987.
      It lists alphabetically each artist and their records
that hit the charts. It tells when the record hit the
charts, its highest position, and how long charted. An
alphabetical song listing is made and there are several
achievement sections.

B456. <u>Who's Who in America</u>-39th Edition. 2 Volumes.
      Illinois: Marquis Who's Who, 1976-1977.
      Profiles persons from all walks of life.

B457. Willis, John. <u>Screen World</u>-Volume 33. N.Y.: Crown,
      1982.
      Credits, cast and picture of THE PILOT.

B458. _____. Screen World-Volume 38. London: Frederick
       Muller, 1987.
       Covers every film released in 1986. It includes
MacRae's obituary with picture.

B459. _____. Theatre World-Volume 24. N.Y.: Crown, 1968.
       Profiles the 1967-68 season and gives all the
information on Broadway's I DO! I DO! MacRae and Carol
Lawrence are pictured.

B460. _____. Theatre World-Volume 42. N.Y.: Crown, 1987
       Covers the 1985-1986 theatre season and includes
MacRae's obituary with picture.

B461. Wilson, Arthur. The Warner Brothers Golden
       Anniversary Book. N.Y.: Dell Special, 1973.
       This illustrated paperback lists every film by year,
with credits, cast and release date. MacRae and Kathryn
Grayson are picture in DESERT SONG.

B462. Young, Christopher. The Films of Doris Day. Secaucus,
       N.J.: Citadel Press, 1977.
       Covers Doris Day's life and career in words and
pictures, and details her films with MacRae.

ADDENDA

B463. Hardy, Phil and Laing, Dave. The Faber Companion To
       20th-Century Popular Music. London: Faber and Faber,
       1990.
       Gives biographical sketches of performers in all
       areas of music.

B464. Lynch, Richard Chigley. Movie Musicals on Record.
       CT: Greenwood Press, 1989.
       Directory of movie musical recordings, 1927-1987.

B465. Lynch, Richard Chigley. TV and Studio Cast Musicals
       on Record. CT: Greenwood Press, 1990.
       A Discography of television musicals and studio
       recordings of stage and film musicals.

B466. Motion Picture. March 1953.
       Photo story on Gordon.

B467. Motion Picture. June 1953.
       Photo story on Gordon and Sheila.

B468. Pictureqoer. November 1, 1952
       Article on ABOUT FACE. MacRae on cover.

B469. Picture Show & Film Pictorial. June 2, 1956
       Article on CAROUSEL. Shirley Jones & MacRae on
       cover.

B470. Screen Stories. August 1948.
       Article on BIG PUNCH.

Song Index

Numbers without letters preceding them refer to page
numbers. Those preceded by a letter correspond to the
section and entry number: S (Stage), R (Radio), F (Film),
T (Television), D (Discography), SM (Sheet Music), NC (Night
Clubs and Concerts), B (Bibliography).

Glad to Be Mrs. Gordon Mac-
  Rae, NC14
Glory of Love, T11.6
God Bless America, NC6
God Rest Ye Merry Gentleman,
  D158
God's Green Acres, F10
Golden Days, D162, D163
Good News, F20
Goodnight, S12
Goodnight Again, R19.1
Goodnight Sweetheart, D139
Gossips Song, D153
Go Tell It on the Mountain,
  D181
Granada, NC18
Green Acres and Purple
  Mountains, D66
Green Grow the Lilacs, D115
Greensleeves (What Child is
  This), D114
Guys and Dolls, S9
Gypsy, T34

Hair of Gold, Eyes of Blue,
  D24
Half a Heart is All You Left
  Me, D48
Half As Much, R15
Hallelujah, T11.4, D129
Hand Me Down That Can of
  Beans, S16
Hankerin', D22
Happy Anniversary, R10, D151
Happy Birthday Mrs. J.J.
  Brown, S15
Hark the Herald Angels Sing,
  D158
Havana, S9
He, D167
Heartaches, D13, D179
Heather on a Hill, T42
Heavenly Hideaway, 4, D5
He Bought My Soul at Calvary,
  D167
He is Born, D114
Hello, Hello There!, S10
Hello Young Lovers, T75, T77,
  NC45
He Needs Me Now, S13
Here Comes the Springtime, R5
Here I Am Broken Hearted, F20
Here's to Everyone in Love,
  NC42, NC49
Here's to Love, T75, NC45
Here's What I'm Here For, D91
He's in Love, S5
Highest Judge of All, S4

High Hopes, T86
High on a Windy Hill, D89,
  D155
Hold Me Hold Me, D57
Holy, Holy, Holy, D129
Home, D157
Home is Where the Heart is,
  F16, D169, SM10
Homin' Time, D73, D87
Honestly I Love You, D78
Honeymoon is Over, The, S12
Hongi Tongi Honki Poki, D53
Honkey Tonky Ten Cent
  Dance, D79
Hooray For Love, D139
Hot Diggity, T11.15
A House With Love in It,
  D157
How About You, T11.14
How Can I Wait, S16
How Close, D65
How Could I Be So Wrong,
  S13
How Do You Face the Sun-
  Shine, R37
How Do You Speak to an
  Angel, D86, NC11
How Green Was My Valley,
  D115
How High the Moon, R33
How Much is That Doggie in
  the Window, 19, NC8, NC14
Huguette, D170
Hymn to Hymie, S14

I Ain't Down Yet, S15
I Am Free, D137
I Am Loved, D56
I Asked the Lord, T11.14,
  D98, D187
I Believe, D123, D167,
  D219, NC11
I Believe in You, NC42
I Can't Say No, S11, F18,
  D145, SM11
Ich Liebe Dich, 19, R17
I Could Have Danced All
  Night, T11.9
I Didn't Know What Time It
  Was, T11.24
I Didn't Promise You a Rose
  Garden, NC69
I Do! I Do!, S12, T62
I Don't Think I'm in Love,
  D107
I Don't Want to Set the
  World on Fire, D1
I Don't Want to Walk With-

My Blushin' Rose, F4
My Buick, My Love and I, D69
My Cup Runneth Over, S12, T62
My Darling, My Darling, D26
My Defenses Are Down, S8
My Dream is Yours, R37
My Fair Lady Medley, NC20,
  NC38
My Funny Valentine, D156, D196
My Girl is Just Enough Woman
  For Me, S7
My Heart is a Singing Heart,
  F16, D169, SM28
My Heart Runs After You, D2
My Home Town, F14, D112
My Kind of Town, NC62
My Love, D65
My Moonlight Madonna, R19.3
My One and Only Highland
  Fling, D34
My Own Brass Bed, S15
My Own True Love and I, F4
My Sweet Gypsy Rose, NC77
My Time of Day, S9
My Way, NC60, NC61, NC77, NC80

Name's the Same, The, T22
Naughty Marietta, D140
Nearer My God to Thee, D129,
  D167, D219
Need You, D31, D136, SM29
Never Before and Never Again,
  D96
Never in a Million Years,
  D74, D88, D155
Never Till Now, D168
New Clothes, S3
New York, New York, 25, T103
Next to Lovin' I Like
  Fightin', S17
Nice People, NC25
Nice Work If You Can Get It,
  R19.5
Night of My Nights, S5, D132
Nine Hundred Miles, D67
Nob Hill, NC73
Nobody But You, NC11
Nobody's Perfect, S12
Nobody Told Me, R21
Noche Caribe, F10
Nocturn, D170
No No Nanette, F6
No Other Girl For Me, F12, D70
No Other Love, NC14
Nothing Like a Dame, T42
Not Since Nineveh, S5, D132
Now, D168
Now Hear This, F16

Now, Now, Now, D38
Now the Day is Over, D136,
  D165, D173
Now We Know, 14

Obey, D99
O Come All Ye Faithful,
  D158
O Come O Come Emmanuel,
  D158
Of Thee I Sing, R19.3
Oh But I Do, R19.1, D120,
  D125, D127, D128
Oh Come Away, D137
Oh Holy Morning, D167
Oh Me, Oh My, F6
Oh Oh Ophelia, D50
O Holy Night, D114
Oh What a Beautiful
  Morning, 17, S11, R35,
  F18, T7.12, T19, T24,
  T45, T52, T75, D145,
  SM30, NC25, NC30, NC32,
  NC38, NC61, NC73
Oh You're a Wonderful
  Person, S3
Oklahoma, S11, R35,, F18,
  T45, T75, T91, D145,
  SM31, NC32, NC61, NC77,
  NC80,
  Medley, T85, T90, D177,
  NC22, NC26, NC29-NC31,
  NC33, NC36-NC39, NC41,
  NC42, NC45-NC47, NC49,
  NC50, NC56, NC58-NC60,
  NC62, NC66-NC68, NC86,
  NC87
Oklahoma Hills, D115
Oldest Established, The, S9
Old Man River, R18, T93,
  D61, D123
Old Rugged Cross, D173,
  D219
O Little Town of Bethlehem,
  D158
Olive Tree, S5, D132
On a Sunday at Coney
  Island, D61
One Alone, F15, D116, D117,
  D150, NC30-NC32
One Flower Grows Alone in
  Your Garden, F15, D116,
  D117
One For My Baby, T11.7,
  T11.11
100 Days Till June, F7
One Kiss, D143, D144
One Misty Morning, T11.15,

Title Index

Numbers without letters preceding them refer to page
numbers. Those preceded by a letter correspond to the
section and entry number: S (Stage), R (Radio), F (Film),
T (Television), D (Discography), SM (Sheet Music), NC (Night
Clubs and Concerts), B (Bibliography).

R28.226
MLLE. MODISTE, R28.27,
  R28.74, R28.163, D204
MOTION PICTURE SOUNDSTAGE,
  D139, D205
MUSICAL CHAIRS, T93
MUSIC IN THE AIR, R28.55,
  R28.134, R28.276, R30.7,
  D183
MUSIC OF SIGMUND ROMBERG,
  D206
MY MARYLAND, R28.189
MY ROMANCE, R28.221
MY THREE SONS, 21

NAUGHTY MARIETTA, R28.16,
  R28.80, R28.210, D140-D142,
  D207
NAVY STAR TIME, R25
NBC HOLLYWOOD CALLING, R26
NECKLACE, THE, R28.196
NEW ALBUM PREVIEW, D189
NEW MOON, R28.9, R28.54,
  R28.121, R28.297, D143,
  D144, D171, D206, D208,
  D209
NEW WINE, R28.245
NEW YEARS EVE BIG BAND
  CELEBRATION, 25, T104
N.H. BROWN SALUTE, R28.51
NIGHT MUSIC, R28.256
NINA ROSA, R28.136
1947 ACADEMY AWARDS 7, R1
1948 ACADEMY AWARDS 8, R2
1948 CHRISTMAS SEAL PARTY, 8,
  R11, 52
NO NO NANETTE, 9, R28.60, F6
NO PLACE LIKE HOME, 19, T31,
  B157

OKLAHOMA, 6, 15, 17, 19, 21,
  25, S11, R28.36, F18, D145,
  D146, D210, 121, NC18, NC80,
  B25, B51, B59, B72, B76,
  B95, B98, B107, B124, B131,
  B155, B188, B216, B245,
  B257, B284, B325, B363,
  B436
OLD ACQUAINTANCES, T13.7
OLD RUGGED CROSS, D147, D211
100 YEARS OF GOLDEN HITS, 24,
  T101
ONE SUNDAY AFTERNOON, T13.15,
  B89
1001 NIGHTS, R28.148
ONE TOUCH OF VENUS, R28.132
ONE WAY PASSAGE, T13.20
ONE WAY STREET, T13.18

ONLY GIRL, THE, R28.77
ONLY LOVE, 21, D148
ON MOONLIGHT BAY, 10, 12,
  26, F9, F14, D149, B35,
  B189, B210, B242, B361,
  B362
ON THE WINGS OF A SONG,
  R28.251
ON YOUR TOES, R28.214
OPERATION STARLIFT, F10
OPERETTA FAVORITES, D150
ORANGE BLOSSOMS, R28.110,
  R28.174
OUR BETTERS, B417
OUR LOVE STORY, 19, T37,
  D151, B157
OVER EASY, 24, T95, T97,
  T99

PAINT YOUR WAGON, 23, S16
PARIS CALLING, T13.31
PASSWORD, T57
PAY CARDS, T59
PAYMENT IN KIND, T13.32
PENNY WHISTLE, R28.247,
  R28.293
PENROD, F9, F14
PENROD & SAM, F9, F14
PERRY COMO SHOW, T3
PERSONALITY, T61, T68
PERSON TO PERSON, T36
PETER LUPUS' BODY SHOP, T82
PETTICOAT JUNCTION, 20
PILOT, THE, 24, F21, T96,
  B150, B357, B458
PINK LADY, R28.84, R28.185,
  R28.237, R28.296
PIRATES OF NEW ORLEANS,
  R28.198
PIRATES OF PENSANCE,
  R28.114
PIRATES OF PICADILLY,
  R28.146, R28.203
PLAYHOUSE 90, B285
PORGY AND BESS, R28.34
POSSESSED, T13.19
PREMIERE OF A STAR IS BORN,
  T4
PRIMAL STORY, R28.248
PRINCE OF PILSEN, R28.82
PRINCESS PAT, R28.86,
  R28.233, D212
PRISONER OF LOVE, D152

QUALITY STREET, R28.242

RAILROAD HOUR, 8, 9, 13,
  22, R27, R28, 52, D109,

General Index

Numbers without letters preceding them refer to page numbers. Those preceded by a letter correspond to the section and entry number: S (Stage), R (Radio), F (Film), T (Television), D (Discography), SM (Sheet Music), NC (Night Clubs and Concerts), B (Bibliography).

R28.173, R28.215, R28.217,
R28.230, R28.232, R28.274,
R28.276, R28.286
Bergen, Edgar, R8
Berger, Richard, 19, 20, B91,
  B116, B172
Bergman, Ingrid, R1
Berle, Milton, 6, R6, R34
Berlin, Irving, S8
Berstein, Bob, B9
Bersten, G.W., F5, F10, F16
Bert Farber Orchestra, NC59
Best, Marjorie, F2, F7, F9,
  F15
Beverly Hills Hotel, NC30,
  NC330
Big Band Almanac, The, B448
Big Broadcast 1920-1950, The,
  B386
Billboard, NC26, B9, B12, B13
Billboard Book of Top 40 Hits,
  The, B451
Bill Snyder Orchestra, NC42,
  NC56
Bingham, Mary Alice, S3
Binns, Ed, 24, F21
Biographical Dictionary of
  American Music, B388
Birch, Miriam, S9
Bishop, Bunny, D132
Bishop, Joey, T71, T72, T79
Bissell, Whit, T87
Bixby, Bill, 20
Black, Arthur, F18
Blackstone, Jay, F18, D145
Blackwell, Earl, B379
Blaine, Vivian, S9, T13.16
Blair, Janet, T42, T86
Blake, Amanda, T4
Blane, Paul, NC86
Bleyer, Archie, R31
Block, Martin, R10
Block, Paul, 19
Block, Ray, 5, T58
Blue, Monty, F3
Blue Mouse Theatre, B77, B168
Blum, Daniel, B383
Blyden, Larry, T61, T68
Blyth, Anne, R2
Bob Cross Orchestra, NC40
Bob Devaye Trio, NC35
Bob Ellis Orchestra, NC14
Bogart, Humphrey, NC11, NC20
Bolen, Murray, R28
Boles, John, 12
Bolger, Ray, 6, S3, F2, T4,
  B203
Bond, David, F16

Bond, Raymond, F5
Bonoff, Buster, S9
Boone, Debbie, T103
Borden, Eugene, F20
Borgnine, Ernest, 18, 27,
  F20
Borg, Veda Ann, F16
Borzago, Frank, R2
Bosler, Virginia, F18
Boston Post TV Eye, B277
Bowd, Robert, S9
Bowers, William, F20
Bowman, John, B382
Bowman, Harry, B14
Boxoffice, B15-B17
Boyden, Dr. Frank, 2
Boyle, Johnny Jr., F7
Boys Town Choir, 23, D114
Brace, Linda, F20
Bracken, Eddie, 11, R28.5,
  F12
Brady, William, 7
Brando, Marlon, NC20
Brennan, Terry, T7.3
Brennan, Walter Jr., F10
Bresler, Jerry, NC41, NC42,
  NC51
Brian Farnon Orchestra,
  NC57
Brice, Fanny, 6, R19
Bridges Auditorium, NC80,
  B110
Brigade Records, D179
Briggs, Matt, S2
Brinkley, David, NC41
Britt, Jacqueline, S13
Broadcasting, B290
Broadhurst Theatre, S3
Broadmoor Hotel, 19, NC15
Broadway Musical-A Complete
  LP Discography, The, B402
Brookhouser, Frank, NC60,
  B18
Brook, Sara, S11, S13
Brooks, Carolyn, B19
Brooks, Foster, T103
Brooks, Norman, F20
Brooks, Tim, B384, B385
Brothers, Dr. Joyce, T81
Brother Turyananda, 22
Brown, George C., F1
Brown, Helen Gurley, T65
Brown, James, F10
Brown, Kelly, F18
Brown, Les, 3, T103
Brown, Lew, 18
Brubeck, Dave, T63
Bruce, Jon, B20

About the Author

BRUCE R. LEIBY earned his B.S. degree in Business Administration from Tusculum College in Greeneville, Tennessee, and currently teaches in the Upper Darby School District in Upper Darby, Pennsylvania.

Lightning Source UK Ltd.
Milton Keynes UK
UKOW052048121111

181919UK00005B/28/P